DAN-83   DANTES SUBJECT STANDARDIZED TESTS (DSST)

This is your
PASSBOOK for...

Health and Human Development

Test Preparation Study Guide
Questions & Answers

COPYRIGHT NOTICE

This book is SOLELY intended for, is sold ONLY to, and its use is RESTRICTED to individual, bona fide applicants or candidates who qualify by virtue of having seriously filed applications for appropriate license, certificate, professional and/or promotional advancement, higher school matriculation, scholarship, or other legitimate requirements of education and/or governmental authorities.

This book is NOT intended for use, class instruction, tutoring, training, duplication, copying, reprinting, excerption, or adaptation, etc., by:

1) Other publishers
2) Proprietors and/or Instructors of "Coaching" and/or Preparatory Courses
3) Personnel and/or Training Divisions of commercial, industrial, and governmental organizations
4) Schools, colleges, or universities and/or their departments and staffs, including teachers and other personnel
5) Testing Agencies or Bureaus
6) Study groups which seek by the purchase of a single volume to copy and/or duplicate and/or adapt this material for use by the group as a whole without having purchased individual volumes for each of the members of the group
7) Et al.

Such persons would be in violation of appropriate Federal and State statutes.

PROVISION OF LICENSING AGREEMENTS – Recognized educational, commercial, industrial, and governmental institutions and organizations, and others legitimately engaged in educational pursuits, including training, testing, and measurement activities, may address request for a licensing agreement to the copyright owners, who will determine whether, and under what conditions, including fees and charges, the materials in this book may be used them. In other words, a licensing facility exists for the legitimate use of the material in this book on other than an individual basis. However, it is asseverated and affirmed here that the material in this book CANNOT be used without the receipt of the express permission of such a licensing agreement from the Publishers. Inquiries re licensing should be addressed to the company, attention rights and permissions department.

All rights reserved, including the right of reproduction in whole or in part, in any form or by any means, electronic or mechanical, including photocopying, recording, or by any information storage and retrieval system, without permission in writing from the Publisher.

Copyright © 2024 by
National Learning Corporation

212 Michael Drive, Syosset, NY 11791
(516) 921-8888 • www.passbooks.com
E-mail: info@passbooks.com

PUBLISHED IN THE UNITED STATES OF AMERICA

PASSBOOK® SERIES

THE *PASSBOOK® SERIES* has been created to prepare applicants and candidates for the ultimate academic battlefield – the examination room.

At some time in our lives, each and every one of us may be required to take an examination – for validation, matriculation, admission, qualification, registration, certification, or licensure.

Based on the assumption that every applicant or candidate has met the basic formal educational standards, has taken the required number of courses, and read the necessary texts, the *PASSBOOK® SERIES* furnishes the one special preparation which may assure passing with confidence, instead of failing with insecurity. Examination questions – together with answers – are furnished as the basic vehicle for study so that the mysteries of the examination and its compounding difficulties may be eliminated or diminished by a sure method.

This book is meant to help you pass your examination provided that you qualify and are serious in your objective.

The entire field is reviewed through the huge store of content information which is succinctly presented through a provocative and challenging approach – the question-and-answer method.

A climate of success is established by furnishing the correct answers at the end of each test.

You soon learn to recognize types of questions, forms of questions, and patterns of questioning. You may even begin to anticipate expected outcomes.

You perceive that many questions are repeated or adapted so that you can gain acute insights, which may enable you to score many sure points.

You learn how to confront new questions, or types of questions, and to attack them confidently and work out the correct answers.

You note objectives and emphases, and recognize pitfalls and dangers, so that you may make positive educational adjustments.

Moreover, you are kept fully informed in relation to new concepts, methods, practices, and directions in the field.

You discover that you are actually taking the examination all the time: you are preparing for the examination by "taking" an examination, not by reading extraneous and/or supererogatory textbooks.

In short, this PASSBOOK®, used directedly, should be an important factor in helping you to pass your test.

NONTRADITIONAL EDUCATION

Students returning to school as adults bring more varied experience to their studies than do the teenagers who begin college shortly after graduating from high school. As a result, there are numerous programs for students with nontraditional learning curves. Hundreds of colleges and universities grant degrees to people who cannot attend classes at a regular campus or have already learned what the college is supposed to teach.

You can earn nontraditional education credits in many ways:
- Passing standardized exams
- Demonstrating knowledge gained through experience
- Completing campus-based coursework, and
- Taking courses off campus

Some methods of assessing learning for credit are objective, such as standardized tests. Others are more subjective, such as a review of life experiences.

With some help from four hypothetical characters – Alice, Vin, Lynette, and Jorge – this article describes nontraditional ways of earning educational credit. It begins by describing programs in which you can earn a high school diploma without spending 4 years in a classroom. The college picture is more complicated, so it is presented in two parts: one on gaining credit for what you know through course work or experience, and a second on college degree programs. The final section lists resources for locating more information.

Earning High School Credit

People who were prevented from finishing high school as teenagers have several options if they want to do so as adults. Some major cities have back-to-school programs that allow adults to attend high school classes with current students. But the more practical alternatives for most adults are to take the General Educational Development (GED) tests or to earn a high school diploma by demonstrating their skills or taking correspondence classes.

Of course, these options do not match the experience of staying in high school and graduating with one's friends. But they are viable alternatives for adult learners committed to meeting and, often, continuing their educational goals.

GED Program

Alice quit high school her sophomore year and took a job to help support herself, her younger brother, and their newly widowed mother. Now an adult, she wants to earn her high school diploma – and then go on to college. Because her job as head cook and her family responsibilities keep her busy during the day, she plans to get a high school equivalency diploma. She will study for, and take, the GED tests. Every year, about half a million adults earn their high school credentials this way. A GED diploma is accepted in lieu of a high school one by more than 90 percent of employers, colleges, and universities, so it is a good choice for someone like Alice.

The GED testing program is sponsored by the American Council on Education and State and local education departments. It consists of examinations in five subject areas: Writing, science, mathematics, social studies, and literature and the arts. The tests also measure skills such as analytical ability, problem solving, reading comprehension, and ability to understand and apply information. Most of the questions are multiple choice; the writing test includes an essay section on a topic of general interest.

Eligibility rules for taking the exams vary, but some states require that you must be at least 18. Tests are given in English, Spanish, and French. In addition to standard print, versions in large print, Braille, and audiocassette are also available. Total time allotted for the tests is 7 1/2 hours.

The GED tests are not easy. About one-fourth of those who complete the exams every year do not pass. Passing scores are established by administering the tests to a sample of graduating high school seniors. The minimum standard score is set so that about one-third of graduating seniors would not pass the tests if they took them.

Because of the difficulty of the tests, people need to prepare themselves to take them. Often, they start by taking the Official GED Practice Tests, usually available through a local adult education center. Centers are listed in your phone book's blue pages under "Adult Education," "Continuing Education," or "GED." Adult education centers also have information about GED preparation classes and self-study materials. Classes are generally arranged to accommodate adults' work schedules. National Learning Corporation publishes several study guides that aim to thoroughly prepare test-takers for the GED.

School districts, colleges, adult education centers, and community organizations have information about GED testing schedules and practice tests. For more information, contact them, your nearest GED testing center, or:

GED Testing Service
One Dupont Circle, NW, Suite 250
Washington, DC 20036-1163
1(800) 62-MY GED (626-9433)
(202) 939-9490

Skills Demonstration

Adults who have acquired high school level skills through experience might be eligible for the National External Diploma Program. This alternative to the GED does not involve any direct instruction. Instead, adults seeking a high school diploma must demonstrate mastery of 65 competencies in 8 general areas: Communication; computation; occupational preparedness; and self, social, consumer, scientific, and technological awareness.

Mastery is shown through the completion of the tasks. For example, a participant could prove competency in computation by measuring a room for carpeting, figuring out the amount of carpet needed, and computing the cost.

Before being accepted for the program, adults undergo an evaluation. Tests taken at one of the program's offices measure reading, writing, and mathematics abilities. A take-home segment includes a self-assessment of current skills, an individual skill evaluation, and an occupational interest and aptitude test.

Adults accepted for the program have weekly meetings with an assessor. At the meeting, the assessor reviews the participant's work from the previous week. If the task has not been completed properly, the assessor explains the mistake. Participants continue to correct their errors until they master each competency. A high school diploma is awarded upon proven mastery of all 65 competencies.

Fourteen States and the District of Columbia now offer the External Diploma Program. For more information, contact:
External Diploma Program
One Dupont Circle, NW, Suite 250
Washington, DC 20036-1193
(202) 939-9475

Correspondence and Distance Study

Vin dropped out of high school during his junior year because his family's frequent moves made it difficult for him to continue his studies. He promised himself at the time he dropped out that he would someday finish the courses needed for his diploma. For people like Vin, who prefer to earn a traditional diploma in a nontraditional way, there are about a dozen accredited courses of study for earning a high school diploma by correspondence, or distance study. The programs are either privately run, affiliated with a university, or administered by a State education department.

Distance study diploma programs have no residency requirements, allowing students to continue their studies from almost any location. Depending on the course of study, students need not be enrolled full time and usually have more flexible schedules for finishing their work. Selection of courses ranges from vo-tech to college prep, and some programs place different emphasis on the types of diplomas offered. University affiliated schools, for example, allow qualified students to take college courses along with their high school ones. Students can then apply the college credits toward a degree at that university or transfer them to another institution.

Taking courses by distance study is often more challenging and time consuming than attending classes, especially for adults who have other obligations. Success depends on each student's motivation. Students usually do reading assignments on their own. Written exercises, which they complete and send to an instructor for grading, supplement their reading material.

A list of some accredited high schools that offer diplomas by distance study is available free from the Distance Education and Training Council, formerly known as the National Home Study Council. Request the "DETC Directory of Accredited Institutions" from:
The Distance Education and Training Council
1601 18th Street, NW.
Washington, DC 20009-2529
(202) 234-5100

Some publications profiling nontraditional college programs include addresses and descriptions of several high school correspondence ones. See the Resources section at the end of this article for more information.

Getting College Credit For What You Know

Adults can receive college credit for prior coursework, by passing examinations, and documenting experiential learning. With help from a college advisor, nontraditional students should assess their skills, establish their educational goals, and determine the number of college credits they might be eligible for.

Even before you meet with a college advisor, you should collect all your school and training records. Then, make a list of all knowledge and abilities acquired through experience, no matter how irrelevant they seem to your chosen field. Next, determine your educational goals: What specific field do you wish to study? What kind of a degree do you want? Finally, determine how your past work fits into the field of study. Later on, you will evaluate educational programs to find one that's right for you.

People who have complex educational or experiential learning histories might want to have their learning evaluated by the Regents Credit Bank. The Credit Bank, operated by Regents College of the University of the State of New York, allows people to consolidate credits earned through college, experience, or other methods. Special assessments are available for Regents College enrollees whose knowledge in a specific field cannot be adequately evaluated by standardized exams. For more information, contact the Regents Credit Bank at:

Regents College
7 Columbia Circle
Albany, NY 12203-5159
(518) 464-8500

Credit For Prior College Coursework

When Lynette was in college during the 1970s, she attended several different schools and took a variety of courses. She did well in some classes and poorly in others. Now that she is a successful business owner and has more focus, Lynette thinks she should forget about her previous coursework and start from scratch. Instead, she should start from where she is.

Lynette should have all her transcripts sent to the colleges or universities of her choice and let an admissions officer determine which classes are applicable toward a degree. A few credits here and there may not seem like much, but they add up. Even if the subjects do not seem relevant to any major, they might be counted as elective credits toward a degree. And comparing the cost of transcripts with the cost of college courses, it makes sense to spend a few dollars per transcript for a chance to save hundreds, and perhaps thousands, of dollars in books and tuition.

Rules for transferring credits apply to all prior coursework at accredited colleges and universities, whether done on campus or off. Courses completed off campus, often called extended learning, include those available to students through independent study and correspondence. Many schools have extended learning programs; Brigham Young University, for example, offers more than 300 courses through its Department of Independent Study. One type of extended learning is distance learning, a form of correspondence study by technological means such as television, video and audio, CD-ROM, electronic mail, and computer tutorials. See the Resources section at the end of this article for more information about publications available from the National University Continuing Education Association.

Any previously earned college credits should be considered for transfer, no matter what the subject or the grade received. Many schools do not accept the transfer of courses graded below a C or ones taken more than a designated number of years ago. Some colleges and universities also have limits on the number of credits that can be transferred and applied toward a degree. But not all do. For example, Thomas Edison State College, New Jersey's State college for adults, accepts the transfer of all 120 hours of credit required for a baccalaureate degree – provided all the credits are transferred from regionally accredited schools, no more than 80 are at the junior college level, and the student's grades overall and in the field of study average out to C.

To assign credit for prior coursework, most schools require original transcripts. This means you must complete a form or send a written, signed request to have your transcripts released directly to a college or university. Once you have chosen the schools you want to apply to, contact the schools you attended before. Find out how much each transcript costs, and ask them to send your transcripts to the ones you are applying to. Write a letter that includes your name (and names used during attendance, if different) and dates of attendance, along with the names and addresses of the schools to which your transcripts should be sent. Include payment and mail to the registrar at the schools you have attended. The registrar's office will process your request and send an official transcript of your coursework to the colleges or universities you have designated.

Credit For Noncollege Courses

Colleges and universities are not the only ones that offer classes. Volunteer organizations and employers often provide formal training worth college credit. The American Council on Education has two programs that assess thousands of specific courses and make recommendations on the amount of college credit they are worth. Colleges and universities accept the recommendations or use them as guidelines.

One program evaluates educational courses sponsored by government agencies, business and industry, labor unions, and professional and voluntary organizations. It is the Program on Noncollegiate Sponsored Instruction (PONSI). Some of the training seminars Alice has participated in covered topics such as food preparation, kitchen safety, and nutrition. Although she has not yet earned her GED, Alice can earn college credit because of her completion of these formal job-training seminars. The number of credits each seminar is worth does not hinge on Alice's current eligibility for college enrollment.

The other program evaluates courses offered by the Army, Navy, Air Force, Marines, Coast Guard, and Department of Defense. It is the Military Evaluations Program. Jorge has never attended college, but the engineering technology classes he completed as part of his military training are worth college credit. And as an Army veteran, Jorge is eligible for a service that takes the evaluations one step further. The Army/American Council on Education Registry Transcript System (AARTS) will provide Jorge with an individualized transcript of American Council on Education credit recommendations for all courses he completed, the military occupational specialties (MOS's) he held, and examinations he passed while in the Army. All Army and National Guard enlisted personnel and veterans who enlisted after October 1981 are eligible for the transcript. Similar services are being considered by the Navy and Marine Corps.

To obtain a free transcript, see your Army Education Center for a 5454R transcript request form. Include your name, Social Security number, basic active service date, and complete address where you want the transcript sent. Mail your request to:

AARTS Operations Center
415 McPherson Ave.
Fort Leavenworth, KS 66027-1373

Recommendations for PONSI are published in *The National Guide to Educational Credit for Training Programs;* military program recommendations are in *The Guide to the Evaluation of Educational Experiences in the Armed Forces.* See the Resources section at the end of this article for more information about these publications.

Former military personnel who took a foreign language course through the Defense Language Institute may request course transcripts by sending their name, Social Security number, course title, duration of the course, and graduation date to:

> Commandant, Defense Language Institute
> Attn: ATFL-DAA-AR
> Transcripts
> Presidio of Monterey
> Monterey, CA 93944-5006

Not all of Jorge's and Alice's courses have been assessed by the American Council on Education. Training courses that have no Council credit recommendation should still be assessed by an advisor at the schools they want to attend. Course descriptions, class notes, test scores, and other documentation may be helpful for comparing training courses to their college equivalents. An oral examination or other demonstration of competency might also be required.

There is no guarantee you will receive all the credits you are seeking – but you certainly won't if you make no attempt.

Credit By Examination

Standardized tests are the best-known method of receiving college credit without taking courses. These exams are often taken by high school students seeking advanced placement for college, but they are also available to adult learners. Testing programs and colleges and universities offer exams in a number of subjects. Two U.S. Government institutes have foreign language exams for employees that also may be worth college credit.

It is important to understand that receiving a passing score on these exams does not mean you get college credit automatically. Each school determines which test results it will accept, minimum scores required, how scores are converted for credit, and the amount of credit, if any, to be assigned. Most colleges and universities accept the American Council on Education credit recommendations, published every other year in the 250-page *Guide to Educational Credit by Examination*. For more information, contact:

> The American Council on Education
> Credit by Examination Program
> One Dupont Circle, Suite 250
> Washington, DC 20036-1193
> (202) 939-9434

Testing programs:

You might know some of the five national testing programs by their acronyms or initials: CLEP, ACT PEP: RCE, DANTES, AP, and NOCTI. (The meanings of these initialisms are explained below.) There is some overlap among programs; for example, four of them have introductory accounting exams. Since you will not be awarded credit more than once for a specific subject, you should carefully evaluate each program for the subject exams you wish to take. And before taking an exam, make sure you will be awarded credit by the college or university you plan to attend.

CLEP (College-Level Examination Program), administered by the College Board, is the most widely accepted of the national testing programs; more than 2,800 accredited schools award credit for passing exam scores. Each test covers material taught in basic undergraduate courses. There are five general exams – English composition, humanities, college mathematics, natural sciences, and social sciences and history – and many subject exams. Most exams are entirely multiple-choice, but English composition exams may include an essay section. For more information, contact:

    CLEP
    P.O. Box 6600
    Princeton, NJ 08541-6600
    (609) 771-7865

ACT PEP: RCE (American College Testing Proficiency Exam Program: Regents College Examinations) tests are given in 38 subjects within arts and sciences, business, education, and nursing. Each exam is recommended for either lower- or upper-level credit. Exams contain either objective or extended response questions, and are graded according to a standard score, letter grade, or pass/fail. Fees vary, depending on the subject and type of exam. For more information or to request free study guides, contact:

    ACT PEP: Regents College Examinations
    P.O. Box 4014
    Iowa City, IA 52243
    (319) 337-1387
    (New York State residents must contact Regents College directly.)

DANTES (Defense Activity for Nontraditional Education Support) standardized tests are developed by the Educational Testing Service for the Department of Defense. Originally administered only to military personnel, the exams have been available to the public since 1983. About 50 subject tests cover business, mathematics, social science, physical science, humanities, foreign languages, and applied technology. Most of the tests consist entirely of multiple-choice questions. Schools determine their own administering fees and testing schedules. For more information or to request free study sheets, contact:

    DANTES Program Office
    Mail Stop 31-X
    Educational Testing Service
    Princeton, NJ 08541
    1(800) 257-9484

The AP (Advanced Placement) Program is a cooperative effort between secondary schools and colleges and universities. AP exams are developed each year by committees of college and high school faculty appointed by the College Board and assisted by consultants from the Educational Testing Service. Subjects include arts and languages, natural sciences, computer science, social sciences, history, and mathematics. Most tests are 2 or 3 hours long and include both multiple-choice and essay questions. AP courses are available to help students prepare for exams, which are offered in the spring. For more information about the Advanced Placement Program, contact:

    Advanced Placement Services
    P.O. Box 6671
    Princeton, NJ 08541-6671
    (609) 771-7300

NOCTI (National Occupational Competency Testing Institute) assessments are designed for people like Alice, who have vocational-technical skills that cannot be evaluated by other tests. NOCTI assesses competency at two levels: Student/job ready and teacher/experienced worker. Standardized evaluations are available for occupations such as auto-body repair, electronics, mechanical drafting, quantity food preparation, and upholstering. The tests consist of multiple-choice questions and a performance component. Other services include workshops, customized assessments, and pre-testing. For more information, contact:

NOCTI
500 N. Bronson Ave.
Ferris State University
Big Rapids, MI 49307
(616) 796-4699

Colleges and universities:

Many colleges and universities have credit-by-exam programs, through which students earn credit by passing a comprehensive exam for a course offered by the institution. Among the most widely recognized are the programs at Ohio University, the University of North Carolina, Thomas Edison State College, and New York University.

Ohio University offers about 150 examinations for credit. In addition, you may sometimes arrange to take special examinations in non-laboratory courses offered at Ohio University. To take a test for credit, you must enroll in the course. If you plan to transfer the credit earned, you also need written permission from an official at your school. Books and study materials are available, for a cost, through the university. Exams must be taken within 6 months of the enrollment date; most last 3 hours. You may arrange to take the exam off campus if you do not live near the university.

Ohio University is on the quarter-hour system; most courses are worth 4 quarter hours, the equivalent of 3 semester hours. For more information, contact:

Independent Study
Tupper Hall 302
Ohio University
Athens, OH 45701-2979
1(800) 444-2910
(614) 593-2910

The University of North Carolina offers a credit-by-examination option for 140 independent study (correspondence) courses in foreign languages, humanities, social sciences, mathematics, business administration, education, electrical and computer engineering, health administration, and natural sciences. To take an exam, you must request and receive approval from both the course instructor and the independent studies department. Exams must be taken within six months of enrollment, and you may register for no more than two at a time. If you are not near the University's Chapel Hill campus, you may take your exam under supervision at an accredited college, university, community college, or technical institute. For more information, contact:

Independent Studies
CB #1020, The Friday Center
UNC-Chapel Hill
Chapel Hill, NC 27599-1020
1(800) 862-5669 / (919) 962-1134

The Thomas Edison College Examination Program offers more than 50 exams in liberal arts, business, and professional areas. Thomas Edison State College administers tests twice a month in Trenton, New Jersey; however, students may arrange to take their tests with a proctor at any accredited American college or university or U.S. military base. Most of the tests are multiple choice; some also include short answer or essay questions. Time limits range from 90 minutes to 4 hours, depending on the exam. For more information, contact:

Thomas Edison State College
TECEP, Office of Testing and Assessment
101 W. State Street
Trenton, NJ 08608-1176
(609) 633-2844

New York University's Foreign Language Program offers proficiency exams in more than 40 languages, from Albanian to Yiddish. Two exams are available in each language: The 12-point test is equivalent to 4 undergraduate semesters, and the 16-point exam may lead to upper level credit. The tests are given at the university's Foreign Language Department throughout the year.

Proof of foreign language proficiency does not guarantee college credit. Some colleges and universities accept transcripts only for languages commonly taught, such as French and Spanish. Nontraditional programs are more likely than traditional ones to grant credit for proficiency in other languages.

For an informational brochure and registration form for NYU's foreign language proficiency exams, contact:

New York University
Foreign Language Department
48 Cooper Square, Room 107
New York, NY 10003
(212) 998-7030

Government institutes:

The Defense Language Institute and Foreign Service Institute administer foreign language proficiency exams for personnel stationed abroad. Usually, the tests are given at the end of intensive language courses or upon completion of service overseas. But some people – like Jorge, who knows Spanish – speak another language fluently and may be allowed to take a proficiency exam in that language before completing their tour of duty. Contact one of the offices listed below to obtain transcripts of those scores. Proof of proficiency does not guarantee college credit, however, as discussed above.

To request score reports from the Defense Language Institute for Defense Language Proficiency Tests, send your name, Social Security number, language for which you were tested, and, most importantly, when and where you took the exam to:

Commandant, Defense Language Institute
Attn: ATFL-ES-T
DLPT Score Report Request
Presidio of Monterey
Monterey, CA 93944-5006

To request transcripts of scores for Foreign Service Institute exams, send your name, Social Security number, language for which you were tested, and dates or year of exams to:

Foreign Service Institute
Arlington Hall
4020 Arlington Boulevard
Rosslyn, VA 22204-1500
Attn: Testing Office (Send your request to the attention of the testing office of the foreign language in which you were tested)

Credit For Experience

Experiential learning credit may be given for knowledge gained through job responsibilities, personal hobbies, volunteer opportunities, homemaking, and other experiences. Colleges and universities base credit awards on the knowledge you have attained, not for the experience alone. In addition, the knowledge must be college level; not just any learning will do. Throwing horseshoes as a hobby is not likely to be worth college credit. But if you've done research on how and where the sport originated, visited blacksmiths, organized tournaments, and written a column for a trade journal — well, that's a horseshoe of a different color.

Adults attempting to get credit for their experience should be forewarned: Having your experience evaluated for college credit is time-consuming, tedious work — not an easy shortcut for people who want quick-fix college credits. And not all experience, no matter how valuable, is the equivalent of college courses.

Requesting college credit for your experiential learning can be tricky. You should get assistance from a credit evaluations officer at the school you plan to attend, but you should also have a general idea of what your knowledge is worth. A common method for converting knowledge into credit is to use a college catalog. Find course titles and descriptions that match what you have learned through experience, and request the number of credits offered for those courses.

Once you know what credit to ask for, you must usually present your case in writing to officials at the college you plan to attend. The most common form of presenting experiential learning for credit is the portfolio. A portfolio is a written record of your knowledge along with a request for equivalent college credit. It includes an identification and description of the knowledge for which you are requesting credit, an explanatory essay of how the knowledge was gained and how it fits into your educational plans, documentation that you have acquired such knowledge, and a request for college credit. Required elements of a portfolio vary by schools but generally follow those guidelines.

In identifying knowledge you have gained, be specific about exactly what you have learned. For example, it is not enough for Lynette to say she runs a business. She must identify the knowledge she has gained from running it, such as personnel management, tax law, marketing strategy, and inventory review. She must also include brief descriptions about her knowledge of each to support her claims of having those skills.

The essay gives you a chance to relay something about who you are. It should address your educational goals, include relevant autobiographical details, and be well organized, neat, and convey confidence. In his essay, Jorge might first state his goal of becoming an engineer. Then he would explain why he joined the Army, where he got hands-on training and experience in developing and servicing electronic equipment.

This, he would say, led to his hobby of creating remote-controlled model cars, of which he has built 20. His conclusion would highlight his accomplishments and tie them to his desire to become an electronic engineer.

Documentation is evidence that you've learned what you claim to have learned. You can show proof of knowledge in a variety of ways, including audio or video recordings, letters from current or former employers describing your specific duties and job performance, blueprints, photographs or artwork, and transcripts of certifying exams for professional licenses and certification – such as Alice's certification from the American Culinary Federation. Although documentation can take many forms, written proof alone is not always enough. If it is impossible to document your knowledge in writing, find out if your experiential learning can be assessed through supplemental oral exams by a faculty expert.

Earning a College Degree

Nontraditional students often have work, family, and financial obligations that prevent them from quitting their jobs to attend school full time. Can they still meet their educational goals? Yes.

More than 150 accredited colleges and universities have nontraditional bachelor's degree programs that require students to spend little or no time on campus; over 300 others have nontraditional campus-based degree programs. Some of those schools, as well as most junior and community colleges, offer associate's degrees nontraditionally. Each school with a nontraditional course of study determines its own rules for awarding credit for prior coursework, exams, or experience, as discussed previously. Most have charges on top of tuition for providing these special services.

Several publications profile nontraditional degree programs; see the Resources section at the end of this article for more information. To determine which school best fits your academic profile and educational goals, first list your criteria. Then, evaluate nontraditional programs based on their accreditation, features, residency requirements, and expenses. Once you have chosen several schools to explore further, write to them for more information. Detailed explanations of school policies should help you decide which ones you want to apply to.

Get beyond the printed word – especially the glowing words each school writes about itself. Check out the schools you are considering with higher education authorities, alumni, employers, family members, and friends. If possible, visit the campus to talk to students and instructors and sit in on a few classes, even if you will be completing most or all of your work off campus. Ask school officials questions about such things as enrollment numbers, graduation rate, faculty qualifications, and confusing details about the application process or academic policies. After you have thoroughly investigated each prospective college or university, you can make an informed decision about which is right for you.

Accreditation

Accreditation is a process colleges and universities submit to voluntarily for getting their credentials. An accredited school has been investigated and visited by teams of observers and has periodic inspections by a private accrediting agency. The initial review can take two years or more.

Regional agencies accredit entire schools, and professional agencies accredit either specialized schools or departments within schools. Although there are no national accrediting standards, not just any accreditation will do. Countless "accreditation associations" have been invented by schools, many of which have no academic programs and sell phony degrees, to accredit themselves. But 6 regional and about 80 professional accrediting associations in the United States are recognized by the U.S. Department of Education or the Commission on Recognition of Postsecondary Accreditation. When checking accreditation, these are the names to look for. For more information about accreditation and accrediting agencies, contact:

    Institutional Participation Oversight Service Accreditation and State Liaison Division
    U.S. Department of Education
    ROB 3, Room 3915
    600 Independence Ave., SW
    Washington, DC 20202-5244
    (202) 708-7417

Because accreditation is not mandatory, lack of accreditation does not necessarily mean a school or program is bad. Some schools choose not to apply for accreditation, are in the process of applying, or have educational methods too unconventional for an accrediting association's standards. For the nontraditional student, however, earning a degree from a college or university with recognized accreditation is an especially important consideration. Although nontraditional education is becoming more widely accepted, it is not yet mainstream. Employers skeptical of a degree earned in a nontraditional manner are likely to be even less accepting of one from an unaccredited school.

Program Features

Because nontraditional students have diverse educational objectives, nontraditional schools are diverse in what they offer. Some programs are geared toward helping students organize their scattered educational credits to get a degree as quickly as possible. Others cater to those who may have specific credits or experience but need assistance in completing requirements. Whatever your educational profile, you should look for a program that works with you in obtaining your educational goals.

A few nontraditional programs have special admissions policies for adult learners like Alice, who plan to earn their GEDs but want to enroll in college in the meantime. Other features of nontraditional programs include individualized learning agreements, intensive academic counseling, cooperative learning and internship placement, and waiver of some prerequisites or other requirements – as well as college credit for prior coursework, examinations, and experiential learning, all discussed previously.

Lynette, whose primary goal is to finish her degree, wants to earn maximum credits for her business experience. She will look for programs that do not limit the number of credits awarded for equivalency exams and experiential learning. And since well-documented proof of knowledge is essential for earning experiential learning credits, Lynette should make sure the program she chooses provides assistance to students submitting a portfolio.

Jorge, on the other hand, has more credits than he needs in certain areas and is willing to forego some. To become an engineer, he must have a bachelor's degree; but because he is accustomed to hands-on learning, Jorge is interested in getting experience as he gains more technical skills. He will concentrate on finding schools with strong cooperative education, supervised fieldwork, or internship programs.

Residency Requirements

Programs are sometimes deemed nontraditional because of their residency requirements. Many people think of residency for colleges and universities in terms of tuition, with in-state students paying less than out-of-state ones. Residency also may refer to where a student lives, either on or off campus, while attending school.

But in nontraditional education, residency usually refers to how much time students must spend on campus, regardless of whether they attend classes there. In some nontraditional programs, students need not ever step foot on campus. Others require only a very short residency, such as one day or a few weeks. Many schools have standard residency requirements of several semesters but schedule classes for evenings or weekends to accommodate working adults.

Lynette, who previously took courses by independent study, prefers to earn credits by distance study. She will focus on schools that have no residency requirement. Several colleges and universities have nonresident degree completion programs for adults with some college credit. Under the direction of a faculty advisor, students devise a plan for earning their remaining credits. Methods for earning credits include independent study, distance learning, seminars, supervised fieldwork, and group study at arranged sites. Students may have to earn a certain number of credits through the degree-granting institution. But many programs allow students to take courses at accredited schools of their choice for transfer toward their degree.

Alice wants to attend lectures but has an unpredictable schedule. Her best course of action will be to seek out short residency programs that require students to attend seminars once or twice a semester. She can take courses that are televised and videotape them to watch when her schedule permits, with the seminars helping to ensure that she properly completes her coursework. Many colleges and universities with short residency requirements also permit students to earn some credits elsewhere, by whatever means the student chooses.

Some fields of study require classroom instruction. As Jorge will discover, few colleges and universities allow students to earn a bachelor's degree in engineering entirely through independent study. Nontraditional residency programs are designed to accommodate adults' daytime work schedules. Jorge should look for programs offering evening, weekend, summer, and accelerated courses.

Tuition and Other Expenses

The final decisions about which schools Alice, Jorge, and Lynette attend may hinge in large part on a single issue: Cost. And rising tuition is only part of the equation. Beginning with application fees and continuing through graduation fees, college expenses add up.

Traditional and nontraditional students have some expenses in common, such as the cost of books and other materials. Tuition might even be the same for some courses, especially for colleges and universities offering standard ones at unusual times. But for nontraditional programs, students may also pay fees for services such as credit or transcript review, evaluation, advisement, and portfolio assessment.

Students are also responsible for postage and handling or setup expenses for independent study courses, as well as for all examination and transcript fees for transferring credits. Usually, the more nontraditional the program, the more detailed the fees. Some schools charge a yearly enrollment fee rather than tuition for degree completion candidates who want their files to remain active.

Although tuition and fees might seem expensive, most educators tell you not to let money come between you and your educational goals. Talk to someone in the financial aid department of the school you plan to attend or check your library for publications about financial aid sources. The U.S. Department of Education publishes a guide to Federal aid programs such as Pell Grants, student loans, and work-study. To order the free 74-page booklet, *The Student Guide: Financial Aid from the U.S. Department of Education,* contact:

Federal Student Aid Information Center
P.O. Box 84
Washington, DC 20044
1 (800) 4FED-AID (433-3243)

Resources

Information on how to earn a high school diploma or college degree without following the usual routes is available from several organizations and in numerous publications. Information on nontraditional graduate degree programs, available for master's through doctoral level, though not discussed in this article, can usually be obtained from the same resources that detail bachelor's degree programs.

National Learning Corporation publishes study guides for all of these exams, for both general examinations and tests in specific subject areas. To order study guides, or to browse their catalog featuring more than 5,000 titles, visit NLC online at www.passbooks.com, or contact them by phone at (800) 632-8888.

Organizations

Adult learners should always contact their local school system, community college, or university to learn about programs that are readily available. The following national organizations can also supply information:

American Council on Education
One Dupont Circle
Washington, DC 20036-1193
(202) 939-9300

Within the American Council on Education, the Center for Adult Learning and Educational Credentials administers the National External Diploma Program, the GED Program, the Program on Noncollegiate Sponsored Instruction, the Credit by Examination Program, and the Military Evaluations Program.

DANTES Subject Standardized Tests

INTRODUCTION

The DANTES (Defense Activity for Non-Traditional Education Support) subject standardized tests are comprehensive college and graduate level examinations given by the Armed Forces, colleges and graduate schools as end-of-subject course evaluation final examinations or to obtain college equivalency credits in the various subject areas tested.

The DANTES Examination Program enables students to obtain college credit for what they have learned on the job, through self-study, personal interest, correspondence courses or by any other means. It is used by colleges and universities to award college credit to students who demonstrate that they know as much as students completing an equivalent college course. It is a cost-efficient, time-saving way for students to use their knowledge to accomplish their educational goals.

Most schools accept the American Council on Education (ACE) recommendations for the minimum score required and the amount of credit awarded, but not all schools do. Be sure to check the policy regarding the score level required for credit and the number of credits to be awarded.

Not all tests are accepted by all institutions. Even when a test is accepted by an institution, it may not be acceptable for every program at that institution. Before considering testing, ascertain the acceptability of a specific test for a particular course.

Colleges and universities that administer DANTES tests may administer them to any applicant – or they may administer the tests only to students registered at their institution. Decisions about who will be allowed to test are made by the school. Students should contact the test center to determine current policies and schedules for DANTES testing.

Colleges and universities authorized to administer DANTES tests usually do so throughout the calendar year. Each school sets its own fee for test administration and establishes its own testing schedule. Contact the representative at the administering school directly to make arrangements for testing.

Checklist
For Students

✓ Visit **www.getcollegecredit.com** to obtain a list of tests, fact sheets, test preparation materials, participating colleges and universities, and much more.

✓ Contact your school advisor to confirm that the DSST you selected will fit into your curriculum.

✓ Consult the ***DSST Candidate Information Bulletin*** for answers to specific questions.

✓ Contact the test site to schedule your test.

✓ Prepare for your examination by using the fact sheet as a guide.

✓ Take the test.

If you would like a score report sent to your college or university, it is a good idea to bring the four-digit code with you. You must write the DSST Test Center Code for that institution on your answer sheet at the time of testing. DSST Test Center Codes are noted in the DSST Participating Colleges and Universities listing on the Web site.

If you prefer to send a score report to an institution at a later date, there is a transcript fee of $20 for each transcript ordered.

Thomson Prometric
DSST Program
2000 Lenox Drive, Third Floor
Lawrenceville, NJ 08648

Toll-free: 877-471-9860
609-895-5011

E-mail: pnj-dsst@thomson.com

MAKING A COLLEGE DEGREE WITHIN YOUR REACH

Today, there are many educational alternatives to the classroom—you can learn from your job, your reading, your independent study, and special interests you pursue. You may already have learned the subject matter covered by some college-level courses.

The DSST Program is a nationally recognized testing program that gives you the opportunity to receive college credit for learning acquired outside the traditional college classroom. Colleges and universities throughout the United States administer the program, developed by Thomson Prometric, year-round. Annually, over 90,000 DSSTs are administered to individuals who are interested in continuing their education. Take advantage of the DSST testing program; it speeds the educational process and provides the flexibility adults need, making earning a degree more feasible.

Since requirements differ from college to college, please check with the credit-awarding institution before taking a DSST. More than 1,800 colleges and universities currently award credit for DSSTs, and the number is growing every day. You can choose from 37 test titles in the areas of Social Science, Business, Mathematics, Applied Technology, Humanities, and Physical Science. A brief description of each examination is found on the pages that follow.

Reach Your Career Goals Through DSSTs

Use DSSTs to help you earn your degree, get a promotion, or simply demonstrate that you have college-level knowledge in subjects relevant to your work.

Save Time...

You don't have to sit through classes when you have previously acquired the knowledge or experience for most of what is being taught and can learn the rest yourself. You might be able to bypass introductory-level courses in subject areas you already know.

Save Money...

DSSTs save you money because the classes you bypass by earning credit through the DSST Program are classes you won't have to pay for on your way to earning your degree. You can use the money instead to take more advanced courses that can be more challenging and rewarding.

Improve Your Chances for Admission to College

Each college has its own admission policies; however, having passing scores for DSSTs on your transcript can provide strong evidence of how well you can perform at the college level.

Gain Confidence Performing at a College Level

Many adults returning to college find that lack of confidence is often the greatest hurdle to overcome. Passing a DSST demonstrates your ability to perform on a college level.

Make Up for Courses You May Have Missed

You may be ready to graduate from college and find that you are a few credits short of earning your degree. By using semester breaks, vacation time, or leisure time to study independently, you can prepare to take one or more DSSTs, fulfill your academic requirements, and graduate on time.

If You Cannot Attend Regularly Scheduled Classes...

If your lifestyle or responsibilities prevent you from attending regularly scheduled classes, you can earn your college degree from a college offering an external degree program. The DSST Program allows you to earn your degree by study and experience outside the traditional classroom.

Many colleges and universities offer external degree or distance learning programs. For additional information, contact the college you plan to attend or:

Center for Lifelong Learning
American Council on Education
One DuPont Circle NW, Suite 250
Washington, DC 20036
202-939-9475
www.acenet.edu
(Select "Center for Lifelong Learning" under "Programs & Services"
for more information)

Fact Sheets

For each test, there is a Fact Sheet that outlines the topics covered by each test and includes a list of sample questions, a list of recommended references of books that would be useful for review, and the number of credits awarded for a passing score as recommended by the American Council on Education (ACE). *Please note that some schools require scores that are higher than the minimum ACE-recommended passing score.* It is suggested that you check with your college or university to determine what score they require in order to earn credit. You can obtain Fact Sheets by:
- Downloading them from www.getcollegecredit.com
- E-mailing a request to pnj-dsst@thomson.com
- Completing a Candidate Publications Order Form

DSST Online Practice Tests

DSST online practice tests contain items that reflect a *partial range of difficulty* identified in the Content Outline section on each Fact Sheet. There is an online DSST Practice Test in the following categories:
- Mathematics
- Social Science
- Business
- Physical Science
- Applied Technology
- Humanities

Although the online DSST Practice Test questions do not indicate the full range of difficulty you would find in an actual DSST test, they will help you assess your knowledge level. Each online DSST Practice Test can be purchased by visiting www.getcollegecredit.com and clicking on DSST Practice Exams.

TAKING DSST EXAMINATIONS

Earning College Credit for DSST Examinations

To find out if the college of your choice awards credit for passing DSST scores, contact the admissions office or counseling and testing office. The college can also provide information on the scores required for awarding credit, the number of credit hours awarded, and any courses that can be bypassed with satisfactory scores.

It is important that you contact the institution of your choice as early as possible since credit-awarding policies differ among colleges and universities.

Where to Take DSSTs

DSSTs are administered at colleges and universities nationwide. Each location determines the frequency and scheduling of test administrations. To obtain the most current list of participating DSST colleges and universities:
- Visit and download the information from www.getcollegecredit.com
- E-mail pnj-dsst@thomson.com

Scheduling Your Examination

Please be aware that some colleges and universities provide DSST testing services to enrolled students only. After you have selected a college or university that administers DSSTs, you will need to contact them to schedule your test date.

The fee to take a DSST is $60 per test. This fee entitles you to two score reports after the test is scored. One will be sent directly to you and the other will be sent to the college or university that you designate on your answer sheet. You may pay the test fee with a certified check or U.S. money order made payable to Thomson Prometric or you may charge the test fee to your Visa, MasterCard or American Express credit card. Note: The credit card statement will reflect a charge from Thomson Prometric for all DSST examinations. *(Declined credit card charges will be assessed an additional $25 processing fee.)*

In addition, the test site may also require a test administration fee for each examination, to be paid directly to the institution. Contact the test site to determine its administration fee and payment policy.

Other Testing Arrangements

If you are unable to find a participating DSST college or university in your area, you may want to contact the testing office of a local accredited college or university to determine whether a representative from that office will agree to administer the test(s) for you.

The school's representative should then contact the DSST Program at 866-794-3497 to arrange for this administration. If you are unable to locate a test site, contact Thomson Prometric for assistance at pnj-dsst@thomson.com or 866-794-3497.

Testing Accommodations for Students with Disabilities

Thomson Prometric is committed to serving test takers with disabilities by providing services and reasonable testing accommodations as set forth in the provisions of the *Americans with Disabilities Act* (ADA). If you have a disability, as prescribed by the ADA, and require special testing services or arrangements, please contact the test administrator at the test site. You will be asked to submit to the test administrator documentation of your disability and your request for special accommodations. The test administrator will then forward your documentation along with your request for testing accommodations to Thomson Prometric for approval.

Please submit your request as far in advance of your test date as possible so that the necessary accommodations can be made. Only test takers with documented disabilities are eligible for special accommodations.

On the Day of the Examination

It is important to review this information and to have the correct identification present on the day of the examination:
- Arrive on time as a courtesy to the test administrator.
- Bring a valid form of government-issued identification that includes a current photo and your signature (acceptable documents include a driver's license, passport, state-issued identification card or military identification). *Anyone who fails to present valid identification will not be allowed to test.*
- Bring several No. 2 (soft-lead) sharpened pencils with good erasers, a watch, and a black pen if you will be writing an essay.
- Do not bring books or papers.
- Do not bring an alarm watch that beeps, a telephone, or a phone beeper into the testing room.
- The use of nonprogrammable calculators, slide rules, scratch paper and/or other materials is permitted for some of the tests.

DSST SCORING POLICIES

Your DSST examination scores are reported only to you, unless you request that they be sent elsewhere. If you want your scores sent to your college, you must provide the correct DSST code number of the school on your answer sheet at the time you take the test. See the *DSST Directory of Colleges and Universities* on the Web site www.getcollegecredit.com.

If your institution is not listed, contact Thomson Prometric at 866-794-3497 to establish a code number. (Some schools may require a student to be enrolled prior to receiving a score report.)

Receiving Your Score Report

Allow approximately four weeks after testing to receive your score report.

Calling DSST Customer Service before the required four-week score processing time has elapsed will not expedite the processing of your scores. Due to privacy and security requirements, scores will not be reported to students over the telephone under any circumstance.

Scoring of Principles of Public Speaking Speeches

The speech portion of the *Principles of Public Speaking* examination will be sent to speech raters who are faculty members at accredited colleges that currently teach or have previously taught the course. Scores for the *Principles of Public Speaking* examination are available six to eight weeks from receipt by Thomson Prometric. If you take the *Principles of Public Speaking* examination and fail (either the objective, speech portion, or both), you must follow the retesting policy waiting period of six months (180 days) before retaking the entire exam.

Essays

The essays for *Ethics in America* and *Technical Writing* are <u>optional</u> and thus are not scored by raters. The essays are forwarded to the college or university that you designate, along with your score report, for their use in determining the award of credit. <u>Before taking the *Ethics in America* or *Technical Writing* examinations, check with your college or university to determine whether the essay is required.</u>

NOTE: *Principles of Public Speaking* speech topic cassette tapes and essays are kept on file at Thomson Prometric for one year from the date of administration.

How to Get Transcripts

There is a $20 fee for each transcript you request. Payment must be in the form of a certified check, U.S. money order payable to Thomson Prometric, or credit card. Personal checks and debit cards are NOT an acceptable method of payment. One transcript may include scores for one or more examinations taken. To request a transcript, download the Transcript Order Form from www.getcollegecredit.com.

DESCRIPTION OF THE DSST EXAMINATIONS

Mathematics

- **Fundamentals of College Algebra** covers mathematical concepts such as fundamental algebraic operations; linear, absolute value; quadratic equations, inequalities, radials, exponents and logarithms, factoring polynomials and graphing. The use of a nonprogrammable, handheld calculator is permitted.

- **Principles of Statistics** tests the understanding of the various topics of statistics, both qualitatively and quantitatively, and the ability to apply statistical methods to solve a variety of problems. The topics included in this test are descriptive statistics; correlation and regression; probability; chance models and sampling and tests of significance. The use of a nonprogrammable, handheld calculator is permitted.

Social Science

- **Art of the Western World** deals with the history of art during the following periods: classical; Romanesque and Gothic; early Renaissance; high Renaissance, Baroque; rococo; neoclassicism and romanticism; realism, impressionism and post-impressionism; early twentieth century; and post-World War II.

- **Western Europe Since 1945** tests the knowledge of basic facts and terms and the understanding of concepts and principles related to the areas of the historical background of the aftermath of the Second World War and rebuilding of Europe; national political systems; issues and policies in Western European societies; European institutions and processes; and Europe's relations with the rest of the world.

- **An Introduction to the Modern Middle East** emphasizes core knowledge (including geography, Judaism, Christianity, Islam, ethnicity); nineteenth-century European impact; twentieth-century Western influences; World Wars I and II; new nations; social and cultural changes (1900-1960) and the Middle East from 1960 to present.

- **Human/Cultural Geography** includes the Earth and basic facts (coordinate systems, maps, physiography, atmosphere, soils and vegetation, water); culture and environment, spatial processes (social processes, modern economic systems, settlement patterns, political geography); and regional geography.

- **Rise and Fall of the Soviet Union** covers Russia under the Old Regime; the Revolutionary Period; New Economic Policy; Pre-war Stalinism; The Second World War; Post-war Stalinism; The Khrushchev Years; The Brezhnev Era; and reform and collapse.

- **A History of the Vietnam War** covers the history of the roots of the Vietnam War; the First Vietnam War (1946-1954); pre-war developments (1954-1963); American involvement in the Vietnam War; Tet (1968); Vietnamizing the War (1968-1973); Cambodia and Laos; peace; legacies and lessons.

- **The Civil War and Reconstruction** covers the Civil War from presecession (1861) through Reconstruction. It includes causes of the war; secession; Fort Sumter; the war in the east and in the west; major battles; the political situation; assassination of Lincoln; end of the Confederacy; and Reconstruction.

- **Foundations of Education** includes topics such as contemporary issues in education; past and current influences on education (philosophies, democratic ideals, social/economic influences); and the interrelationships between contemporary issues and influences.

- **Life-span Developmental Psychology** covers models and theories; methods of study; ethical issues; biological development; perception, learning and memory; cognition and language; social, emotional, and personality development; social behaviors, family life cycle, extrafamilial settings; singlehood and cohabitation; occupational development and retirement; adjustment to life stresses; and bereavement and loss.

- **Drug and Alcohol Abuse** includes such topics as drug use in society; classification of drugs; pharmacological principles; alcohol (types, effects of, alcoholism); general principles and use of sedative hypnotics, narcotic analgesics, stimulants, and hallucinogens; other drugs (inhalants, steroids); and prevention/treatment.

- **General Anthropology** deals with anthropology as a discipline; theoretical perspectives; physical anthropology; archaeology; social organization; economic organization; political organization; religion; and modernization and application of anthropology.

- **Introduction to Law Enforcement** includes topics such as history and professional movement of law enforcement; overview of the U.S. criminal justice system; police systems in the U.S.; police organization, management, and issues; and U.S. law and precedents.

- **Criminal Justice** deals with criminal behavior (crime in the U.S., theories of crime, types of crime); the criminal justice system (historical origins, legal foundations, due process); police; the court system (history and organization, adult court system, juvenile court, pre-trial and post-trial processes); and corrections.

- **Fundamentals of Counseling** covers historical development (significant influences and people); counselor roles and functions; the counseling relationship; and theoretical approaches to counseling.

Business
- **Principles of Finance** deals with financial statements and planning; time value of money; working capital management; valuation and characteristics; capital budgeting; cost of capital; risk and return; and international financial management. The use of a nonprogrammable, handheld calculator is permitted.

- **Principles of Financial Accounting** includes topics such as general concepts and principles, accounting cycle and classification; transaction analysis; accruals and deferrals; cash and internal control; current accounts; long- and short-term liabilities; capital stock; and financial statements. The use of a nonprogrammable, handheld calculator is permitted.

- **Human Resource Management** covers general employment issues; job analysis; training and development; performance appraisals; compensation issues; security issues; personnel legislation and regulation; labor relations and current issues; an overview of the Human Resource Management Field; Human Resource Planning; Staffing; training and development; compensation issues; safety and health; employee rights and discipline; employment law; labor relations and current issues and trends.

- **Organizational Behavior** deals with the study of organizational behavior (scientific approaches, research designs, data collection methods); individual processes and characteristics; interpersonal and group processes and characteristics; organizational processes and characteristics; and change and development processes.

- **Principles of Supervision** deals with the roles and responsibilities of the supervisor; management functions (planning, organization and staffing, directing at the supervisory level); and other topics (legal issues, stress management, union environments, quality concerns).

- **Business Law II** covers topics such as sales of goods; debtor and creditor relations; business organizations; property; and commercial paper.

- **Introduction to Computing** includes topics such as history and technological generations; hardware/software; applications to information technology; program development; data management; communications and connectivity; and computing and society. The use of a nonprogrammable, handheld calculator is permitted.

- **Management Information Systems** covers systems theory, analysis and design of systems, hardware and software; database management; telecommunications; management of the MIS functional area and informational support.

- **Introduction to Business** deals with economic issues affecting business; international business; government and business; forms of business ownership; small business, entrepreneurship and franchise; management process; human resource management; production and operations; marketing management; financial management; risk management and insurance; and management and information systems.

- **Money and Banking** covers the role and kinds of money; commercial banks and other financial intermediaries; central banking and the Federal Reserve system; money and macroeconomics activity; monetary policy in the U.S.; and the international monetary system.

- **Personal Finance** includes topics such as financial goals and values; budgeting; credit and debt; major purchases; taxes; insurance; investments; and retirement and estate planning. The use of auxiliary materials, such as calculators and slide rules, is NOT permitted.

- **Business Mathematics** deals with basic operations with integers, fractions, and decimals; round numbers; ratios; averages; business graphs; simple interest; compound interest and annuities; net pay and deductions; discounts and markups; depreciation and net worth; corporate securities; distribution of ownership; and stock and asset turnover.

Physical Science
• **Astronomy** covers the history of astronomy, celestial mechanics; celestial systems; astronomical instruments; the solar system; nature and evolution; the galaxy; the universe; determining astronomical distances; and life in the universe.

• **Here's to Your Health** covers mental health and behavior; human development and relationships; substance abuse; fitness and nutrition; risk factors, disease, and disease prevention; and safety, consumer awareness, and environmental concerns.

• **Environment and Humanity** deals with topics such as ecological concepts (ecosystems, global ecology, food chains and webs); environmental impacts; environmental management and conservation; and political processes and the future.

• **Principles of Physical Science I** includes physics: Newton's Laws of Motion; energy and momentum; thermodynamics; wave and optics; electricity and magnetism; chemistry: properties of matter; atomic theory and structure; and chemical reactions.

• **Physical Geology** covers Earth materials; igneous, sedimentary, and metamorphic rocks; surface processes (weathering, groundwater, glaciers, oceanic systems, deserts and winds, hydrologic cycle); internal Earth processes; and applications (mineral and energy resources, environmental geology).

Applied Technology
• **Technical Writing** covers topics such as theory and practice of technical writing; purpose, content, and organizational patterns of common types of technical documents; elements of various technical reports; and technical editing. Students have the option to write a short essay on one of the technical topics provided. Thomson Prometric will not score the essay; however, for determining the award of credit, a copy of the essay will be forwarded to the college or university you've designated along with the score report or transcript.

Humanities
• **Ethics in America** deals with ethical traditions (Greek views, Biblical traditions, moral law, consequential ethics, feminist ethics); ethical analysis of issues arising in interpersonal and personal-societal relationships and in professional and occupational roles; and relationships between ethical traditions and the ethical analysis of situations. Students have the option to write an essay to analyze a morally problematic situation in terms of issues relevant to a decision and arguments for alternative positions. Thomson Prometric will not score the essay; however, for determining the award of credit, a copy of the essay will be forwarded to the college or university you've designated along with the score report or transcript.

• **Introduction to World Religions** covers topics such as dimensions and approaches to religion; primal religions; Hinduism; Buddhism; Confucianism; Taoism; Judaism; Christianity; and Islam.

• **Principles of Public Speaking** consists of two parts: Part One consists of multiple-choice questions covering considerations of Principles of Public Speaking; audience analysis; purposes of speeches; structure/organization; content/supporting materials; research; language and style; delivery; communication apprehension; listening and feedback; and criticism and evaluation. Part Two requires the student to record an impromptu persuasive speech that will be scored.

FREQUENTLY ASKED QUESTIONS ABOUT DSSTs

In order to pass the test, must I study from one of the recommended references?

The recommended references are a listing of books that were being used as textbooks in college courses of the same or similar title at the time the test was developed. Appropriate textbooks for study are not limited to those listed in the fact sheet. If you wish to obtain study resources to prepare for the examination, you may reference either the current edition of the listed titles or textbooks currently used at a local college or university for the same class title. It is recommended that you reference more than one textbook on the topics outlined in the fact sheet. You should begin by checking textbook content against the content outline included on the front page of the DSST fact sheet before selecting textbooks that cover the text content from which to study. Textbooks may be found at the campus bookstore of a local college or university offering a course on the subject.

Is there a penalty for guessing on the tests?

There is no penalty for guessing on DSSTs, so you should mark an answer for each question.

How much time will I have to complete the test?

Many DSSTs can be completed within 90 minutes; however, additional time can be allowed if necessary.

What should I do if I find a test question irregularity?

Continue testing and then report the irregularity to the test administrator after the test. This may be done by asking that the test administrator note the irregularity on the Supervisor's Irregularity Report or you can write to Thomson Prometric, DSST Program, 2000 Lenox Drive, Third Floor, Lawrenceville, NJ 08648, and indicate the form and question number(s) or circumstances as well as your name and address.

When will I receive my score report?

Allow approximately four weeks from the date of testing to receive your score report. Allow six to eight weeks to receive a score report for the *Principles of Public Speaking* examination.

Will my test scores be released without my permission?

Your test score will not be released to anyone other than the school you designate on your answer sheet unless you write to us and ask us to send a transcript elsewhere. Instructions about how to do this can be found on your score report. Your scores may be used for research purposes, but individual scores are never made public nor are individuals identified if research findings are made public.

If I do not achieve a passing score on the test, how long must I wait until I can take the test again?

If you do not receive a score on the test that will enable you to obtain credit for the course, you may take the test again after six months (180 days). Please do not attempt to take the test before six months (180 days) have passed because you will receive a score report marked <u>invalid</u> and your test fee will not be refunded.

Can my test scores be canceled?

The test administrator is required to report any irregularities to Thomson Prometric. <u>The consequence of bringing unauthorized materials into the testing room, or giving or receiving help, will be the forfeiture of your test fee and the invalidation of test scores.</u> The DSST Program reserves the right to cancel scores and not issue score reports in such situations.

What can I do if I feel that my test scores were not accurately reported?

Thomson Prometric recognizes the extreme importance of test results to candidates and has a multi-step quality-control procedure to help ensure that reported scores are accurate. If you have reason to believe that your score(s) were not accurately reported, you may request to have your answer sheet reviewed and hand scored.

The fees for this service are:
- $20 fee if requested within six months of the test date
- $30 fee if requested more than six months from the test date
- $30 fee if a re-evaluation of the *Principles of Public Speaking* speech is requested

The fee for this service can be paid by credit card or by certified check or U.S. money order payable to Thomson Prometric. Submit your request for score verification along with the appropriate fee or credit card information (credit card number and expiration date) to Thomson Prometric, DSST Program, 2000 Lenox Drive, Third Floor, Lawrenceville, NJ 08648. Include your full name, the test title, the date you took the test, and your Social Security number. Candidates will be notified if a scoring discrepancy is discovered within four weeks of receipt of the request.

What does ACE recommendation mean?

The ACE recommendation is the minimum passing score recommended by the American Council on Education for any given test. It is equivalent to the average score of students in the DSST norming sample who received a grade of C for the course. Some schools require a score higher than the ACE recommendation.

Who is NLC?

National Learning Corporation (NLC) has been successfully preparing candidates for 40 years for over 5,000 exams. NLC publishes Passbook® study guides to help candidates prepare for all DANTES and CLEP exams and almost every other type of exam from high school through adult career.

Go to our website — www.passbooks.com — or call (800) 632-8888 for information about ordering our Passbooks.

To get detailed information on the DSST program and DSST preparation materials, visit www.getcollegecredit.com.

If you are interested in taking the DSST exams, call 877-471-9860 or e-mail pnj-dsst@thomson.com.

HEALTH AND HUMAN DEVELOPMENT

EXAM INFORMATION

This Health and Human Development exam (formerly known as Here's to Your Health) was developed to enable schools to award credit to students for knowledge equivalent to that learned by students taking the course. This exam covers human development and relationships; fitness and nutrition, disease and prevention; consumer awareness; psychological disorders and addictive behaviors; intentional injuries; and violence. The exam contains 100 questions to be answered in 2 hours.

CREDIT RECOMMENDATIONS

The American Council on Education's College Credit Recommendation Service (ACE CREDIT) has evaluated the DSST test development process and content of this exam. It has made the following recommendations:

Area or Course Equivalent: Health and Human Development
Level: Lower-level baccalaureate
Amount of Credit: 3 Semester Hours
Minimum Score: 400
Source: www.acenet.edu

EXAM CONTENT OUTLINE

The following is an outline of the content areas covered in the examination. The approximate percentage of the examination devoted to each content area is also noted.

I. **Health, Wellness, and Mind/Body Connection – 20%**
   a. Dimensions of wellness, health and lifestyles
   b. Healthy People 2020
   c. Prevention
   d. Mental health and mental illness

II. **Human Development and Relationships – 15%**
   a. Reproduction
   b. Sexuality
   c. Intimate relationships
   d. Healthy aging
   e. Death and bereavement

III. **Addiction – 15%**
   a. Addictive behavior
   b. Alcohol
   c. Tobacco
   d. Other drugs
   e. Other addictions

IV. **Fitness and Nutrition – 20%**
   a. Components of physical fitness
   b. Nutrition and its effect

V. **Risk Factors, Disease and Disease Prevention – 20%**
   a. Infectious diseases
   b. The cardiovascular system
   c. Types of cancer
   d. Immune disorders
   e. Diabetes, arthritis and genetic-related disorders

f. Stress management and coping mechanisms
   g. Common neurological disorders
VI. **Safety, Consumer Awareness and Environmental Concerns – 10%**
   a. Safety
   b. Intentional injuries and violence
   c. Consumer awareness
   d. Environmental concerns

REFERENCES
Below is a list of reference publications that were either used as a reference to create the exam, or were used as textbooks in college courses of the same or similar title at the time the test was developed. You may reference either the current edition of these titles or textbooks currently used at a local college or university for the same class title. It is recommended that you reference more than one textbook on the topics outlined in this fact sheet.

You should begin by checking textbook content against the content outline provided before selecting textbooks that cover the test content from which to study.

Sources for study material are suggested but not limited to the following:

1. *Core Concepts in Health,* Brief 13th Edition, 2013, Paul Insel and Walton Roth, McGraw-Hill.

2. *Focus on Health,* Loose Leaf Edition, 11th Edition, 2012, Dale Hahn, Wayne Payne, Ellen Lucas, McGraw-Hill.

SAMPLE QUESTIONS
All test questions are in a multiple-choice format, with one correct answer and three incorrect options. The following are samples of the types of questions that may appear on the exam.

1. The primary stage of Dr. Hans Seyle's general adaption syndrome during which the body prepares to fight or flee is known as

    a. resistance
    b. alarm
    c. exhaustion
    d. compulsion

2. The heart and the network of blood vessels leading to and from it comprise the

    a. cardiovascular system
    b. respiratory system
    c. endocrine system
    d. reproductive system

3. Which of the following abnormalities in a developing fetus can be detected by the use of amniocentesis?

    a. Cleft palate
    b. Tay-Sachs disease
    c. Phocomelia
    d. Diabetes

4. The primary pollutant that forms acid rain after entering the atmosphere is

    a. fluorocarbon
    b. ozone

c. sulphur dioxide
   d. dioxin

5. Which of the following is a barrier form of birth control?

   a. oral contraceptive
   b. intrauterine device
   c. diaphragm
   d. rhythm method

6. A cancer of the connective tissues is known as a?

   a. carcinoma
   b. Leukemia
   c. sarcoma
   d. melanoma

7. The intoxicating ingredient in beer, wine and distilled liquor is called?

   a. methanol
   b. isopropanol
   c. butanol
   d. ethanol

8. Drugs made from opium or its synthetic equivalent are classified as

   a. narcotic analgesics
   b. hallucinogens
   c. sedative-hypnotics
   d. major tranquilizers

9. The lowest level of Abraham Maslow's "hierarchy of needs is

   a. self-actualization
   b. esteem
   c. physiological needs
   d. love

Answers to sample questions:

1-B, 2-A, 3-B, 4-C, 5-C, 6-C, 7-D, 8-A, 9-C

HOW TO TAKE A TEST

You have studied long, hard and conscientiously.

With your official admission card in hand, and your heart pounding, you have been admitted to the examination room.

You note that there are several hundred other applicants in the examination room waiting to take the same test.

They all appear to be equally well prepared.

You know that nothing but your best effort will suffice. The "moment of truth" is at hand: you now have to demonstrate objectively, in writing, your knowledge of content and your understanding of subject matter.

You are fighting the most important battle of your life—to pass and/or score high on an examination which will determine your career and provide the economic basis for your livelihood.

What extra, special things should you know and should you do in taking the examination?

I. YOU MUST PASS AN EXAMINATION

A. WHAT EVERY CANDIDATE SHOULD KNOW
    Examination applicants often ask us for help in preparing for the written test. What can I study in advance? What kinds of questions will be asked? How will the test be given? How will the papers be graded?

B. HOW ARE EXAMS DEVELOPED?
    Examinations are carefully written by trained technicians who are specialists in the field known as "psychological measurement," in consultation with recognized authorities in the field of work that the test will cover. These experts recommend the subject matter areas or skills to be tested; only those knowledges or skills important to your success on the job are included. The most reliable books and source materials available are used as references. Together, the experts and technicians judge the difficulty level of the questions.
    Test technicians know how to phrase questions so that the problem is clearly stated. Their ethics do not permit "trick" or "catch" questions. Questions may have been tried out on sample groups, or subjected to statistical analysis, to determine their usefulness.
    Written tests are often used in combination with performance tests, ratings of training and experience, and oral interviews. All of these measures combine to form the best-known means of finding the right person for the right job.

II. HOW TO PASS THE WRITTEN TEST

A. BASIC STEPS

1) Study the announcement

How, then, can you know what subjects to study? Our best answer is: "Learn as much as possible about the class of positions for which you've applied." The exam will test the knowledge, skills and abilities needed to do the work.

Your most valuable source of information about the position you want is the official exam announcement. This announcement lists the training and experience qualifications. Check these standards and apply only if you come reasonably close to meeting them. Many jurisdictions preview the written test in the exam announcement by including a section called "Knowledge and Abilities Required," "Scope of the Examination," or some similar heading. Here you will find out specifically what fields will be tested.

2) Choose appropriate study materials

If the position for which you are applying is technical or advanced, you will read more advanced, specialized material. If you are already familiar with the basic principles of your field, elementary textbooks would waste your time. Concentrate on advanced textbooks and technical periodicals. Think through the concepts and review difficult problems in your field.

These are all general sources. You can get more ideas on your own initiative, following these leads. For example, training manuals and publications of the government agency which employs workers in your field can be useful, particularly for technical and professional positions. A letter or visit to the government department involved may result in more specific study suggestions, and certainly will provide you with a more definite idea of the exact nature of the position you are seeking.

3) Study this book!

III. KINDS OF TESTS

Tests are used for purposes other than measuring knowledge and ability to perform specified duties. For some positions, it is equally important to test ability to make adjustments to new situations or to profit from training. In others, basic mental abilities not dependent on information are essential. Questions which test these things may not appear as pertinent to the duties of the position as those which test for knowledge and information. Yet they are often highly important parts of a fair examination. For very general questions, it is almost impossible to help you direct your study efforts. What we can do is to point out some of the more common of these general abilities needed in public service positions and describe some typical questions.

1) General information

Broad, general information has been found useful for predicting job success in some kinds of work. This is tested in a variety of ways, from vocabulary lists to questions about current events. Basic background in some field of work, such as sociology or economics, may be sampled in a group of questions. Often these are principles which have become familiar to most persons through exposure rather than through formal training. It is difficult to advise you how to study for these questions; being alert to the world around you is our best suggestion.

2) Verbal ability

An example of an ability needed in many positions is verbal or language ability. Verbal ability is, in brief, the ability to use and understand words. Vocabulary and grammar tests are typical measures of this ability. Reading comprehension or paragraph interpretation questions are common in many kinds of civil service tests. You are given a paragraph of written material and asked to find its central meaning.

IV. KINDS OF QUESTIONS

1. Multiple-choice Questions

Most popular of the short-answer questions is the "multiple choice" or "best answer" question. It can be used, for example, to test for factual knowledge, ability to solve problems or judgment in meeting situations found at work.

A multiple-choice question is normally one of three types:
- It can begin with an incomplete statement followed by several possible endings. You are to find the one ending which best completes the statement, although some of the others may not be entirely wrong.
- It can also be a complete statement in the form of a question which is answered by choosing one of the statements listed.
- It can be in the form of a problem – again you select the best answer.

Here is an example of a multiple-choice question with a discussion which should give you some clues as to the method for choosing the right answer:

When an employee has a complaint about his assignment, the action which will best help him overcome his difficulty is to
- A. discuss his difficulty with his coworkers
- B. take the problem to the head of the organization
- C. take the problem to the person who gave him the assignment
- D. say nothing to anyone about his complaint

In answering this question, you should study each of the choices to find which is best. Consider choice "A" – Certainly an employee may discuss his complaint with fellow employees, but no change or improvement can result, and the complaint remains unresolved. Choice "B" is a poor choice since the head of the organization probably does not know what assignment you have been given, and taking your problem to him is known as "going over the head" of the supervisor. The supervisor, or person who made the assignment, is the person who can clarify it or correct any injustice. Choice "C" is, therefore, correct. To say nothing, as in choice "D," is unwise. Supervisors have and interest in knowing the problems employees are facing, and the employee is seeking a solution to his problem.

2. True/False

3. Matching Questions

Matching an answer from a column of choices within another column.

V. RECORDING YOUR ANSWERS

Computer terminals are used more and more today for many different kinds of exams.

For an examination with very few applicants, you may be told to record your answers in the test booklet itself. Separate answer sheets are much more common. If this separate answer sheet is to be scored by machine – and this is often the case – it is highly important that you mark your answers correctly in order to get credit.

VI. BEFORE THE TEST

YOUR PHYSICAL CONDITION IS IMPORTANT

If you are not well, you can't do your best work on tests. If you are half asleep, you can't do your best either. Here are some tips:

1) Get about the same amount of sleep you usually get. Don't stay up all night before the test, either partying or worrying—DON'T DO IT!
2) If you wear glasses, be sure to wear them when you go to take the test. This goes for hearing aids, too.
3) If you have any physical problems that may keep you from doing your best, be sure to tell the person giving the test. If you are sick or in poor health, you relay cannot do your best on any test. You can always come back and take the test some other time.

Common sense will help you find procedures to follow to get ready for an examination. Too many of us, however, overlook these sensible measures. Indeed, nervousness and fatigue have been found to be the most serious reasons why applicants fail to do their best on civil service tests. Here is a list of reminders:

- Begin your preparation early – Don't wait until the last minute to go scurrying around for books and materials or to find out what the position is all about.
- Prepare continuously – An hour a night for a week is better than an all-night cram session. This has been definitely established. What is more, a night a week for a month will return better dividends than crowding your study into a shorter period of time.
- Locate the place of the exam – You have been sent a notice telling you when and where to report for the examination. If the location is in a different town or otherwise unfamiliar to you, it would be well to inquire the best route and learn something about the building.
- Relax the night before the test – Allow your mind to rest. Do not study at all that night. Plan some mild recreation or diversion; then go to bed early and get a good night's sleep.
- Get up early enough to make a leisurely trip to the place for the test – This way unforeseen events, traffic snarls, unfamiliar buildings, etc. will not upset you.
- Dress comfortably – A written test is not a fashion show. You will be known by number and not by name, so wear something comfortable.
- Leave excess paraphernalia at home – Shopping bags and odd bundles will get in your way. You need bring only the items mentioned in the official notice you received; usually everything you need is provided. Do not bring reference books to the exam. They will only confuse those last minutes and be taken away from you when in the test room.

- Arrive somewhat ahead of time – If because of transportation schedules you must get there very early, bring a newspaper or magazine to take your mind off yourself while waiting.
- Locate the examination room – When you have found the proper room, you will be directed to the seat or part of the room where you will sit. Sometimes you are given a sheet of instructions to read while you are waiting. Do not fill out any forms until you are told to do so; just read them and be prepared.
- Relax and prepare to listen to the instructions
- If you have any physical problem that may keep you from doing your best, be sure to tell the test administrator. If you are sick or in poor health, you really cannot do your best on the exam. You can come back and take the test some other time.

VII. AT THE TEST

The day of the test is here and you have the test booklet in your hand. The temptation to get going is very strong. Caution! There is more to success than knowing the right answers. You must know how to identify your papers and understand variations in the type of short-answer question used in this particular examination. Follow these suggestions for maximum results from your efforts:

1) Cooperate with the monitor

The test administrator has a duty to create a situation in which you can be as much at ease as possible. He will give instructions, tell you when to begin, check to see that you are marking your answer sheet correctly, and so on. He is not there to guard you, although he will see that your competitors do not take unfair advantage. He wants to help you do your best.

2) Listen to all instructions

Don't jump the gun! Wait until you understand all directions. In most civil service tests you get more time than you need to answer the questions. So don't be in a hurry. Read each word of instructions until you clearly understand the meaning. Study the examples, listen to all announcements and follow directions. Ask questions if you do not understand what to do.

3) Identify your papers

Civil service exams are usually identified by number only. You will be assigned a number; you must not put your name on your test papers. Be sure to copy your number correctly. Since more than one exam may be given, copy your exact examination title.

4) Plan your time

Unless you are told that a test is a "speed" or "rate of work" test, speed itself is usually not important. Time enough to answer all the questions will be provided, but this does not mean that you have all day. An overall time limit has been set. Divide the total time (in minutes) by the number of questions to determine the approximate time you have for each question.

5) Do not linger over difficult questions

If you come across a difficult question, mark it with a paper clip (useful to have along) and come back to it when you have been through the booklet. One caution if you do this – be sure to skip a number on your answer sheet as well. Check often to be sure that you have not lost your place and that you are marking in the row numbered the same as the question you are answering.

6) Read the questions

Be sure you know what the question asks! Many capable people are unsuccessful because they failed to read the questions correctly.

7) Answer all questions

Unless you have been instructed that a penalty will be deducted for incorrect answers, it is better to guess than to omit a question.

8) Speed tests

It is often better NOT to guess on speed tests. It has been found that on timed tests people are tempted to spend the last few seconds before time is called in marking answers at random – without even reading them – in the hope of picking up a few extra points. To discourage this practice, the instructions may warn you that your score will be "corrected" for guessing. That is, a penalty will be applied. The incorrect answers will be deducted from the correct ones, or some other penalty formula will be used.

9) Review your answers

If you finish before time is called, go back to the questions you guessed or omitted to give them further thought. Review other answers if you have time.

10) Return your test materials

If you are ready to leave before others have finished or time is called, take ALL your materials to the monitor and leave quietly. Never take any test material with you. The monitor can discover whose papers are not complete, and taking a test booklet may be grounds for disqualification.

VIII. EXAMINATION TECHNIQUES

1) Read the general instructions carefully. These are usually printed on the first page of the exam booklet. As a rule, these instructions refer to the timing of the examination; the fact that you should not start work until the signal and must stop work at a signal, etc. If there are any special instructions, such as a choice of questions to be answered, make sure that you note this instruction carefully.

2) When you are ready to start work on the examination, that is as soon as the signal has been given, read the instructions to each question booklet, underline any key words or phrases, such as least, best, outline, describe and the like. In this way you will tend to answer as requested rather than discover on reviewing your paper that you listed without describing, that you selected the worst choice rather than the best choice, etc.

3) If the examination is of the objective or multiple-choice type – that is, each question will also give a series of possible answers: A, B, C or D, and you are called upon to select the best answer and write the letter next to that answer on your answer paper – it is advisable to start answering each question in turn. There may be anywhere from 50 to 100 such questions in the three or four hours allotted and you can see how much time would be taken if you read through all the questions before beginning to answer any. Furthermore, if you

come across a question or group of questions which you know would be difficult to answer, it would undoubtedly affect your handling of all the other questions.

4) If the examination is of the essay type and contains but a few questions, it is a moot point as to whether you should read all the questions before starting to answer any one. Of course, if you are given a choice – say five out of seven and the like – then it is essential to read all the questions so you can eliminate the two that are most difficult. If, however, you are asked to answer all the questions, there may be danger in trying to answer the easiest one first because you may find that you will spend too much time on it. The best technique is to answer the first question, then proceed to the second, etc.

5) Time your answers. Before the exam begins, write down the time it started, then add the time allowed for the examination and write down the time it must be completed, then divide the time available somewhat as follows:
    - If 3-1/2 hours are allowed, that would be 210 minutes. If you have 80 objective-type questions, that would be an average of 2-1/2 minutes per question. Allow yourself no more than 2 minutes per question, or a total of 160 minutes, which will permit about 50 minutes to review.
    - If for the time allotment of 210 minutes there are 7 essay questions to answer, that would average about 30 minutes a question. Give yourself only 25 minutes per question so that you have about 35 minutes to review.

6) The most important instruction is to read each question and make sure you know what is wanted. The second most important instruction is to time yourself properly so that you answer every question. The third most important instruction is to answer every question. Guess if you have to but include something for each question. Remember that you will receive no credit for a blank and will probably receive some credit if you write something in answer to an essay question. If you guess a letter – say "B" for a multiple-choice question – you may have guessed right. If you leave a blank as an answer to a multiple-choice question, the examiners may respect your feelings but it will not add a point to your score. Some exams may penalize you for wrong answers, so in such cases only, you may not want to guess unless you have some basis for your answer.

7) Suggestions
    a. Objective-type questions
        1. Examine the question booklet for proper sequence of pages and questions
        2. Read all instructions carefully
        3. Skip any question which seems too difficult; return to it after all other questions have been answered
        4. Apportion your time properly; do not spend too much time on any single question or group of questions
        5. Note and underline key words – all, most, fewest, least, best, worst, same, opposite, etc.
        6. Pay particular attention to negatives
        7. Note unusual option, e.g., unduly long, short, complex, different or similar in content to the body of the question
        8. Observe the use of "hedging" words – probably, may, most likely, etc.

9. Make sure that your answer is put next to the same number as the question
10. Do not second-guess unless you have good reason to believe the second answer is definitely more correct
11. Cross out original answer if you decide another answer is more accurate; do not erase until you are ready to hand your paper in
12. Answer all questions; guess unless instructed otherwise
13. Leave time for review

b. Essay questions
   1. Read each question carefully
   2. Determine exactly what is wanted. Underline key words or phrases.
   3. Decide on outline or paragraph answer
   4. Include many different points and elements unless asked to develop any one or two points or elements
   5. Show impartiality by giving pros and cons unless directed to select one side only
   6. Make and write down any assumptions you find necessary to answer the questions
   7. Watch your English, grammar, punctuation and choice of words
   8. Time your answers; don't crowd material

8) Answering the essay question

Most essay questions can be answered by framing the specific response around several key words or ideas. Here are a few such key words or ideas:

M's: manpower, materials, methods, money, management
P's: purpose, program, policy, plan, procedure, practice, problems, pitfalls, personnel, public relations
a. Six basic steps in handling problems:
   1. Preliminary plan and background development
   2. Collect information, data and facts
   3. Analyze and interpret information, data and facts
   4. Analyze and develop solutions as well as make recommendations
   5. Prepare report and sell recommendations
   6. Install recommendations and follow up effectiveness

   b. Pitfalls to avoid
   1. Taking things for granted – A statement of the situation does not necessarily imply that each of the elements is necessarily true; for example, a complaint may be invalid and biased so that all that can be taken for granted is that a complaint has been registered
   2. Considering only one side of a situation – Wherever possible, indicate several alternatives and then point out the reasons you selected the best one
   3. Failing to indicate follow up – Whenever your answer indicates action on your part, make certain that you will take proper follow-up action to see how successful your recommendations, procedures or actions turn out to be
   4. Taking too long in answering any single question – Remember to time your answers properly

EXAMINATION SECTION

EXAMINATION SECTION
TEST 1

DIRECTIONS: Each question or incomplete statement is followed by several suggested answers or completions. Select the one the BEST answers the question or completes the statement. *PRINT THE LETTER OF THE CORRECT ANSWER IN THE SPACE AT THE RIGHT.*

1. Among men in their late forties and early fifties, impotence is most often associated with _____ than with any other single factor.   1.____

    A. prescription drugs for hypertension
    B. anxiety or stress
    C. alcohol consumption
    D. smoking

2. Physical and physiological effects of cigarette smoking include   2.____
    I. increased arterial cholesterol deposits
    II. skin wrinkles
    III. increased blood pressure and heart rate
    IV. impaired liver function

    A. I and III
    B. I, II, and III
    C. III and IV
    D. I, II, III and IV

3. Which of the following is a water-soluble vitamin?   3.____

    A. A
    B. C
    C. D
    D. K

4. Overall, the most common method of preventing unwanted pregnancies in the United States is   4.____

    A. abstinence
    B. oral contraceptives
    C. the diaphragm
    D. sterilization

5. Mind-altering drugs appear to have their most significant effects on the brain's   5.____

    A. limbic system
    B. cerebrum
    C. medulla oblongata
    D. cerebellum

6. Which of the following is the most accurate description of the typical sleep patterns of elderly people?   6.____

    A. Longer, more restful periods of sleep.
    B. More wakefulness at night, with missed sleep made up in daytime naps

1

C. Overall reduced amounts of sleep, achieved in shorter periods of rest.
D. A later bedtime followed by a brief period of deep sleep.

7. Signs of shock include
   I. Staring, lusterless eyes
   II. Hyperventilation
   III. Weak, rapid heartbeat
   IV. Sweating

   A. I and II
   B. I and III
   C. II, III and IV
   D. I, II, III and IV

7.___

8. Research has shown that among family-or job-related factors associated with stress-related illness, the most critical factor tends to be the

   A. the degree of physical exertion involved in tasks
   B. the activity level associated with daily routines
   C. overall pressure to perform in individual roles
   D. the person's sense of control over events and circumstances

8.___

9. Which of the following valves of the heart allows oxygenated blood to move into the left ventricle from the left atrium?

   A. Tricuspid
   B. Aortic
   C. Mitral
   D. Pulmonary

9.___

10. Which of the following activities will be most useful in improving a person's flexibility?

    A. Rowing
    B. Cross-country skiing
    C. Weight lifting
    D. Swimming

10.___

11. Which of the following is NOT typically an element of hospice care?

    A. All care decisions are made by a collaborative hospice-care team.
    B. Counseling continues for the patient's family after death.
    C. Care is given in the patient's home or in a home-like environment.
    D. Pain management is used to keep the patient as comfortable and alert as possible.

11.___

12. Which of the following substances, found in the urine, may be an indicator of kidney disease?

    A. Albumin
    B. Cortisone
    C. Bilirubin
    D. Hemoglobin

12.___

13. Which of the following is NOT an advantage associated with the use of oral contraceptives?   13.____

    A. Lighter, more regular periods
    B. Decreased HDL cholesterol
    C. Protection against ovarian cancer
    D. Decreased risk of fibrocystic breast disease

14. The most important risk factor associated with bladder cancer is   14.____

    A. Multiple sexual partners
    B. Smoking
    C. Diabetes
    D. Alcoholism

15. What is the term for a deficiency of blood within an organ or part of an organ?   15.____

    A. Ischemia
    B. Aneurysm
    C. Infarct
    D. Occlusion

16. Which of the following may cause liver spots on the skin of older people?   16.____

    A. A retraction of pigment from the skin
    B. A high-fat diet
    C. Overproduction of liver secretions such as bile
    D. Prolonged overexposure to the sun

17. Which of the following is NOT a body fluid that is considered to be a mode of transmission for human immunodeficiency virus (HIV)?   17.____

    A. Semen
    B. Breast milk
    C. Vaginal fluids
    D. Saliva

18. For the purpose of bone maintenance, it is recommended that poslmenopausal women who are not on hormone therapy should increase their daily calcium intake to around _____ mg per day.   18.____

    A. 800
    B. 1000
    C. 1500
    D. 2500

19. The most severe form of chronic inflammatory joint disease is   19.____

    A. ankylosing spondylitis
    B. osteoarthritis
    C. gout
    D. rheumatoid arthritis

20. A postmenopausal woman should wait about _____ after her last period before she can safely stop using contraceptives.

    A. 8 to 12 weeks
    B. 6 to 8 months
    C. 1 to 2 years
    D. 2 to 3 years

21. The most significant source of radiation exposure in the United States is

    A. radon gas
    B. consumer products
    C. nuclear medicine
    D. chemicals within the human body

22. Which of the following occupations is classified as a "high strain" job-that is, one that is most likely to result in stress-related illness?

    A. Doctor
    B. Janitor
    C. Farmer
    D. Waiter/waitress

23. Of the following, which is NOT a defense against a consumer pleading negligence on the part of a manufacturer?

    A. Disclaimer
    B. Contributory negligence
    C. State of the art in design
    D. Undetectable defect

24. Which of the following should consider taking a calcium supplement?
    I. Adolescents who play contact sports
    II. The elderly
    III. Lactose-intolerant people
    IV. Women and teenage girls

    A. I, II and IV
    B. II and III
    C. II, III and IV
    D. I, II, III and IV

25. It is generally recommended that men _____ and older should undergo a rectal exam and PSA test as part of their regular checkups.

    A. 30
    B. 40
    C. 50
    D. 60

26. Which of the following is/are pancreatic hormones?

    I. Insulin
    II. Corticosteroid
    III. Glucagon
    IV. Globulin

    A. I only
    B. I and III
    C. II and IV
    D. I, III and IV

26.____

27. A person who weighs 180 pounds, walking 2 miles in an hour, will most likely expend about _____ calories.

    A. 80
    B. 140
    C. 210
    D. 450

27.____

28. Which of the following elements of personality is MOST likely to change as a person moves through middle age (40s through 60s)?

    A. Introversion/extroversion
    B. Impulsiveness
    C. Perceived locus of control
    D. Aggression

28.____

29. It is generally believed by health professionals that any diet program that makes a person lose weight at a sustained overall rate of more than _____ pound(s) a week is a possible health risk.

    A. 1
    B. 2
    C. 5
    D. 10

29.____

30. Which of the following metals has the highest toxicity on acute exposures?

    A. Manganese
    B. Lead
    C. Cadmium
    D. Zinc

30.____

31. Which of the following is a pituitary hormone that stimulates the release of breast milk?

    A. Colostrum
    B. Prolactin
    C. Oxytocin
    D. Progesterone

31.____

32. Which of the following is NOT one of the American Cancer Society's warning signs of cancer?

    A. Excessive thirst
    B. Unusual bleeding or discharge
    C. Marked change in bladder or bowel habits
    D. Nagging hoarseness or coughing

33. Withdrawal symptoms from chronic use of marijuana include
      I. diarrhea
      II. vomiting
      III. tremors
      IV. sleep difficulties

    A. I and II
    B. I, II, III and IV
    C. IV only
    D. There are no proven withdrawal symptoms associated with marijuana

34. What is the term for the uterine lining that as sloughed off each month during menstruation is pregnancy does not occur?

    A. Prostaglandin
    B. Placenta
    C. Endometrium
    D. Perinium

35. Which of the following diseases typically breaks out every 10-40 years as a pandemic that affects people all over the world?

    A. Measles
    B. Typhoid fever
    C. Influenza
    D. Scarlet fever

36. Which of the following is a primary symptom of syphilis?

    A. Painless sores on genitals
    B. Soreness and aching in bones and joints
    C. Burning, frequent urination
    D. Vaginal or urethral discharge

37. Which of the following is a symptom of hypoglycemia?

    A. Slowed heart rhythm
    B. Bluish lips and tongue
    C. Extreme thirst
    D. Tingling around the mouth

38. Which of the following statements is TRUE?

    A. Among adolescents, about three times as many boys as girls suffer from depression.
    B. Across all age groups, males and females suffer from depression at about the same rate.
    C. Among adults, about twice as many women as men suffer from depression
    D. Among the elderly, depression is most likely to be associated with substance abuse.

39. The main consumer advantage to outpatient care is

    A. greater choice of services
    B. lower cost
    C. professional collaboration on individual cases
    D. supervised recovery

40. A man is 40 years old. Assuming no limiting factors, the target heart rate for his exercise sessions should be about _____ beats per minute.

    A. 80
    B. 95
    C. 125
    D. 180

41. Which of the following behaviors on the part of the FATHER may affect the well-being of a child at the time of conception?

    A. Smoking
    B. Heavy caffeine use
    C. Heavy drinking
    D. Moderate exercise

42. The principal site for alcohol absorption by the body is the

    A. liver
    B. stomach
    C. small intestine
    D. spleen

43. Siderosis is a lung-scarring condition caused by inhalation of

    A. beryllium
    B. iron oxide
    C. lead oxide
    D. free silica

44. A woman taking oral contraceptives who wants to conceive should switch to another form of birth control for a period of _____ before trying to conceive.

    A. 8 weeks
    B. 3 months
    C. 6 months
    D. 1 year

45. Which of the following terms is used to describe the abnormal development of a tissue?

    A. Aplastic
    B. Metastasis
    C. Dysplasia
    D. Lithiasis

46. Generally, low-fat or skim milk is recommended over whole milk, EXCEPT for

    A. children under age 2
    B. older people
    C. nursing mothers
    D. people with osteoporosis

47. During the third trimester of a pregnancy, a woman can expect

    A. a slight drop in body temperature
    B. very short, scant bleeding
    C. Braxton-Hicks contractions
    D. a return of energy

48. According to Shontz, a person's first emergency reaction to a diagnosis of a serious illness is marked by each of the following characteristics, EXCEPT

    A. being stunned or bewildered
    B. thinking of alternatives
    C. behaving automatically
    D. feeling a sense of detachment

49. In the first stage of the General Adaptation Syndrome,

    A. the immune system is heavily taxed
    B. a person's resistance suddenly spikes
    C. a disease of adaptation becomes apparent
    D. a person becomes more susceptible to infection and disease

50. What is the term for the class of drugs used to treat allergies, asthma, nausea, motion sickness, nasal congestion, coughing, and itching?

    A. Antihistamines
    B. Salicylates
    C. Analgesics
    D. Corticosteroids

51. A person who has just begun an attempt to quit smoking should expect to experience withdrawal symptoms for a period of

    A. 48-36 hours
    B. 3-10 days
    C. 8-16 days
    D. 14-24 days

52. When a sunscreen has a sun protection factor (SPF) of 45, it means the user

    A. offers 15 times the protection of regular mineral oil
    B. may stay in the sun safely 45 times longer than without sunscreen.
    C. screens out 45% of the sun's harmful ultraviolet (UV) rays
    D. will be protected from the sun for a period of 45 minutes between applications

53. Common signs or symptom of adolescent depression include 53.____
    I. Marked loss of interest in activities
    II. Changes in appetite and weight
    III. Gastrointestinal upset
    IV. Hypertension

    A. I only
    B. I and II
    C. I, II and III
    D. I, II, III and IV

54. Which of the following is a condition in which the walls of arteries thicken and harden, 54.____
    sometimes interfering with blood flow?

    A. Angioedema
    B. Arteriosclerosis
    C. Aneurysm
    D. Atherosclerosis

55. Research suggests that the rate of urinary tract infections among uncircumcised infant 55.____
    boys

    A. is slightly higher than that of circumcised infants
    B. is about 10 times higher than that of circumcised infants
    C. is slightly lower than that of circumcised infants
    D. is about 3 times lower than that of circumcised infants

56. Which of the following is NOT typically a physiological response to stress? 56.____

    A. Muscle tension
    B. Increased heart rate
    C. Stomach/intestinal upset
    D. Dopamine release

57. Likely mental effects of a regular exercise program include 57.____
    I. Improved sleep
    II. Better concentration
    III. Reduced anxiety and stress
    IV. Overall feeling of well-being

    A. I, II and IV
    B. II and III
    C. III and IV
    D. I, II, III and IV

58. Starting at approximately age 20, a woman should examine her breasts 58.____

    A. weekly
    B. monthly
    C. every 6 months
    D. annually

59. The first goal in the treatment of most alcoholics is to

    A. separate the alcoholic from all sources of alcohol
    B. separate the alcoholic from all sources of emotional support
    C. penetrate the alcoholic's personal defenses
    D. obtain concrete evidence of the person's alcohol abuse

60. Generally, it is recommended that women refrain from sexual intercourse for a period of _____ after the delivery of a baby.

    A. 24 weeks
    B. 4-6 weeks
    C. 8-12 weeks
    D. 3-6 months

61. A full-scale stroke may be foreshadowed by a(n)

    A. brain aneurysm
    B. coronary thrombosis
    C. transient ischemic attack (TIA)
    D. embolism

62. According to Erikson, the most important issue for people who reach middle age is

    A. whether their lives have had meaning or have been wasted
    B. forming a clear self-image from a complex set of roles
    C. the choice between a preoccupation with self and a concern for others
    D. the ability to share one's self with another without fearing the loss of identity

63. To maintain good health, a person should consume about _____ of polyunsaturated fat in a single day

    A. 1 teaspoon
    B. 1 tablespoon
    C. 3 tablespoons
    D. 1/2 cup

64. Valium, Nembutal, and Quaalude belong to the class of drugs known as

    A. amphetamines
    B. sedative-hypnotics
    C. major tranquilizers
    D. narcotic analgesics

65. Brief, rhythmic cries that intensify over a period of time typically indicate that an infant

    A. is hungry
    B. has colic
    C. is tired
    D. is teething

66. Which of the following is a term for pain in the muscles during exercise, caused by inadequate arterial blood flow?

    A. Claudication
    B. Prolapse
    C. Micturition
    D. Senescence

67. Other than physiological needs, which of the following is most basic in Maslow's Hierarchy of Needs?

    A. Safety
    B. Self-actualization
    C. Belongingness
    D. Esteem

68. Which of the following is NOT a risk factor for breast cancer?

    A. Late childbearing
    B. Childlessness
    C. Family history of breast cancer
    D. Formula feeding of children

69. When talking to children about the death of a friend or family member, it's important to remember that most children don't develop a real understanding of death until around the age of

    A. 5
    B. 7
    C. 9
    D. 11

70. The central element in the definition of "addiction" is

    A. a loss of control
    B. increased tolerance
    C. denial
    D. impaired functioning

71. Hormone replacement therapy (HRT) for post-menopausal women

    A. helps to protect women from heart attacks.
    B. alleviates symptoms of cardiovascular problems such as heart disease or asthma.
    C. accelerates the rate at which women acquire the symptoms of osteoporosis.
    D. slows the growth rate of breast cancer.

72. Which of the following is an example of secondary prevention?

    A. Wearing a seat belt
    B. Getting a mammogram
    C. Exercising
    D. Getting a flu vaccination

73. After it is fertilized by a sperm cell, an egg is known as a(n)

    A. gamete
    B. dicot
    C. zygote
    D. embryo

74. Which of the following is a symptom of hepatitis?

    A. Aching joints
    B. Hunger
    C. Sweating
    D. Jerky movements

75. For a healthy diet, a person's overall fat intake should generally be limited to _____ % of all calories.

    A. 5
    B. 15
    C. 30
    D. 50

KEY (CORRECT ANSWERS)

1. C	16. D	31. C	46. A	61. C
2. B	17. D	32. A	47. C	62. C
3. B	18. C	33. B	48. C	63. B
4. D	19. D	34. C	49. D	64. B
5. A	20. C	35. C	50. A	65. A
6. B	21. A	36. A	51. B	66. A
7. B	22. D	37. D	52. B	67. A
8. D	23. A	38. C	53. B	68. D
9. C	24. C	39. B	54. B	69. C
10. D	25. B	40. C	55. B	70. A
11. A	26. B	41. C	56. D	71. A
12. A	27. C	42. C	57. D	72. B
13. B	28. C	43. B	58. B	73. C
14. B	29. B	44. B	59. C	74. A
15. A	30. C	45. C	60. B	75. C

TEST 2

DIRECTIONS: Each question or incomplete statement is followed by several suggested answers or completions. Select the one the BEST answers the question or completes the statement. *PRINT THE LETTER OF THE CORRECT ANSWER IN THE SPACE AT THE RIGHT.*

1. Research suggests that postponing a pregnancy until after the age of 35 increases the risk of each of the following, EXCEPT

    A. miscarriage
    B. low birth weight
    C. congenital abnormalities
    D. toxoplasmosis

2. Which of the following mineral nutrients helps to regulate the fluids of the body?

    A. Sodium
    B. Calcium
    C. Potassium
    D. Phosphorus

3. The most common cause of vision loss in older people is

    A. age-related macular degeneration (ARMD)
    B. glaucoma
    C. presbyopia
    D. cataract

4. Which of the following is NOT a physical effect that can be consistently attributed to a regular exercise program?

    A. Muscles require less oxygen
    B. Improved muscle and joint strength/flexibility
    C. For women, improved chance of avoiding osteoporosis
    D. Stronger, more resilient heart

5. The term "platelets" is often used to denote

    A. thrombocytes
    B. leukocytes
    C. erythrocytes
    D. lymphocytes

6. A definition of "mental health" would typically include each of the following, EXCEPT

    A. the ability to sustain relationships with family and friends
    B. the ability to control emotional reactions to conflicts or distressful events until they can be better understood
    C. a realistic perception of the motivations of others
    D. the ability to cope with life's transitions and traumas in a way that allows one's personality to remain intact

7. Effective electrical grounding in a home or other building may be accomplished by use of

   A. a metal framework or metal structures with negligible resistance to ground or grounding electrodes
   B. three-conductor cords with polarized plug-in receptacles
   C. transformer isolation with a low resistance path to ground
   D. a ground fault interrupter for every circuit with proper cross-connection.

8. Which of the following statements regarding exercise during pregnancy is TRUE?

   A. Inactive women should start a fitness program while pregnant.
   B. Exercise should be severely limited or avoided altogether after the seventh month.
   C. Active women should increase the length of workouts during the first two trimesters.
   D. Women should avoid exercises done lying on the back after the fourth month.

9. According to the current definition, physical dependence on a drug is characterized by
   I. tolerance—larger doses to achieve the same high
   II. withdrawal symptoms
   III. cravings for the drug
   IV. interference with daily functioning

   A. I only
   B. I and II
   C. II and III
   D. I, II, III and IV

10. Which of the following methods of contraception has the highest estimated effectiveness?

    A. Cervical cap
    B. Diaphrarn with spermicide
    C. Vaginal sponge
    D. Condom

11. The leading cause of death among alcoholics is

    A. cirrhosis of the liver
    B. cancer
    C. Wernicke-Korsakoff's syndrome
    D. cardiovascular disease

12. The largest preventable cause of premature death and disability in the United States is

    A. workplace accidents
    B. smoking
    C. alcohol abuse
    D. traffic accidents

13. Signs and symptoms of HIV infection include   13._____
    I. Chronic diarrhea
    II. Difficulties with speech, memory, or concentration
    III. Soaking night sweats
    IV. Muscular aches and pains

    A. I and IV
    B. I, II, and III
    C. II and III
    D. I, II, III and IV

14. Which of the following is a NOT a stage of the General Adaptation Syndrome?   14._____

    A. appraisal
    B. resistance
    C. exhaustion
    D. alarm reaction

15. Which of the following methods of contraception may increase a woman's chance of hav-   15._____
    ing an ectopic pregnancy?

    A. Cervical cap
    B. Vaginal spermicide
    C. Intrauterine device (IUD)
    D. Tubal ligation

16. Substitution of a less harmful substance for a toxic material is a practical method of elim-   16._____
    inating an industrial health hazard. Substitution should be the primary method of control
    for which one of the following solvents used in open cleaning?

    A. Hexane
    B. Carbon tetrachloride
    C. Toluene
    D. Xylene

17. Which of the following is administered as an evaluation of an infant's overall condition   17._____
    immediately after birth?

    A. Apgar score
    B. Foot stick
    C. Tonic reflex
    D. Grant's score

18. Which of the following is probably a person's best defense against the common cold?   18._____

    A. Frequent hand washing
    B. Annual flu shots
    C. Staying warm and dry
    D. High doses of vitamin C

19. To reduce stress, a patient is taught to concentrate on the self-suggestion of warmth and heavy limbs. This is an example of

    A. biofeedback
    B. hypnosis
    C. autogenic training
    D. meditation

20. Tachycardia is defined as a heart rate that

    A. exceeds 100 beats per minute
    B. is irregular
    C. is lower than 60 beats per minute
    D. is syncopated

21. Which of the following is NOT an opiate?

    A. Heroin
    B. Meperidine
    C. Cocaine
    D. Codeine

22. Which of the following is NOT an arterial pressure point commonly used to stop bleeding?

    A. Beneath the jaw
    B. Inside the elbow
    C. Behind the knee
    D. At the base of the neck

23. To be usable as fuel, carbohydrates must be broken down into

    A. constituent amino acids
    B. lactose
    C. polyunsaturated fats
    D. glucose

24. Within a period of _____ years, a person who quits smoking today will eventually experience a risk of developing heart disease and lung cancer that is equal to that of a non-smoker.

    A. 1-3
    B. 5-9
    C. 10-15
    D. 15-20

25. At the highest level of Kohlberg's moral development, a person conforms to society's idea of moral behavior in order to

    A. maintain the respect of spectators
    B. avoid self-condemnation
    C. avoid censure and guilt
    D. obtain rewards

26. Hypertension is usually defined as a consistent systolic pressure of at least _____ mm Hg and a consistent diastolic pressure of at least _____ mm Hg.

   A. 60, 150
   B. 80, 120
   C. 110, 75
   D. 140, 90

27. Research suggests that the dietary element most closely related to kidney disease is

   A. carbohydrate
   B. sugar
   C. protein
   D. fat

28. Which of the following conditions should older men expect to encounter regarding their sexuality?
   I. Frequent impotence
   II. Less sexual urgency
   III. Delayed or partial erections
   IV. Less well-defined moment of ejaculation

   A. I and II
   B. I and III
   C. I, III and IV
   D. I, II, III and IV

29. For real benefit, it is important for a person to maintain a schedule of higher-intensity exercise sessions at a rate of

   A. two sessions of at least 40 minutes every week
   B. three sessions of at least 20 minutes every week
   C. five sessions of at least 30 minutes every week
   D. five sessions of at least 45 minutes every week

30. An infant is restless and draws up her legs. She has severe crying spells that do not respond to any efforts to comfort her. The most likely cause of these crying spells is

   A. colic
   B. a soiled diaper
   C. illness
   D. hunger

31. According to Erikson, the most important developmental task for elementary school children is

   A. forming a sense of initiative in deciding on many activities
   B. developing and maintaining an interest in how things work
   C. establishing a sense of autonomy
   D. forming a clear self-image from a complex set of roles

32. In general, the "correct" intensity of exercise requires that a person (who has been exercising for a period of weeks) reach an ideal of _____ percent of his or her maximum heart rate.

    A. 30
    B. 50
    C. 70
    D. 90

33. Most treatment programs for alcoholism make use of each of the following, EXCEPT

    A. aversion therapy
    B. medical treatment
    C. a 12-step or similar program
    D. insistence on abstinence

34. Which of the following is a substance that has a role in stimulating uterine contractions during birth?

    A. Prolactin
    B. Progesterone
    C. Estrogen
    D. Prostaglandin

35. Generally, most cases of multiple sclerosis (MS) begin with a first attack between the ages of

    A. 5 and 8
    B. 12 and 35
    C. 20 and 40
    D. 45 and 65

36. The leading cause of accidental death for people over age 65 is

    A. falling
    B. injury-related infection
    C. traffic accidents
    D. accidental poisoning

37. The main symptom of urinary tract infection (UTI) in women is

    A. blood, pus, or a strong odor in the urine
    B. pain and burning while urinating
    C. pain above the pubic bone
    D. a frequent, urgent need to urinate but with only a small amount fluid passed

38. Risk factors for pancreatic cancer include
    I. smoking
    II. a high-fat diet
    III. regular and heavy use of alcohol
    IV. being over 50

    A. I and II
    B. I, II and III
    C. III and IV
    D. I, II, III and IV

39. A child will typically show signs that he is ready to begin toilet training between _____ months of age

    A. 12 and 18
    B. 18 and 24
    C. 24 and 28
    D. 28 and 32

40. Which of the following is NOT a class A carcinogen, according to the Environmental Protection Agency (EPA)?

    A. Radon
    B. Asbestos
    C. Secondhand cigarette smoke
    D. Dioxin

41. Which of the following neurotransmitters is NOT commonly associated with depression?

    A. Serotonin
    B. Acetylcholine
    C. Norepinephrine
    D. Dopamine

42. The area of the body containing the highest concentration of macrophages is the

    A. lymph nodes
    B. spleen
    C. liver
    D. bone marrow

43. On Monday, a person notices that he has a cough. On Wednesday he concludes that he is ill. On Saturday he decides to seek medical treatment, and on Sunday he sees the doctor. In this example the illness delay is _____ day(s).

    A. 1
    B. 2
    C. 3
    D. 6

44. Typically, a menstrual period that ranges in frequency from _____ days is considered normal

    A. 14 to 40
    B. 18 to 32
    C. 22 to 35
    D. 25 to 45

45. Which of the following activities is likely to expend the greatest number of calories in an hour?

    A. Swimming
    B. Jogging
    C. Tennis
    D. Bicycling

46. Which of the following is a category of blood proteins of which antibodies are formed?

    A. Globulin
    B. Prostaglandin
    C. Bilirubin
    D. Albumin

47. Most psychologists and family therapists suggest that a realistic timetable for a stepfamily to blend comfortably is at least

    A. 6 months
    B. 1 year
    C. 2 years
    D. 4 years

48. Which of the following does NOT occupy the "top" of the Food Guide Pyramid?

    A. Cheese
    B. Oils
    C. Sweets
    D. Fats

49. The class of drugs known as hallucinogens (psychedelics) includes each of the following, EXCEPT

    A. psilocybin
    B. LSD
    C. mescaline
    D. Ecstasy (MDMA)

50. During the first trimester of a pregnancy, a woman can expect

    A. increased blood volume
    B. ankle swelling
    C. leg cramps
    D. heartburn

51. High blood levels of _____ are associated with a lower risk of heart disease.

    A. Triglycerides
    B. High-density lipoprotein (HDL)
    C. Low-density lipoprotein (LDL)
    D. Very low-density lipoprotein (VLDL)

52. The two major problems faced by consumers in the modern health care system are

    A. access and cost
    B. overregulation and generalization
    C. overuse of drug treatments and bias toward surgical interventions
    D. overspecialization and availability

53. Initially, drinking alcohol effects each of the following, EXCEPT

    A. thoughts
    B. muscle coordination
    C. emotions
    D. judgement

54. Which of the following groups has a higher risk of developing glaucoma than the general population?
    I. Diabetics
    II. Those with a family history of glaucoma
    III. African Americans
    IV. Those with light-colored (blue or green) eyes

    A. I and II
    B. I, II and III
    C. III and IV
    D. I, II, III and IV

55. Tetanus booster shots should generally be administered once every

    A. 5 years
    B. 10 years
    C. 15 years or every major injury
    D. 20 years

56. "Angina pectoris" is an episodic pain in the chest that is caused by

    A. inadequate blood supply to the heart
    B. a variation or disruption in the heart's normal rhythm
    C. allergic swelling of the chest's mucous membranes
    D. a sudden rush of blood through the pulmonary vein

57. Which of the following tests/procedures can easily be performed at home by couples who want to assess their fertility?

    A. BBT charting
    B. Postcoital test (PCI)
    C. Semen analysis
    D. Blood tests

58. In recent years, fitness experts have recommended that in addition to regular workout sessions, people should choose moderate-intensity activities that will burn about _____ calories each day.

    A. 50
    B. 100
    C. 200
    D. 400

59. The main distinction between chest pains caused by a heart attack and those associated with other conditions (heartburn, pulled muscle, etc.) is that chest pain caused by a heart attack

    A. is sharp and burning
    B. radiates from the center of the chest to the jaw, neck, and arms
    C. worsens when the person bends over or lies down
    D. is localized and tender to the touch

60. Which of the following hormones is an androgen?

    A. Estrogen
    B. Aldosterone
    C. Calcitonin
    D. Testosterone

61. Hypertension can be alleviated by
    I. stopping smoking
    II. reducing alcohol consumption
    III. regular exercise
    IV. lowering sodium intake

    A. I and II
    B. I and III
    C. II, III, and IV
    D. I, II, III and IV

62. Which of the following is a bronchodilator?

    A. Digoxin
    B. Lisinopryl
    C. Cephalexin
    D. Theophylline

63. Biofeedback has proven to be an effective means of accomplishing each of the following, EXCEPT

    A. lowering blood pressure
    B. decreasing blood lactate
    C. slowing metabolism
    D. reducing heart rate

64. According to researcher Howard Leventhal, one of the basic common sense components of how people think about disease is

    A. health definition
    B. illness history
    C. illness identity
    D. prevalence rates

65. Around age 45, many people begin to have trouble reading fine print. This is most likely caused by a condition known as

    A. presbyopia
    B. retinopathy
    C. macular degeneration
    D. myopia

66. Generally, a T-helper cell count of less than _____ is enough to diagnose AIDS. 66._____

   A. 100
   B. 200
   C. 500
   D. 750

67. Which of the following is NOT an element of the "relaxation response" designed by Herbert Benson and his associates? 67._____

   A. Decreased muscle tension
   B. An active, participatory attitude
   C. A quiet environment
   D. A constant stimulus or mental device

68. Medicare is available to 68._____
   I. all persons in a particular state whose income falls below a certain level
   II. all Americans aged 65 or older
   III. some persons with kidney disease
   IV. some handicapped persons

   A. I only
   B. I and II
   C. II, III and IV
   D. I, II, III and IV

69. According to the American Heart Association, a person's daily salt intake should be limited to 69._____

   A. 1.5 tablespoons
   B. 3 teaspoons
   C. 1.5 teaspoons
   D. 0.5 teaspoon

70. Which of the following is an antianxiety drug? 70._____

   A. Loperamide
   B. Fluoxitine
   C. Lorazepam
   D. Zolpedim

71. Which of the following personality traits is MOST likely to be associated with heart disease or other stress-related illnesses? 71._____

   A. Hostility or cynicism
   B. Passivity or hopelessness
   C. Competitiveness
   D. Aggression

72. The period during the heart cycle in which the cardiac muscle relaxes is known as

    A. sinus rhythm
    B. diastole
    C. discontracture
    D. systole

73. Which of the following statements about Type II (non-insulin-dependent) diabetes is TRUE?

    A. It comprises 10 percent of all diabetes cases.
    B. The onset is usually sudden and dramatic.
    C. It occurs mainly in adults over the age of 40 who are overweight
    D. Typically, daily insulin injections are required as treatment.

74. The most serious form of hepatitis is

    A. A
    B. B
    C. C
    D. D

75. Jaundice is a condition caused by an excess of _____ in the blood.

    A. albumin
    B. gamma globulin
    C. bilirubin
    D. lymph

KEY (CORRECT ANSWERS)

1.	D	16.	B	31.	B	46.	A	61.	D
2.	A	17.	A	32.	C	47.	D	62.	D
3.	A	18.	A	33.	A	48.	A	63.	A
4.	A	19.	C	34.	D	49.	D	64.	C
5.	A	20.	A	35.	C	50.	D	65.	A
6.	B	21.	C	36.	A	51.	B	66.	B
7.	A	22.	B	37.	D	52.	A	67.	B
8.	D	23.	D	38.	A	53.	B	68.	C
9.	B	24.	C	39.	B	54.	B	69.	C
10.	D	25.	B	40.	D	55.	B	70.	C
11.	D	26.	D	41.	B	56.	A	71.	A
12.	B	27.	C	42.	B	57.	A	72.	B
13.	B	28.	C	43.	C	58.	C	73.	C
14.	A	29.	B	44.	C	59.	B	74.	B
15.	C	30.	A	45.	D	60.	D	75.	C

EXAMINATION SECTION
TEST 1

DIRECTIONS: Each question or incomplete statement is followed by several suggested answers or completions. Select the one that BEST answers the question or completes the statement. *PRINT THE LETTER OF THE CORRECT ANSWER IN THE SPACE AT THE RIGHT.*

1. A highly complex compound containing nitrogen essential for building and repairing of body cells and tissue is
    A. carbohydrates
    B. fats
    C. proteins
    D. vitamins
    E. minerals

    1._____

2. Which of the following is *generally* considered superior to other sources of basic amino acids?
    A. Fats
    B. Green leafy vegetables
    C. Poultry
    D. Fruits
    E. Milk, eggs and meat

    2._____

3. The building blocks for the manufacture of proteins in the body are
    A. amino acids
    B. carbohydrates
    C. fats
    D. thyroxin
    E. bile

    3._____

4. A *more highly* concentrated source of energy than either proteins or carbohydrates is
    A. hemoglobin
    B. vitamins
    C. sugars
    D. antibodies
    E. fats

    4._____

5. Two minerals related to the health of the bones are _____ and _____.
    A. calcium; phosphorus
    B. copper; zinc
    C. chloride; iodine
    D. fluorine; manganese
    E. sodium; iron

    5._____

6. A condition in which the blood is deficient in either quality or quantity of red blood cells is
    A. arteriosclerosis
    B. goiter
    C. schizophrenia
    D. anemia
    E. myxedema

    6._____

7. The CORRECT percentage of adult body weight in regard to water is most closely
    A. 35%   B. 45%   C. 50%   D. 60%   E. 75%

    7._____

8. The ability to do better physical labor may be achieved as a result of eating a breakfast containing both _____ and carbohydrates.
    A. vegetables
    B. minerals
    C. vitamins
    D. fats
    E. fruits

    8._____

9. The CHIEF reason for obesity is
   A. heredity
   B. overeating
   C. glandular
   D. psychological
   E. eating proteins only

10. The MOST effective method of determining sensitivity to food allergies is the _____ test.
    A. elimination
    B. patch
    C. skin
    D. Minnesota
    E. Salmonellosis

11. Of the following, the MOST sensible way to approach weight loss is to
    A. cut out breakfast
    B. cut out midday meals
    C. cut out dinner or evening meals
    D. discuss diet or weight-loss options with your physician
    E. drink less water

12. Control of bodily activities and movements is the responsibility of the
    A. nervous system
    B. endocrine system
    C. thyroid gland
    D. parathyroid gland
    E. skeletal system

13. The products of the endocrine glands are called
    A. hormones
    B. chromosomes
    C. eugenics
    D. pneumococcus
    E. toxins

14. Olfactory cells are important to us in regard to
    A. tasting
    B. touching
    C. hearing
    D. smelling
    E. production

15. The taste buds are embedded in the
    A. throat
    B. tongue
    C. teeth
    D. roof of the mouth
    E. esophagus

16. Excessive amounts of caffeine may result in
    A. indigestion
    B. nervousness
    C. sleeplessness
    D. irritability
    E. all of the above

17. On a camping trip, the BEST way to purify drinking water is to
    A. boil the water
    B. filter the water
    C. store the water in reservoirs and allow the impurities to settle
    D. chlorinate the water

18. Trichinosis is a disease that may result from eating insufficiently cooked
    A. veal
    B. pork
    C. mutton
    D. fowl

19. The normal temperature of the human body is _____ degrees.
    A. 68.0
    B. 90.6
    C. 98.6
    D. 99.4

20. The BEST treatment for a cold is to
    A. take a laxative
    B. go to bed
    C. exercise vigorously to work up a sweat
    D. gargle with salt water or mouthwash

    20.____

21. If sugar is found regularly in the urine, the disease that may be present is
    A. diabetes   B. anthrax   C. rheumatism   D. beriberi

    21.____

22. A psychiatrist specializes in the field of
    A. psychology
    B. infectious diseases
    C. high blood pressure and other circulatory diseases
    D. mental or emotional problems

    22.____

23. A person with persistent bad breath should
    A. clean his or her teeth several times daily to kill the odor
    B. have a medical examination to determine the cause
    C. gargle several times daily to kill the odor
    D. chew gum when with other people

    23.____

24. The BEST way for students to learn about health is by
    A. listening to their family and friends
    B. personal experience
    C. studying scientific facts
    D. seeking medical information on the internet

    24.____

25. Sensitivity to proteins contained in pollen, feathers, etc. may be the cause of
    A. tuberculosis   B. pyorrhea   C. arthritis   D. hay fever

    25.____

26. Identify the FALSE statement.
    A. Ability to drive a car is directly related to maturity and judgment.
    B. It is safe for a good swimmer to swim alone in a regular swimming pool.
    C. A pedestrian should walk on the left side of the road so that he will face the cars coming from the opposite direction.
    D. Carrying a passenger on a bicycle is not a safe practice.

    26.____

27. When a person who has been sick is recovering, he or she is said to be
    A. regenerating   B. anemic   C. convalescing   D. infectious

    27.____

28. The tuberculin test is helpful in determining which
    A. people are immune to tuberculosis
    B. people have been infected with tuberculosis germs and need additional tests
    C. people have recovered from tuberculosis
    D. part of the body is infected

    28.____

29. Of the following, the disease MOST likely to be fatal is
    A. mumps
    B. chicken pox
    C. scurvy
    D. tetanus (lockjaw)

30. Identify the TRUE statement regarding treatment of a fever by drinking whiskey.
    A. There is neither harm nor value in this method.
    B. The use of whiskey to treat a fever is standard medical practice.
    C. It is a little-known method but one that is frequently of value.
    D. It is more dangerous than helpful.

31. Food groups and the Food Pyramid are concepts related to
    A. the cultural significance of popular foods and beverages
    B. the nutritional value of eating different cuisines
    C. healthy eating and nutrition
    D. reducing calories

32. Identify the MOST accurate statement about the effect of alcohol on muscular coordination.
    A. An alcoholic drink just before playing a round of golf will increase a player's muscular coordination.
    B. The effect of alcohol on muscular coordination depends largely on the health of the individual.
    C. An alcoholic drink just before leaving a party will NOT decrease one's muscular coordination in driving an automobile.
    D. There is considerable evidence that the use of alcohol affects muscular coordination.

33. If an artery in the lower forearm has been cut, the pressure should be applied
    A. between the cut and the wrist
    B. either at the wrist or the elbow
    C. between the cut and the elbow
    D. both at the wrist and the elbow

34. Which of the following statements about posture is FALSE?
    A. Poor posture makes one appear less conspicuous.
    B. Carelessness is the cause of MOST poor posture.
    C. Poor posture increases fatigue.
    D. *Stand tall*, *Walk tall* and *Sit tall* are the chief rules for good posture.

35. Beriberi, rickets, scurvy and pellagra are examples of _____ diseases.
    A. circulatory
    B. nutritional
    C. communicable
    D. occupational

36. Which of the following statements about nutrition is FALSE?
    A. Most leafy vegetables are rich in vitamins and minerals.
    B. There is no harm in drinking orange juice and milk at the same meal.
    C. Eating fish is associated with improved brain function.
    D. Drinking more than six glasses of water daily is fattening.

37. Historically, another term used for poliomyelitis is
    A. tonsillitis
    B. goiter
    C. infantile paralysis
    D. spina bifida

38. The mineral needed by red corpuscles in the blood to help them carry oxygen is 38.____
    A. iron   B. calcium   C. fluorine   D. phosphorus

39. Emotional instability in adults is MOST frequently attributed to 39.____
    A. heredity   B. heart conditions
    C. head injuries   D. childhood home life

40. Accidents due to _____ occur MOST often in the home. 40.____
    A. falls
    B. poisoning from drugs and cleansing materials
    C. burns and scalds
    D. gas poisoning

KEY (CORRECT ANSWERS)

1.	C	11.	D	21.	A	31.	C
2.	E	12.	A	22.	D	32.	D
3.	A	13.	A	23.	B	33.	C
4.	E	14.	D	24.	C	34.	A
5.	A	15.	B	25.	D	35.	B
6.	D	16.	E	26.	B	36.	D
7.	D	17.	A	27.	C	37.	C
8.	D	18.	B	28.	B	38.	A
9.	B	19.	C	29.	D	39.	D
10.	C	20.	B	30.	D	40.	A

TEST 2

DIRECTIONS: Each question or incomplete statement is followed by several suggested answers or completions. Select the one that BEST answers the question or completes the statement. *PRINT THE LETTER OF THE CORRECT ANSWER IN THE SPACE AT THE RIGHT.*

1. Athlete's foot is caused by
   A. streptococcus   B. oxides   C. bacillus
   D. fungi   E. streptomycin

2. An adult has _____ permanent teeth.
   A. 26   B. 28   C. 30   D. 32   E. 36

3. Although some digested foods are absorbed by the bloodstream in the stomach, MOST absorption takes place in the
   A. liver   B. pancreas   C. gall bladder
   D. large intestine   E. small intestine

4. The LARGEST gland in the body is said to be the
   A. liver   B. brain   C. heart
   D. stomach   E. large intestine

5. Jaundice results from
   A. excessive amounts of bile being produced
   B. a shortage of lymph
   C. bile ducts being blocked
   D. an improper diet
   E. none of the above

6. When the feces is slowed down in its passage through the colon, a condition of _____ is the result.
   A. diarrhea   B. hemorrhoids   C. indigestion
   D. constipation   E. jaundice

7. Most stomach ulcers are caused by
   A. irregularities in heart beat
   B. varicose veins
   C. rapid peristaltic movement
   D. bacterial infection
   E. preference for spicy or acidic foods

8. Sleeping pills typically contain
   A. marijuana   B. cocaine   C. antitoxin
   D. agglutinines   E. hypnotics

9. The Schick test was a procedure used to determine if a person was immune to
   A. diphtheria   B. scarlet fever   C. typhoid fever
   D. tuberculosis   E. none of the above

10. Most vaccines are made up of
    A. botulism
    B. trichinosis
    C. dead or weakened viruses or germs
    D. anthrax
    E. material from chicken eggs

    10.____

11. Tuberculosis is caused by a
    A. virus   B. toxin   C. bacteria
    D. genetic defect   E. toxoid

    11.____

12. Hydrophobia is a condition that has historically been associated with
    A. abnormal desire for water   B. rabies
    C. abnormal fear of darkness   D. drowning
    E. fear of heights

    12.____

13. Poor posture among school-age children is a(n)
    A. orthopedic defect   B. poliomyelitis defect
    C. osteomyelitis defect   D. epidemiologist defect
    E. none of the above

    13.____

14. _____ are generally not used for the diagnosis and/or treatment of cancer.
    A. X-rays   B. Radiation   C. Hormones
    D. Anticoagulants   E. Chemotherapy

    14.____

15. Hypochondria describes a person who
    A. fears the dark   B. daydreams
    C. imagines illnesses   D. fears water
    E. enjoys burning things

    15.____

16. Alcohol is one type of
    A. tranquilizer   B. pep pill   C. depressant
    D. stimulant   E. all of the above

    16.____

17. Ophthalmology is the medical field concerned with the
    A. ears   B. nose   C. throat   D. eyes   E. feet

    17.____

18. A basal metabolism test is taken to determine if
    A. the heartbeat is normal   B. the thyroid is functioning properly
    C. constipation exists   D. blood pressure is normal
    E. barbiturates exist in the blood

    18.____

19. The astigmatism test will determine a person's ability to
    A. see   B. hear   C. write   D. speak   E. reason

    19.____

20. A skin specialist may also be called a
    A. chiropodist   B. epidemiologist   C. dermatologist
    D. podiatrist   E. none of the above

    20.____

21. An electro-cardiograph
    A. photographs the kidneys
    B. charts heartbeats
    C. records blood pressure
    D. records reaction time
    E. photographs the lungs

22. Regular vigorous physical exercise will gradually
    A. increase the number of body muscles
    B. develop good character traits
    C. develop a heart condition
    D. increase heart efficiency
    E. weaken a person

23. Another name for hernia is
    A. laceration   B. groin   C. rupture   D. incision

24. All of the following are treatments for sudden onset of kidney stones EXCEPT
    A. surgery
    B. analgesics
    C. Flomax
    D. blood thinners

25. _____ is acted upon by bacteria in the mouth to produce acids that dissolve tooth enamel.
    A. Protein
    B. Ascorbic acid
    C. Sugar
    D. Phosphorus

26. Hemochromatosis is a condition in which excess _____ is stored in the _____.
    A. iron; liver
    B. calcium; kidneys
    C. lymph; pancreas
    D. bile; liver

27. An approved first-aid treatment would be to
    A. remove a foreign body from the ear with a match stick
    B. use a tourniquet to stop bleeding from a minor wound
    C. treat heat exhaustion with drinks that are high in salts or electrolytes
    D. apply absorbent cotton directly to a burn or scald

28. A blood count of a person suspected of having appendicitis reveals that the number of white corpuscles is normal.
    It may be concluded that the person
    A. probably has appendicitis
    B. probably does not have appendicitis
    C. is developing no resistance to fight a possible infection
    D. needs a blood transfusion

29. Artificial respiration is NOT applied for
    A. drowning
    B. gas poisoning
    C. corrosive poisoning
    D. electric shock

30. The term "enriched," as used on food labels, generally refers to bread made of white flour to which has been added
    A. milk, butter or eggs
    B. nutrients like thiamine, niacin and riboflavin
    C. protein, fiber and fat
    D. calcium, vitamin C and sugar

31. Fatigue due to sedentary or mental work is usually BEST relieved at the end of one's working hours by
    A. several cups of coffee
    B. eight hours of sleep
    C. a tepid shower
    D. recreational activity of a physical type

32. Which statement on alcohol and its uses is FALSE?
    A. Alcoholic beverages are useful in preventing and curing colds.
    B. Alcohol is to be avoided in the treatment of snake or spider bites.
    C. It is a mistake to take an alcoholic drink before going out in bitter cold weather.
    D. Alcohol has limited use as a medicine.

33. Normally, constipation is BEST avoided through the use or consumption of
    A. mineral oil   B. yeast
    C. laxatives   D. foods containing fiber

34. Though rare, tuberculosis cases should be considered primarily a result of
    A. poor nutrition   B. infection
    C. emotional ailment   D. hereditary disease

35. Gonorrhea is frequently a cause of
    A. stomach ulcers   B. insanity
    C. baldness   D. sterility

36. One purpose of a periodic health examination is the detection of all of the following conditions EXCEPT
    A. memory loss   B. heart disease
    C. cancer   D. high blood pressure

37. These hormones help to regulate various body functions. _____ is involved when we get excited or angry.
    A. Thyroxin   B. Adrenalin   C. Insulin   D. Pituitrin

38. To a person driving a car or riding a bicycle, peripheral vision is MOST useful for
    A. seeing better at night
    B. reading traffic signs more easily
    C. detecting moving objects at the sides
    D. judging more accurately the speed of approaching vehicles

39. Beer, wine and whiskey should be considered   39.____
    A. foods   B. tonics   C. stimulants   D. depressants

40. A good substitute for oranges as a source of vitamin C is/are   40.____
    A. tomatoes   B. beef
    C. cod liver oil   D. whole wheat bread

KEY (CORRECT ANSWERS)

1.	D	11.	C	21.	B	31.	D
2.	D	12.	B	22.	D	32.	A
3.	E	13.	A	23.	C	33.	D
4.	A	14.	D	24.	D	34.	B
5.	C	15.	C	25.	C	35.	D
6.	D	16.	C	26.	A	36.	A
7.	D	17.	D	27.	C	37.	B
8.	E	18.	B	28.	B	38.	C
9.	A	19.	A	29.	C	39.	D
10.	C	20.	C	30.	B	40.	A

TEST 3

DIRECTIONS: Each question or incomplete statement is followed by several suggested answers or completions. Select the one that BEST answers the question or completes the statement. *PRINT THE LETTER OF THE CORRECT ANSWER IN THE SPACE AT THE RIGHT.*

1. Digestion actually begins in the
   A. mouth
   B. pharynx or throat
   C. trachea
   D. stomach
   E. small intestine

   1.____

2. Vomiting is USUALLY an indication that there is also a disturbance in some part of the body other than the
   A. stomach
   B. mouth
   C. throat
   D. small intestine
   E. large intestine

   2.____

3. The normal breathing rate per minute for an adult is about
   A. 11 to 13
   B. 14 to 16
   C. 16 to 18
   D. 19 to 21
   E. 21 to 23

   3.____

4. The MOST important to life is
   A. milk
   B. meat
   C. vegetables
   D. water
   E. fruits

   4.____

5. Pneumonia causes an inflammation of the
   A. throat
   B. lungs
   C. stomach
   D. nose
   E. kidneys

   5.____

6. The circulatory system does NOT involve the body's
   A. blood
   B. heart
   C. lymphatic vessels
   D. spinal cord
   E. blood vessels

   6.____

7. To protect the body from infection and disease is the function of
   A. platelets
   B. white blood cells
   C. red blood cells
   D. hemoglobin
   E. gamma globulin

   7.____

8. _____ carry blood away from the heart.
   A. Venules
   B. Veins
   C. Arteries
   D. Capillaries
   E. Descending vena cava

   8.____

9. Defects that a person is born with are called
   A. endocarditis
   B. congenital
   C. cardiac
   D. rheumatic
   E. mutations

   9.____

35

10. The MOST complicated system in the body is the _____ system.   10.____
    A. circulatory   B. respiratory   C. nervous
    D. digestive   E. motor

11. The autonomic nervous system controls   11.____
    A. voluntary muscles   B. smooth muscle
    C. conditioned reflexes   D. sympathetic movements
    E. involuntary muscles

12. *Spastic* is a term generally used in relation to   12.____
    A. nerves   B. muscles   C. emotions
    D. environment E. thoughts

13. The colored portion of the eye is called the   13.____
    A. cornea   B. pupil   C. iris   D. sclera   E. retina

14. Your _____ is NOT one of your body's weapons against germs.   14.____
    A. skin   B. hairs   C. nose
    D. antibodies   E. phagocytes

15. Dizziness or faintness may be associated with a disturbance of the _____ system.   15.____
    A. nervous   B. respiratory
    C. circulatory   D. all of the above

16. The LARGEST number of people are accidentally killed when   16.____
    A. swimming   B. driving   C. walking
    D. falling   E. flying

17. The LARGEST number of accidents occur   17.____
    A. at home   B. in the water   C. on the playground
    D. at airports E. on highways

18. Shock exists because of   18.____
    A. poor circulation of the blood   B. rapid heart beat
    C. nervous tension   D. drop in body temperature
    E. open wound

19. A floor burn would be considered a(n) _____ wound.   19.____
    A. incised   B. abrasion   C. laceration
    D. puncture   E. bruise

20. A doctor uses a sphygmomanometer to test   20.____
    A. reaction time   B. heart beat
    C. pulse rate   D. blood pressure
    E. amount of sugar in urine

21. Stuttering is USUALLY due to   21.____
    A. emotional disturbance   B. nervous tension
    C. high blood pressure   D. lack of muscular control
    E. childhood diseases

22. The capacity of the lungs and heart to carry on their tasks during strenuous   22.____
    activity is called
    A. muscle endurance   B. muscle tone
    C. cardiorespiratory endurance D. respiration

23. A podiatrist is a specialist who treats the   23.____
    A. eyes   B. ears   C. feet   D. nose   E. mouth

24. Malignant tumor is associated with   24.____
    A. tuberculosis   B. heart disease   C. rabies
    D. moles   E. cancer

25. Skin pores can be found on all of the following EXCEPT   25.____
    A. arms   B. legs   C. palms   D. chest   E. feet

26. The chemical salt of _____, when found in drinking water or applied directly   26.____
    to the teeth, seems to help reduce tooth decay.
    A. chlorides   B. fluorides   C. sulphates   D. nitrates

27. When cold air or cold water hits the skin, the body reduces heat loss   27.____
    principally by
    A. expanding the pores in the skin
    B. generating more heat in the muscles
    C. reducing the size of the blood vessels in the skin
    D. making the heart beat faster

28. A cup of coffee with sugar but WITHOUT cream contains only   28.____
    A. vitamin B   B. calories   C. protein   D. fiber

29. A deficiency of _____ is a cause of night blindness.   29.____
    A. iodine   B. protein   C. vitamin A   D. vitamin C

30. MOST authorities believe the usual cause of color blindness is that it   30.____
    A. is an inherited characteristic, and so runs in families
    B. may develop from looking at brightly colored lights, especially red ones
    C. is a contagious infection caused by a filterable virus
    D. is caused by an injury to the eyes

31. Active acquired immunity occurs when a person has a disease and then   31.____
    recovers from it.
    This is common for the diseases of _____ and _____.
    A. tuberculosis; malaria   B. measles; chicken pox
    C. colds; pneumonia   D. diabetes; anemia

32. Fatty liver disease is commonly associated with
    A. alcohol consumption
    B. overproduction of bile
    C. a diet high in eggs and yogurt
    D. an imbalance in hormone production

33. If improperly maintained, forced-air heating systems in the home can cause a person to experience all of the following EXCEPT
    A. runny nose or congestion   B. dry mouth
    C. allergic reaction   D. pink eye

34. Antitoxin pertains to
    A. immunization
    B. sterilization
    C. germ-killing drugs
    D. determination of susceptibility to a disease

35. Someone experiencing hookworm was likely exposed through
    A. eating poorly cooked pork
    B. walking barefoot outdoors for prolonged periods
    C. an inadequate diet
    D. poor ventilation in the home

36. The most common reason a person is overweight is because they
    A. exercise improperly
    B. have inherited a tendency to be overweight
    C. have an underactive thyroid gland
    D. consume a high-calorie diet

37. A meal that consists of bread, macaroni, rice pudding and cake contains an excess of
    A. protein   B. vitamins
    C. carbohydrates   D. fats

38. Which statement about sunburn is FALSE?
    A. Sunburn is similar to any other burn and should be treated in the same manner.
    B. If a person who is badly sunburned develops a fever, a doctor should be called.
    C. A severe sunburn may be more serious than other burns of like extent.
    D. There is no danger of getting sunburned on a cloudy day.

39. Goiter may be caused by a lack of _____ in the diet or drinking water.
    A. iodine   B. chlorine   C. fluorine   D. bromine

40. It is FALSE that
    A. secondary sex characteristics generally become evident at adolescence
    B. the female reproductive organs which produce eggs are called ovaries
    C. the male reproductive organs which produce sperm are called testes
    D. girls and boys mature on the average at the same age

KEY (CORRECT ANSWERS)

1.	A	11.	E	21.	A	31.	B
2.	A	12.	B	22.	C	32.	A
3.	C	13.	C	23.	C	33.	D
4.	D	14.	C	24.	E	34.	A
5.	B	15.	D	25.	C	35.	B
6.	D	16.	B	26.	B	36.	D
7.	B	17.	A	27.	C	37.	C
8.	C	18.	A	28.	B	38.	D
9.	B	19.	B	29.	C	39.	A
10.	C	20.	D	30.	A	40.	D

TEST 4

DIRECTIONS: Each question or incomplete statement is followed by several suggested answers or completions. Select the one that BEST answers the question or completes the statement. *PRINT THE LETTER OF THE CORRECT ANSWER IN THE SPACE AT THE RIGHT.*

1. A state health officer is GENERALLY a
   A. specialist
   B. physician
   C. health educator
   D. member of the bar association
   E. nurse

   1.____

2. The SEVEREST forms of mental illnesses are classified as
   A. neurosis
   B. psychosis
   C. sublimations
   D. personality disorders
   E. peristalsis

   2.____

3. A public-health campaign educating people about blood pressure and circulatory health would likely include the definition of
   A. lymph nodes
   B. caloric intake
   C. hypertension
   D. red blood cells, white blood cells and platelets
   E. renal failure

   3.____

4. The appendix
   A. aids in elimination
   B. aids in respiration
   C. serves no function
   D. fights bacteria
   E. aids in digestion

   4.____

5. Diabetes is a disease of the
   A. pancreas
   B. kidney
   C. spleen
   D. gonads
   E. veins

   5.____

6. MOST all children are born
   A. with astigmatism
   B. nearsighted
   C. farsighted
   D. unable to hear
   E. blind

   6.____

7. Alcoholism is considered a
   A. habit
   B. disease
   C. sickness
   D. pleasure
   E. weakness

   7.____

8. Alcohol is absorbed directly from the
   A. small intestine
   B. large intestine
   C. stomach
   D. gall bladder
   E. kidneys

   8.____

9. Anesthetics produce
   A. a feeling of warmth
   B. diseases
   C. a loss of pain
   D. freedom from diseases
   E. tuberculosis

10. The PRIMARY fault of self-prescribed drugs is that they
    A. are too costly
    B. do not cure the cause
    C. are hard to get
    D. are too slow in acting
    E. weaken the taker

11. Disease-producing bacteria form a poison called
    A. pimples   B. toxins   C. inflammation
    D. spores   E. bacilli

12. _____ diseases last for a long period of time.
    A. Chronic   B. Cochlea   C. Anaesthetic
    D. Analgesic E. Acute

13. Rocky Mountain spotted fever is spread by
    A. ants   B. dogs   C. feces   D. ticks   E. flies

14. Which word is NOT related to the others?
    A. Antitoxins   B. Antibodies   C. Phagocytes
    D. Vaccine   E. Intravenous

15. The MOST frequent cause of death is
    A. cancer   B. nephritis   C. tuberculosis
    D. heart disease E. skin disease

16. A group of similar cells working together is called a(n)
    A. organ   B. tissue   C. nucleus   D. nerve   E. bine

17. The contraction of striated muscle cells is controlled by the
    A. person   B. nerves   C. heart   D. tissues   E. cartilages

18. The muscles are fastened to the bones at both ends by
    A. ligament   B. ossification   C. cartilages
    D. tendons   E. coccyx

19. The outer layer of the skin is called the
    A. callus   B. dermis   C. papillae
    D. epidermis   E. cuticle

20. Human eggs are produced in the
    A. vagina   B. uterus   C. ovaries
    D. fallopian tube E. conceptus

21. Heredity plays an important part in the transmission of
    A. cancer B. color blindness C. heart disease
    D. tuberculosis E. streptococcus

22. Fatigue is produced by accumulations of dioxide and lactic acid in
    A. the muscle cells B. lungs C. respiratory system
    D. nerve cells E. cardiac muscles

23. _____ is NOT a function of the bones of the body.
    A. Support B. Attachment of muscles
    C. Manufacture of blood cells D. Protection
    E. Weight control

24. A hernia, or rupture, is more common in
    A. young girls B. middle-aged women
    C. infants D. men
    E. older women

25. The body's _____ glands sit atop the kidneys.
    A. adrenal B. pituitary C. thyroid
    D. parathyroid E. pineal

26. An inflamed area containing pus is called a(n)
    A. blackhead B. impetigo C. pustule
    D. boil E. fever blister

27. _____ is(are) the MOST important concerning vitamin D.
    A. Green vegetables B. Lean meat C. Sunshine
    D. Butter E. Fruits

28. To recover from influenza, it is MOST important to
    A. rest and hydrate B. move to a dry climate
    C. exercise by taking long walks D. take antibiotics

29. Cooking vegetables by boiling decreases their nutritional value in respect to
    A. proteins B. starch C. vitamins D. fats

30. The _____ destroy disease germs by surrounding and devouring them.
    A. red corpuscles B. white corpuscles
    C. blood platelets D. interstitial cells

31. An unconscious person should be given _____ as a first-aid measure.
    A. water B. whiskey or brandy
    C. coffee or tea D. none of these

32. The scientific name for the female reproductive cell is
    A. sperm B. ovum C. gamete D. embryo

33. Little or no fiber is contained in
    A. raw fruits
    B. whole-grain cereals
    C. sugar and candy
    D. vegetables

34. The term *fracture*, as used in first aid, means a(n)
    A. bone out of joint
    B. broken bone
    C. injury to a cartilage
    D. severed tendon

35. A disease in which certain body cells seem to *grow wild*, thereby destroying the regular cells and tissues, is
    A. leprosy   B. ulcers   C. cancer   D. hernia

36. It is NOT advisable to use cathartics and laxatives regularly because they
    A. weaken the muscle tone of the intestines
    B. destroy the enzymes of digestion
    C. cause one to lose appetite
    D. cause one to lose weight

37. Diseases that can be transmitted from one person to another by germs are
    A. infectious
    B. hereditary
    C. allergies
    D. non-communicable

38. From a health perspective, a campaign emphasizing the benefits of home fruit and vegetable gardens should focus primarily on which of the following?
    A. Harvesting techniques and timing for peak fruit ripeness
    B. The importance of properly storing and washing home-grown foods
    C. Amount of money saved on home-grown versus store-bought items
    D. Relationship between vitamin density and quality of soil mixes

39. The soft tissue that underlies the hard outer enamel of a tooth is called
    A. dentine
    B. cement
    C. connective tissue
    D. root

40. Which statement on the reliability and accuracy of health advertising over the internet and social media is TRUE?
    A. It is very reliable since it is vetted before being broadcast.
    B. It may be considered reliable since doctors often prescribe many of the health remedies advertised.
    C. Most of it is reliable and can be believed by the public.
    D. Much of it is of questionable reliability.

41. The *bends* is a(n)
    A. gymnastic movement
    B. disease of the intestinal tract
    C. disease of divers and caisson workers
    D. ailment due to inhaling dust

42. A condition that involves curvature of the spine is 42.____
    A. spinal stenosis B. anemia
    C. rheumatoid arthritis D. scoliosis

43. All of the following are procedures performed during the annual physical check-up 43.____
    of an overweight 30-year-old male EXCEPT
    A. blood test B. urine analysis
    C. blood pressure reading D. prostate exam

44. _____ applies to the destruction of bacteria. 44.____
    A. Quarantine   B. Vaccination   C. Disinfection   D. Inoculation

45. The age period in which lack of proper nutrition results in the MOST harm is 45.____
    A. from birth to 6 years of age
    B. childhood (approximately 6-12 years)
    C. adolescence (approximately 12-18 years)
    D. early maturity (18-24 years)

KEY (CORRECT ANSWERS)

1.	C	11.	B	21.	B	31.	D	41.	C
2.	B	12.	A	22.	A	32.	B	42.	D
3.	C	13.	D	23.	E	33.	C	43.	D
4.	C	14.	E	24.	D	34.	B	44.	C
5.	A	15.	D	25.	A	35.	C	45.	A
6.	C	16.	B	26.	C	36.	A		
7.	B	17.	A	27.	C	37.	A		
8.	C	18.	D	28.	A	38.	B		
9.	C	19.	D	29.	C	39.	A		
10.	B	20.	C	30.	B	40.	D		

EXAMINATION SECTION
TEST 1

DIRECTIONS: Each question or incomplete statement is followed by several suggested answers or completions. Select the one that BEST answers the question or completes the statement. *PRINT THE LETTER OF THE CORRECT ANSWER IN THE SPACE AT THE RIGHT.*

1. Dichloro-diphenyl-trichloroethane was used MOST effectively as a(n)
   A. disinfectant
   B. termite preventative
   C. moth preventative
   D. insecticide

   1.____

2. Learning by constant repetition without being aware of the thought behind what is being learned is
   A. book learning
   B. automation
   C. rationalization
   D. rote learning

   2.____

3. All of the following are common methods for treating drug addiction EXCEPT
   A. detoxification with guidance from healthcare professionals
   B. medication to manage cravings and withdrawal symptoms
   C. behavioral and psychological therapy
   D. institutionalization until the addiction is cured

   3.____

4. The purpose of vaccines is to
   A. reduce the causative organism
   B. develop scar tissue
   C. stimulate growth of antibodies
   D. produce bacteriostasis

   4.____

5. Of the following, the MOST dangerous narcotic is
   A. codeine
   B. opium
   C. heroin
   D. marijuana

   5.____

6. If a teenage girl is careless about putting her clothes away,
   A. put the clothing away for her
   B. tolerate the situation
   C. inspire her to be neat
   D. lecture her

   6.____

7. A two-year-old child that refuses to eat lunch should
   A. be forced to eat
   B. be appeased
   C. not be forced to eat, and the food should be removed without comment after a reasonable amount of time has passed
   D. be scolded

   7.____

8. Thumbsucking should be eliminated by
   A. satisfying the physical and emotional needs
   B. mechanical restraints
   C. applying distatseful compounds
   D. punishment

9. During the first three years, the strongest influence on the personality of a child is
   A. his or her friends
   B. the economic status of the family
   C. the social status of the family
   D. his or her relationships within the family

10. For 12-year-old children, an allowance
    A. may be used as a training device
    B. should be provided
    C. encourages a distorted sense of values
    D. provides a means of disciplinary control

11. When a 10-year-old boy temporarily becomes irritable and boisterous, parents should
    A. divert his attention   B. punish him
    C. cater to his whims   D. ascertain the reason

12. Parents should provide opportunities to habituate control of small muscles of the arms when the child
    A. eats solid food   B. makes an effort to feed himself
    C. eats in restaurant   D. attends school

13. Concerning a six-year-old child, parents who insist on absolute perfection may
    A. hamper future accomplishments
    B. encourage good habits
    C. increase mutual love
    D. destroy imitative performance

14. Lefthandedness
    A. is an individual trait   B. should be corrected
    C. indicates a shortcoming   D. is a conditioned reflex

15. To reduce fears in children, parents should
    A. give affection   B. lecture them
    C. shield them   D. provide safeguards

16. When a new baby is expected, to encourage a sense of belonging, older children should be allowed
    A. to anticipate another playmate
    B. no knowledge of the new baby
    C. to know, but not talk, about the new baby
    D. to share in the preparations

17. First-aid care of a third-degree burn requires 17.____
    A. oil and chalk mixture   B. sterile dressing
    C. antiseptic solution   D. healing ointment

18. Concerning teeth, 18.____
    A. dental caries appear most frequently between ages 12 and 20
    B. dental tartar should not be removed
    C. orthodontia is unimportant
    D. fluorides prevent all decay

19. Heat destroys bacteria by 19.____
    A. enucleation
    B. hemolysis
    C. coagulating protein
    D. making the cell wall permeable

20. The value of antihistaminic compounds lies PRIMARILY in their ability to 20.____
    A. increase intervals between infections
    B. relieve allergic manifestations
    C. immunize
    D. prevent the spread of infection

21. A test program that gives positive proof of drug addiction is through the use of 21.____
    A. hystidine   B. nalline   C. chlorine   D. choline

22. Drug withdrawal symptoms in addicts include vomiting and changes in 22.____
    A. muscular control   B. nerves
    C. color of the skin   D. pupils of the eyes

23. Overuse of NSAIDs like ibuprofen often leads to 23.____
    A. allergic reaction
    B. memory loss or dizziness
    C. sharp decrease in blood pressure
    D. gastrointestinal issues

24. Plantar fasciitis is a condition most likely to be diagnosed by a(n) 24.____
    A. dermatologist   B. hand specialist
    C. oncologist   D. podiatrist

25. Body Mass Index (BMI) is a numeric value used to classify patients as 25.____
    overweight or obese through the measurement of _____ and _____.
    A. height; weight   B. HDL; LDL
    C. pulse rate; breathing rate   D. weight; cholesterol

26. The home can BEST benefit the mental health of its members through 26.____
    A. development of attitudes which result in appropriate emotional expression
    B. an elementary knowledge of psychiatry
    C. a check on the psychosomatics of the older members
    D. regular physical check-ups

4 (#1)

27. When a child expresses fear of darkness on retiring, the BEST procedure is to
    A. make light of his fears
    B. compel him to accept the darkness
    C. provide a dim light
    D. shame him for his fears

28. Active immunity is acquired through
    A. production of antibodies
    B. imperviousness of skin tissue
    C. enzyme activity
    D. washing action of mucous membranes

29. The main criticism of body mass index as a measure of overall health is that it
    A. can cause mental health issues by classifying someone as obese
    B. fails to accurately account for muscle mass and body fat
    C. is too complex to provide an accurate assessment
    D. is too difficult to measure

30. A highly dangerous and addictive synthetic narcotic is
    A. amidol   B. amidone   C. cobalamine   D. pyridoxine

KEY (CORRECT ANSWERS)

1.	D	11.	D	21.	B
2.	D	12.	B	22.	D
3.	D	13.	A	23.	D
4.	C	14.	A	24.	D
5.	C	15.	A	25.	A
6.	C	16.	D	26.	A
7.	C	17.	B	27.	C
8.	A	18.	A	28.	A
9.	D	19.	C	29.	B
10.	A	20.	B	30.	B

TEST 2

DIRECTIONS: Each question or incomplete statement is followed by several suggested answers or completions. Select the one that BEST answers the question or completes the statement. *PRINT THE LETTER OF THE CORRECT ANSWER IN THE SPACE AT THE RIGHT.*

1. The Salk vaccine is administered to prevent
    A. measles
    B. diphtheria
    C. poliomyelitis
    D. whooping cough

    1.____

2. Cancer of the blood is
    A. carcinoma
    B. sarcoma
    C. leukemia
    D. epithelioma

    2.____

3. The accepted treatment in severe and extensive radiation burns is to FIRST
    A. apply tannic acid generously
    B. apply wet sodium bicarbonate dressing
    C. bandage the burned area firmly
    D. put the patient to bed

    3.____

4. A bed cradle is a device for supporting the
    A. back
    B. knees
    C. bed covering
    D. food tray

    4.____

5. Pediculosis Capitus refers to
    A. baldness
    B. athlete's foot
    C. lice
    D. tics

    5.____

6. The MAIN purpose of a good nursing chart is to
    A. aid the nurse's memory
    B. help the doctor in diagnosis and treatment
    C. prevent lawsuits
    D. protect the hospital

    6.____

7. When an ice bag is applied, it should be
    A. kept filled with ice
    B. strapped in place
    C. removed every 15 or 20 minutes
    D. removed every hour

    7.____

8. Hepatitis is a disease of the
    A. renals
    B. spleen
    C. liver
    D. pancreas

    8.____

9. Bones are joined to one another with
    A. sinews
    B. tendons
    C. ligaments
    D. membranes

    9.____

10. Average adult pulse rate for a man is
    A. 64 B. 72 C. 80 D. 96

11. In MOST cases, to get a doctor in an emergency, call the
    A. nearest doctor
    B. nearest hospital
    C. Red Cross
    D. police emergency 911

12. Intravenous injections may be legally administered by the
    A. registered nurse
    B. practical nurse
    C. nursing aide
    D. home nurse

13. Persons who are likely to come in contact with communicable diseases are immunized by
    A. heredity
    B. environment
    C. asepsis
    D. biotics

14. The temperature of water for a hot water bottle should NOT exceed
    A. 100°F B. 150°F C. 125°F D. 175°F

15. The currently accepted treatment for arthritis is
    A. x-ray
    B. cortisone
    C. aureomycin
    D. gold injections

16. The MOST reliable temperature is that found in the
    A. rectum
    B. axilla
    C. mouth
    D. none of the above

17. An antiseptic solution recommended in first aid for slight skin scratches (abrasions) is
    A. concentrated boric acid
    B. tincture of merthiolate 1:1000
    C. iodine 2%
    D. tincture of green soap

18. The MOST frequent cause of death in the United States today is
    A. cancer
    B. tuberculosis
    C. Alzheimer's disease
    D. heart disease

19. Average adult temperature by rectum is ____°F.
    A. 99.6 B. 97.6 C. 98.6 D. 100.6

20. Metaplasia refers to disturbances of the
    A. mucous membranes
    B. epithelial tissues
    C. cartilage
    D. basal metabolism

21. A subjective symptom is one that the patient
    A. feels
    B. hears
    C. sees
    D. smells

22. A bed cradle
    A. keeps the patient's weight off the bed
    B. keeps the knees up
    C. elevates the feet
    D. keeps the weight of the covers off the patient

23. Statistics indicate that MOST youths start the drug habit with
    A. marijuana   B. heroin   C. cocaine   D. morphine

24. A stroke may be caused by
    A. cerebral hemorrhage   B. caecal dilation
    C. aortal thrombosis   D. pleural edema

25. The control of automatic breathing is located in the
    A. cerebrum   B. cerebellum
    C. spinal cord   D. medulla oblongata

26. The water for a baby's bath should be closest to ____°F.
    A. 80   B. 90   C. 100   D. 110

27. The Schick test indicates immunity to
    A. diphtheria   B. smallpox   C. tetanus   D. tuberculosis

28. Difficulty in speaking is known as
    A. asphyxia   B. aphasia   C. amnesia   D. anorexia

29. A water blister should be
    A. opened and drained
    B. left unbroken
    C. painted with iodine and bandaged
    D. soaked in hot Epsom salt solution

30. The FIRST to be affected by the anesthetizing action of alcohol is the exercise of
    A. judgment   B. memory
    C. muscular coordination   D. control of speech

31. To the nervous system, alcohol acts as a
    A. depressant   B. stimulant   C. gratifier   D. agitator

32. Acute alcoholism may properly be labeled a psychosis because it involves
    A. intellectual limitations
    B. a loss of contact with reality
    C. emotional inadequacies
    D. bodily disease

33. Blood alcohol content is a measure of
    A. the amount of alcohol consumed in a 24-hour span
    B. the amount of alcohol in the blood
    C. the amount of alcohol it takes to intoxicate an average adult
    D. the effect of alcohol on blood thinning

34. Characteristic symptoms of chronic alcoholism include
    A. exiccosis
    B. damage to brain tissue
    C. increase in weight
    D. periods of depression

35. Alcohol is MOST often used excessively in order to
    A. induce sleep
    B. stimulate brain action
    C. overcome social inadequacy
    D. furnish temporary release from tensions

KEY (CORRECT ANSWERS)

1.	C	11.	D	21.	A	31.	A
2.	C	12.	A	22.	D	32.	B
3.	C	13.	D	23.	A	33.	B
4.	C	14.	C	24.	A	34.	D
5.	C	15.	B	25.	D	35.	D
6.	B	16.	A	26.	C		
7.	C	17.	C	27.	A		
8.	C	18.	D	28.	B		
9.	C	19.	C	29.	B		
10.	B	20.	C	30.	A		

EXAMINATION SECTION
TEST 1

DIRECTIONS: Each question or incomplete statement is followed by several suggested answers or completions. Select the one that BEST answers the question or completes the statement. *PRINT THE LETTER OF THE CORRECT ANSWER IN THE SPACE AT THE RIGHT.*

1. A specialist is a physician who has restricted his or her practice to a given body system. Which of the statements below is FALSE concerning the various medical specialties? A(n)

    A. internist deals with diseases of the bones
    B. opthamologist deals with diseases of the eye
    C. dermatologist deals with diseases of the skin
    D. neurologist deals with diseases of the brain and nervous system

1.____

2. Alcohol has which of the following effects on the body? Alcohol

    A. causes blood vessels near the skin to constrict
    B. helps the body retain heat
    C. stimulates responses by the brain
    D. stimulates the secretion of acid in the stomach

2.____

3. The term hypertension refers to someone who

    A. has high blood pressure
    B. has overtaxed his muscular system
    C. has stomach ulcers
    D. does not deal effectively with stress

3.____

4. When a person exhibits neurotic behavior, he may

    A. act in a peculiar way or exhibit physical symptoms because of his response to anxiety
    B. hallucinate and perceive objects around him to be different than they really are
    C. perceive reality in such a distorted way that he may be unable to function properly
    D. exhibit two widely different personalities or extremely different moods

4.____

5. Gonorrhea, the MOST frequently reported venereal disease,

    A. has early symptoms that are usually more pronounced in women than in men
    B. may be diagnosed by a blood test and treated with injections of gamma globulin
    C. is normally transmitted through sexual intercourse
    D. is caused and transferred by a virus

5.____

6. Which organ of the body is responsible for the oxidation of alcohol into simpler products? The

    A. heart   B. liver   C. lungs   D. stomach

6.____

7. Ovulation USUALLY occurs in the human female

   A. approximately five days before the end of the menstrual cycle
   B. approximately halfway between menstrual cycles
   C. during menstruation
   D. approximately five days after the beginning of menstruation

8. Which one of the following behaviors on the part of parents could be damaging to developing positive emotional health in children?

   A. Showing their love, support, and acceptance to their children
   B. Listening carefully to what their children have to say
   C. Setting no limits on what type of behaviors and actions are acceptable for their children
   D. Teaching the child to share with others and to consider others

9. When treating a person for shock, you should

   A. give the individual a stimulant to increase the blood pressure
   B. make sure the individual is sitting up to prevent fainting
   C. keep the individual warm and lying still
   D. place a pillow or other soft object under the individual's head to elevate this portion of the body

10. Most people will FIRST feel some effects from drinking alcoholic beverages when the percentage of alcohol in the blood reaches

    A. .02 to .05%   B. .5 to .7%
    C. 1 to 2%   D. .2 to .4%

11. Which drug below probably has the GREATEST tendency to be addictive?

    A. Heroin   B. Benzedrine
    C. Phenobarbital   D. Alcohol

12. It is important to apply a splint to a fractured limb before transporting a person because the splint will

    A. relieve the pain by keeping the limb immobile
    B. prevent the bones from growing together crookedly
    C. allow for limited use of the limb
    D. keep the bones immobile and prevent injury to muscles, blood vessels, and nerves

13. A person will never feel the intoxicating effects of alcohol if

    A. the rate at which alcohol is absorbed into the blood is greater than the rate at which the body oxidizes the alcohol
    B. the consumption of alcohol takes place slowly, but steadily
    C. the rate at which alcohol is absorbed into the blood is equal to the rate at which the body oxidizes the alcohol
    D. only beverages low in alcoholic content are consumed

14. Which of the following statements about the prevention and control of venereal disease is INCORRECT?   14._____

    A. If a person thinks he or she has been exposed to venereal disease, it is important to wait to see what symptoms develop before seeing a doctor.
    B. The probability of contracting venereal disease is greater when a person has many sexual partners.
    C. It is possible for venereal disease to be transmitted by kissing or by contact with open sores or broken skin.
    D. When a case of venereal disease is confirmed, it is important to discover the names of that person's sexual partner or partners.

15. The table below contains the basic information for Mr. Jones' diet on a daily basis. In addition, it is known that a reduction of 3,500 calories is required to lose one pound of fat. Using all this data, how many pounds would Mr. Jones lose in seven days?   15._____

Mr. Jones' basal metabolism	1600 cal/day
On his diet, Mr. Jones eats foods with a calorie content	1200 cal/day
Also on his diet, Mr. Jones has an exercise program in which he *burns up*	600 cal/day

    _____ pound (s).

    A. Almost six   B. Two   C. One   D. Four

16. Which of the following is part of the male reproductive system?   16._____

    A. Fallopian tube   B. Vas deferens
    C. Cervix   D. Pineal gland

17. Under certain conditions, isometric exercise may be used as part of a fitness program to help develop   17._____

    A. strength   B. speed   C. endurance   D. flexibility

18. When considering the purchase of a health insurance policy, one should   18._____

    A. choose a policy that covers all routine costs
    B. avoid a policy that has a deductible clause
    C. choose a policy with the lowest premium cost
    D. choose a policy that covers the cost of medical services you can't afford

19. To aid yourself in developing positive emotional health, you should do all of the following EXCEPT   19._____

    A. attempt to resolve all problems by yourself and not not ask others for help
    B. use your own experiences as learning devices and modify your behavior accordingly
    C. develop a willingness to accept responsibility
    D. attempt to keep your body physically healthy

20. The PRIMARY purpose of Medicare is to help
    A. pay medical costs for the aged
    B. provide financial assistance to community health organizations
    C. pay medical costs of dependent children
    D. pay medical costs for the poor

21. A person who regularly takes narcotics commonly experiences all of the following EXCEPT
    A. reduced sexual drive or impotence
    B. constricted pupils
    C. diarrhea
    D. malnutrition

22. In the case of a severe burn that results in the blistering and charring of the skin, you should
    A. wash the area with soap and water to remove burned skin and prevent infection
    B. cover the burned area with a dry sterile dressing to reduce loss of body fluids
    C. remove fluid from blisters and cover with a clean sterile dressing
    D. cover the burned area with an ointment to reduce pain

23. Which drug or drug type in the list below can BEST be classified as a stimulant?
    A. Barbiturates   B. Amphetamines
    C. Alcohol   D. Opiates

24. The BEST emergency procedure to stop most cases of severe bleeding is to apply
    A. pressure directly over the wound
    B. a clean sterile bandage to the wound
    C. pressure at the closest pressure point
    D. a tourniquet

25. Some terms involving infectious disease are:
    I. Infection
    II. Invasion
    III. Incubation
    What is the CORRECT order or sequence of these terms in regard to how an infectious disease affects the human body?
    A. II, I, III   B. I, II, III
    C. II, III, I   D. I, III, II

26. One of the procedures of CPR (cardio-pulmonary resuscitation) is external heart massage.
    Which of the following statements about external heart massage is FALSE?
    External heart massage
    A. is usually accompanied by mouth-to-mouth resuscitation
    B. squeezes the heart between the sternum and spine
    C. should only be given when there is no apparent carotid pulse
    D. should be given on a soft, unresistant surface to prevent injury to ribs

27. Which of the following is an effect of regular smoking? Smoking

    A. increases the number of stillbirths in pregnant women
    B. tends to make it more difficult for the blood to clot
    C. reduces the chances of developing a stomach ulcer
    D. increases the appetite and stimulates the sense of smell

28. The emergency treatment to be used on a child who has swallowed a strong corrosive substance should include all of the following EXCEPT

    A. treating the child for shock
    B. inducing vomiting
    C. calling a doctor or local hospital
    D. giving the child water or milk to drink

29. Carbon monoxide, one of the substances found in cigarette smoke, is thought to cause shortness of breath because

    A. it is a depressant on the respiratory system
    B. it leaves a deposit of tar in the lungs
    C. it reduces the oxygen-carrying capacity of the blood
    D. hot carbon monoxide tends to singe the lung surfaces

30. The BEST way to choose a family doctor is to

    A. look for a physician closest to home
    B. consult the phone directory for a list of available physicians
    C. ask your local hospital or medical society for recommendations
    D. look in the advertisement section of the newspaper

KEY (CORRECT ANSWERS)

1.	A	16.	B
2.	D	17.	A
3.	A	18.	D
4.	A	19.	A
5.	C	20.	A
6.	B	21.	B
7.	B	22.	B
8.	C	23.	B
9.	C	24.	C
10.	A	25.	C
11.	A	26.	D
12.	D	27.	A
13.	C	28.	B
14.	C	29.	C
15.	B	30.	C

TEST 2

DIRECTIONS: Each question or incomplete statement is followed by several suggested answers or completions. Select the one that BEST answers the question or completes the statement. *PRINT THE LETTER OF THE CORRECT ANSWER IN THE SPACE AT THE RIGHT.*

1. Which of the following physiological changes commonly occurs in women during pregnancy?
   The

   A. size of the heart is slightly reduced
   B. breasts increase in size
   C. position of the diaphragm is lowered
   D. breathing rate is lowered

   1.____

2. The MAIN difference between aerobic and anaerobic exercise is that

   A. aerobic exercise is less suited to older persons than is anaerobic exercise
   B. aerobic exercise involves rapid and vigorous movements, while anaerobic exercise involves rhythmic and more fluid movements
   C. in aerobic exercise sufficient oxygen is present, but in anaerobic exercise, there is an oxygen deficiency
   D. aerobic exercise should be done no more than once a week to be most effective, while anaerobic exercise should be done more often

   2.____

3. Cancer can BEST be defined as a(n)

   A. abnormal growth and spread of cells
   B. elevated white blood cell count
   C. viral infection
   D. fungus infection

   3.____

4. To understand emotional responses, you should realize that

   A. your emotions cannot result in sickness
   B. your emotional responses are like reflexes that involve no thinking
   C. your emotional responses are related to your personal values
   D. you were born with the emotions you have now

   4.____

5. Conception, or fertilization, in the human female

   A. requires implantation of the egg on the wall of the vagina
   B. requires one sperm to penetrate one egg
   C. takes place in the uterus
   D. takes place during menstruation

   5.____

6. The MAJOR importance of fiber in the diet is that it

   A. provides energy for the body
   B. is a source of important minerals
   C. is extremely easy to digest
   D. helps in normal elimination

   6.____

7. The incompatibility of the Rh blood factors in a pregnancy can be a problem when

   A. the mother is Rh positive and the father is Rh negative
   B. both the mother and father are Rh negative
   C. the mother is Rh negative and the baby is Rh positive
   D. both mother and baby are Rh negative

8. Which statement about vitamins is TRUE?

   A. The more vitamins you take, the more healthy your body will be.
   B. Some vitamins may be manufactured by the body.
   C. Vitamins are important sources of energy.
   D. Vitamins are a substitute for fats, proteins, and carbohydrates.

9. Below are listed some characteristics and symptoms of a common infectious disease:
   I. In the United States, its greatest incidence is among young people fifteen to nineteen years old.
   II. Symptoms may include fever, sore throat, nausea, and chills.
   III. A general weakness for three weeks to several months is common after the initial symptoms have passed.
   IV. A blood test can be used to diagnose the disease. From this information, you can diagnose this infectious disease as

   A. measles
   B. mononucleosis
   C. hepatitis
   D. pneumonia

10. Foods that are good sources of protein include

    A. fish, eggs, and cheese
    B. butter, margarine, and corn oil
    C. fruits and vegetables
    D. bread and cereal

11. An unborn human fetus receives nourishment through the

    A. amniotic fluid
    B. digestive system of the fetus
    C. lining of the uterus
    D. placenta

12. The MAJOR reason vegetarians must select a variety of foods is that

    A. vegetables are low in carbohydrates
    B. a wide variety of different enzymes is necessary in the digestive system
    C. eight essential amino acids are needed to build protein
    D. excesses of certain vitamins must be avoided

13. Which one of the following CANNOT be an infectious agent?

    A. Worms   B. Protozoa   C. Platelets   D. Fungus

14. The high consumption of foods that contain large amounts of saturated fats may represent a health hazard because these fats   14.___

    A. seem to increase the probability of developing cancer
    B. cause a build-up of fat-soluble vitamins in the body
    C. are thought to be a factor in heart disease
    D. accumulate in the liver and interfere with the production of bile

15. Which one of the following is considered to be a non-infectious disease?   15.___

    A. Pneumonia   B. Arthritis
    C. The common cold   D. Influenza

16. Defense mechanisms such as rationalization, repression, and escape   16.___

    A. represent responses that help reduce the stress of emotional conflict
    B. are signs of psychosis
    C. are effectively used when the emotional conflicts become overwhelming
    D. represent responses that help reduce the stress of emotional conflict

17. The endocrine glands serve an important function in the body by   17.___

    A. producing substances that carry nerve impulses
    B. producing hormones which regulate many body processes
    C. helping to regulate a person's genetic make-up
    D. releasing disease-fighting agents directly into the bloodstream

18. Which of the statements below is TRUE concerning cancer?   18.___

    A. A *pap smear* is an effective treatment for cancer.
    B. A lump in a woman's breast means she has cancer.
    C. Early diagnosis is important to cure cancer.
    D. Most skin cancers are fatal.

19. In any well-constructed weight-reducing diet, a person should   19.___

    A. only eat foods that contain no calories
    B. eliminate all favorite foods to reduce calorie intake
    C. strive for a weight loss of no more than one or two pounds per week
    D. reduce the amount of strenuous physical activity

20. Since syphilis is a serious venereal disease among young people, it is IMPORTANT to know that   20.___

    A. if left untreated even after many years, syphilis causes only minor physical damage
    B. syphilis is difficult to treat, even with antibiotics
    C. once a person is cured of syphilis, the body's immune system prevents that person from becoming reinfected
    D. the first symptom of the disease is often a sore or lesion in the genital region

21. The health hazards of being overweight include   21.___

    A. increased chances of becoming anemic
    B. severely reduced blood pressure
    C. increased chances of developing heart disease
    D. the likelihood of vitamin deficiencies

22. One of the changes that occurs in both boys and girls during puberty is

    A. improved physical coordination
    B. decreased hormone production
    C. increased amount of body hair
    D. reduced rate of growth

23. Which one of the following statements listed concerning a person's emotional health is TRUE?

    A. Emotionally healthy people do not experience anxiety.
    B. Emotionally healthy people have no psychological needs.
    C. Emotional health is measured by a set of exact standards.
    D. Emotionally healthy people may avoid situations that will cause them to become anxious.

24. Antibodies, which help fight disease in the body, are

    A. proteins manufactured by the body's white cells that react against disease organisms or their toxins
    B. drugs, produced in other living things, which, when injected into the body, help kill disease organisms or their toxins
    C. living infectious agents that are used in vaccines to stimulate the body's immune response
    D. substances from outside the body that stimulate the body's immune response

25. The material found in cigarette smoke that contains the MOST carcinogens is

    A. tar   B. ammonia   C. ash   D. nicotine

26. The MAIN function of the digestive organ indicated by the arrow in the diagram below is

    A. absorption of essential nutrients
    B. absorption of water
    C. secretion of digestive enzymes
    D. secretion of hydrochloric acid

27. To reduce the likelihood of developing cardiovascular disease, one should

    A. keep busy working and only rarely relax
    B. eliminate exercise to avoid straining the heart
    C. eliminate or reduce cigarette smoking
    D. eat plenty of butter, milk, eggs, and cheese

28. When people smoke, the nicotine in tobacco tends to cause a(n) 28.___
    A. sharp decrease in a person's blood pressure
    B. constricting of the blood vessels
    C. decrease in the heartbeat
    D. increase in temperature in the fingers and toes

29. When purchasing a prescription drug, why should you ask the pharmacist whether the drug has a generic equivalent? 29.___
    Generic equivalent drugs
    A. are more pure than the brand-name drug
    B. usually have fewer bad side effects than the brand-name drug
    C. are designed to give you a higher dosage
    D. are usually less expensive than brand-name drugs

30. In any weight-reducing diet, the nutritional calorie is of interest to the dieter. The nutritional calorie is 30.___
    A. found in larger amounts in protein than in any other basic nutrient
    B. a measure of the amount of body fat
    C. found in everything we eat or drink
    D. considered as a unit that measures the amount of fuel entering the body

---

KEY (CORRECT ANSWERS)

1.	B	16.	A
2.	B	17.	B
3.	A	18.	C
4.	C	19.	C
5.	B	20.	D
6.	D	21.	C
7.	C	22.	C
8.	B	23.	D
9.	B	24.	A
10.	A	25.	A
11.	D	26.	B
12.	A	27.	C
13.	C	28.	B
14.	C	29.	D
15.	B	30.	D

EXAMINATION SECTION
TEST 1

DIRECTIONS: Each question or incomplete statement is followed by several suggested answers or completions. Select the one that BEST answers the question or completes the statement. *PRINT THE LETTER OF THE CORRECT ANSWER IN THE SPACE AT THE RIGHT.*

1. Natural resistance is lowered MOST by   1.____
    - A. fatigue
    - B. reduction diet
    - C. cold diet
    - D. lack of immunization

2. Cirrhosis of the liver is USUALLY caused by   2.____
    - A. bacterial contamination of food
    - B. a virus
    - C. excessive use of highly seasoned foods
    - D. extreme malnutrition

3. The true carriers of heredity are   3.____
    - A. neurons
    - B. chromosomes
    - C. sex cells
    - D. genes

4. The MOST serious form of food poisoning is   4.____
    - A. undulant fever
    - B. botulism
    - C. bacterial contamination
    - D. trichinosis

5. The filtering device of the kidneys is the   5.____
    - A. glomerulus
    - B. jejunum
    - C. ileum
    - D. nephron

6. MOST commonly affected by arteriosclerosis are the   6.____
    - A. lungs
    - B. kidneys
    - C. nerves
    - D. senses

7. The Schick test indicates immunity to   7.____
    - A. diphtheria
    - B. smallpox
    - C. tetanus
    - D. tuberculosis

8. Difficulty in speaking is known as   8.____
    - A. axphyxia
    - B. aphasia
    - C. amnesia
    - D. anorexia

9. Heat destroys bacteria by   9.____
    - A. enucleation
    - B. hemolysis
    - C. coagulating protein
    - D. making the cell wall permeable

10. The value of antihistaminic compounds lies PRIMARILY in their ability to

    A. increase intervals between infections
    B. relieve allergic manifestations
    C. immunize
    D. prevent the spread of infection

11. A *stroke* may be caused by

    A. cerebral hemorrhage
    B. caecal dilation
    C. aortal thrombosis
    D. pleural edema

12. The control of automatic breathing is located in the

    A. cerebrum
    B. cerebellum
    C. spinal cord
    D. medulla oblongata

13. Overweight people have less

    A. need for relaxation
    B. resistance to infection
    C. danger of heart disease
    D. inclination to diabetes

14. Rheumatic fever is associated with

    A. infections caused by the hemolytic streptococcus
    B. violent injury to one of the limbs
    C. viral infections of the respiratory tract
    D. bacterial infections of the bones

15. Active immunity is acquired through

    A. production of antibodies
    B. imperviousness of skin tissue
    C. enzyme activity
    D. washing action of mucous membranes

16. The value of antihistaminic compounds lies PRIMARILY in their ability to relieve the effects of

    A. allergies
    B. immunization
    C. infections
    D. nausea

17. The purpose of vaccines is to

    A. reduce the causative organism
    B. develop scar tissue
    C. stimulate growth of antibodies
    D. produce bacteriostasis

18. Hepatitis is a disease of the

    A. renals   B. spleen   C. liver   D. pancreas

19. Salk serum is administered to prevent

    A. measles
    B. diphtheria
    C. poliomyelitis
    D. whooping cough

20. Cancer of the blood is

    A. carcinoma
    B. sarcoma
    C. leukemia
    D. epithelioma

21. Pellagra indicates a deficiency of

    A. ascorbic acid
    B. niacin
    C. thiamine
    D. riboflavin

22. Goiters are caused by lack of

    A. iodine in the food
    B. iron in food
    C. chlorine in the water supply
    D. vitamins in vegetables

23. The MOST frequent cause of death in the United States today is

    A. cancer
    B. tuberculosis
    C. poliomyelitis
    D. heart ailments

24. Average adult temperature by rectum is

    A. 99.6   B. 97.6   C. 98.6   D. 100.6

25. Metaplasia refers to disturbances of the

    A. mucous membranes
    B. epithelial tissues
    C. cartilage
    D. basal metabolism

26. The blood group which is commonly referred to as the *universal recipient* is

    A. A   B. B   C. AB   D. O

27. A contagious disease of the conjunctiva is

    A. glaucoma
    B. xeropthalmia
    C. trachoma
    D. hyperopia

28. Gamma globulins used in the protection against measles and polio contain

    A. toxoids
    B. dead viruses
    C. weakened viruses
    D. antibodies

29. A set of symptoms which usually occur together is known as the

    A. syndrome   B. prognosis   C. synedoche   D. prolan

30. Slow-acting penicillin controls the incidence of

    A. pneumonia
    B. gonorrhea
    C. meningitis
    D. measles

31. Vaccine is a

    A. cure
    B. preventive
    C. remedy
    D. stimulant

32. MOST commonly affected by arteriosclerosis are the

    A. kidneys   B. lungs   C. heart   D. brain

33. A nervous disorder characterized by involuntary action of the muscles which sometimes accompanies rheumatic fever is referred to as

    A. cerebral palsy   B. chorea
    C. neuralgia   D. arthritis

34. When edema is present, sodium intake is restricted because it

    A. slows the heartbeat
    B. causes hardening of the arteries
    C. increases urinary output
    D. holds fluid in the tissues

35. Leukemia is

    A. characterized by an increase in red blood cells
    B. a malignant disease
    C. a disease of the blood vessels
    D. always fatal within six months from the onset of symptoms

36. The child with mumps MUST be considered to be a source of contagion until

    A. his temperature returns to normal
    B. at least four weeks have elapsed since the onset of symptoms
    C. all swelling disappears
    D. the rash has disappeared completely

37. Infectious hepatitis may be transmitted by the patient

    A. for as long as two months after the onset of symptoms
    B. only for the first few days of the illness
    C. until he receives an injection of gamma globulin
    D. only until after the jaundice is no longer noticeable

38. The American Red Cross was founded by

    A. Florence Nightingale   B. Clara Barton
    C. Ellen Richards   D. Anton Leeuwenholk

39. The Schick test is used to determine susceptibility to

    A. poliomyelitis   B. scarlet fever
    C. diphtheria   D. typhoid fever

40. Glorieruli, which help remove impurities from the blood, are found in the

    A. liver   B. gall bladder
    C. lungs   D. kidneys

41. All of the following pertain to skin diseases EXCEPT

    A. glossitis   B. impetigo   C. herpes   D. cheilitis

42. A drug commonly used to treat bronchial infections is

    A. heroin   B. codeine   C. cocaine   D. morphine

43. The relationship between the incidence of cancer and smoking is

    A. inconclusive   B. negative
    C. positive   D. slightly negative

44. Due to advances in immunization, each of the following communicable childhood diseases are rarely found in the United States EXCEPT

    A. diphtheria   B. measles
    C. polio   D. chickenpox

45. A child in the acute stage of rheumatic fever should be given

    A. liquids only
    B. only two meals a day
    C. double servings rich in calories
    D. small frequent feedings

KEY (CORRECT ANSWERS)

1. A	11. A	21. B	31. B	41. A
2. D	12. D	22. A	32. A	42. B
3. D	13. B	23. D	33. B	43. C
4. B	14. A	24. C	34. D	44. D
5. A	15. A	25. C	35. B	45. D
6. B	16. A	26. C	36. C	
7. A	17. C	27. C	37. A	
8. B	18. C	28. D	38. B	
9. C	19. C	29. A	39. C	
10. B	20. C	30. B	40. D	

TEST 2

DIRECTIONS: Each question or incomplete statement is followed by several suggested answers or completions. Select the one that BEST answers the question or completes the statement. *PRINT THE LETTER OF THE CORRECT ANSWER IN THE SPACE AT THE RIGHT.*

1. A malignant disease of the bone marrow is

   A. leukemia
   C. osteoporosis
   B. cirrhosis
   D. nephrosis

2. Dyspnea means difficult

   A. and labored breathing
   B. discharge of urine
   C. or deranged digestion
   D. pronouncing of vocal sounds

3. Underactivity of the thyroid gland in infants may produce the condition known as

   A. gigantism
   C. exophthalmic goiter
   B. Addison's disease
   D. cretinism

4. The number of chromosomes which a person inherits from each of his parents is

   A. 24   B. 35   C. 48   D. 12

5. The four diseases against which an infant should be immunized are smallpox, diphtheria, whooping cough, and

   A. measles
   C. mumps
   B. tetanus
   D. scarlet fever

6. A disease characterized by tender bleeding gums, swollen painful joints, and weakened muscles is

   A. scurvy   B. anemia   C. diabetes   D. carcinoma

7. Of the following diseases, the one that is NOT directly attributable to a specific vitamin deficiency is

   A. scurvy   B. tularemia   C. pellagra   D. rickets

8. A magenta-colored tongue is a symptom indicating a lack of sufficient

   A. vitamin A
   C. niacin
   B. thiamine
   D. riboflavin

9. Diabetic coma is caused by

   A. too much sugar in the diet
   B. too little food intake
   C. imperfect utilization of fat
   D. an overdose of insulin

10. An example of a non-contagious infection is

   A. tetanus
   B. measles
   C. hepatitis
   D. smallpox

11. Infection or irritation of small pouches located along the walls of the small intestines results in a condition called

   A. diverticulitis
   B. nephritis
   C. gastritis
   D. glossitis

12. PKU, a disease in which phenylalanine accumulates in the body, due to faulty metabolism, results in

   A. bone softening in adults
   B. hardening of the corneal tissues
   C. capillary fragility
   D. mental retardation in children

13. Penicillin spores

   A. are present in the air in Northern Alaska
   B. are destroyed by cold storage for two years
   C. germinate in bright sunlight
   D. develop rapidly in dry atmosphere at 30° F

14. Albino rats are used experimentally to determine vitamin C deficiency because

   A. they are allergic to scurvy
   B. they are capable of manufacturing their own ascorbic acid
   C. the symptoms shown do not parallel those in human beings
   D. the effects shown are not clear enough for observation

15. Kyphosis is a term used to designate

   A. angular curvature of the spine
   B. dryness of the mucous membrane
   C. fissures of extreme corners of the mouth
   D. scaly scalp condition

16. The first man to attribute the cause of beri-beri to dietary origin was

   A. Takaki
   B. Eijkman
   C. Funk
   D. Lavoisier

17. An outstanding characteristic of the aging process is

   A. unfavorable reaction to stress
   B. lack of self-reliance
   C. increased irritability
   D. increased heart activity

18. The disease that can be transmitted to human beings by infected rabbits is

   A. undulant fever
   B. tularemia
   C. trichinosis
   D. trichinella

19. All of the following are correct associations EXCEPT
    A. Salk - dead polio vaccine
    B. Sabin - live polio vaccine
    C. Samos - weather satellite
    D. Shepard - suborbital space flight

20. Herpes simplex is an inflammation which affects the
    A. hair   B. skin   C. bones   D. toenails

21. Of the following diseases, the one USUALLY spread by rats and fleas is
    A. typhoid fever   B. sleeping sickness
    C. cholera   D. bubonic plague

22. Of the following, the treatment which would have a diuretic effect is
    A. liquid intake   B. enema
    C. dilantin sodium   D. fluorides

23. Inflammation of the membranes covering the lungs and lining the chest cavity is called
    A. asthma   B. laryngitis
    C. sinusitis   D. pleurisy

24. Hardening of the eyeball, which may lead to blindness in middle-aged or elderly persons, is known as
    A. conjunctivitis   B. trachoma
    C. glaucoma   D. cataract

25. The artery MOST commonly used to count the pulse is the
    A. temporal   B. carotid   C. radial   D. femoral

26. MOST cases of obesity in this country result from
    A. overeating   B. glandular imbalance
    C. heredity   D. economic affluence

27. Observable evidence of vitamin A deficiency in children is
    A. inflammation of eyelids
    B. magenta-colored tongue
    C. sores at angles of lips
    D. coarse, brittle, lusterless hair

28. Cryogenic surgery is a freezing method used in the treatment of
    A. Parkinson's disease   B. xerophthalmia
    C. diabetes   D. pellagra

29. A deficiency of niacin USUALLY results in
    A. osteomalacia   B. rickets
    C. caries   D. pellagra

30. A vaccine is introduced into the body to

   A. develop scar tissue
   B. produce bacteriostasis
   C. stimulate growth of specific antibodies
   D. reduce the causative organism

31. The value of anti-histaminic compounds lies PRIMARILY in their ability to relieve the effects of

   A. athetosis
   B. infections
   C. nausea
   D. allergies

32. The danger of strontium 90 lies in the fact that it

   A. is ultimately concentrated in bone tissue
   B. causes tumors in smooth muscle tissue
   C. is absorbed by the soil
   D. renders the atmosphere unfit for breathing

33. The effect of morphine which is believed to encourage addiction is the

   A. drowsiness, sleep, and dreams
   B. exaggerated feeling of well-being
   C. relief from pain
   D. dulling of perception

34. Ultraviolet rays harm the eyes by

   A. spotting the cornea
   B. enlarging the pupil
   C. destroying the visual purple
   D. drying the retina

35. Cortisone is used to relieve the symptoms of

   A. mental disorders
   B. arthritis
   C. diabetes
   D. heart disease

36. Pigeon-chest, joint enlargements, beaded ribs, and soft bones are symptoms of

   A. beri-beri   B. rickets   C. scurvy   D. pellagra

37. A fatty liver caused by prolonged use of alcohol

   A. raises the riboflavin requirement
   B. delays energy production
   C. contributes to development of cirrhosis
   D. speeds up liver action

38. The deficiency disease associated with ascorbic acid is

   A. beri-beri
   B. scurvy
   C. rickets
   D. night blindness

39. The process by which vital arteries become clogged or narrowed is

    A. atherosclerosis
    B. thrombosis
    C. cirrhosis
    D. scoliosis

40. Artery deposits in atherosclerosis are partially formed by

    A. cholesterol
    B. glycerol
    C. stereols
    D. glycols

41. Heart attacks are MORE common in adults

    A. who are obese
    B. with lung infections
    C. who are underweight
    D. with abdominal injuries

42. Vitamin A deficiency is associated with

    A. keratitis
    B. scurvy
    C. capillary fragility
    D. osteomalacia

43. Vitamin B deficiency is associated with all of the following EXCEPT

    A. blood clotting
    B. pellagra
    C. polyneuritis
    D. anorexia

44. The treatment of alcoholic pellagra is

    A. a balanced diet
    B. oral antibiotics
    C. thiamin injections with an adequate diet
    D. penicillin injections with a balanced diet

45. Aureomycin was developed by

    A. Fleming   B. Waksman   C. Banting   D. Duggar

KEY (CORRECT ANSWERS)

1. A	11. A	21. C	31. D	41. A
2. A	12. D	22. A	32. A	42. A
3. D	13. A	23. D	33. B	43. A
4. A	14. C	24. C	34. C	44. C
5. B	15. A	25. C	35. B	45. D
6. A	16. B	26. A	36. B	
7. B	17. A	27. D	37. C	
8. D	18. B	28. A	38. B	
9. C	19. C	29. D	39. A	
10. A	20. B	30. C	40. A	

EXAMINATION SECTION
TEST 1

DIRECTIONS: Each question or incomplete statement is followed by several suggested answers or completions. Select the one that BEST answers the question or completes the statement. *PRINT THE LETTER OF THE CORRECT ANSWER IN THE SPACE AT THE RIGHT.*

1. A person with simple schizophrenia

    A. has grandiose delusions
    B. withdraws silently to a private world
    C. fears persecution
    D. becomes greatly excited

2. Obsession frequently links a neurosis with

    A. depression
    B. hysteria
    C. amnesia
    D. compulsion

3. Fear of height is

    A. xenophobia
    B. necrophobia
    C. acrophobia
    D. cynophobia

4. If an obese teenager wanted to initiate a self-imposed program of weight control, one good practice would be to

    A. refrain from drinking water with meals
    B. delay eating when very hungry
    C. initiate a "crash diet"
    D. eat slowly and chew food thoroughly

5. The nutritive value of most foods can be BEST preserved by

    A. keeping vegetables hot after they are cooked
    B. storing foods in an opaque container
    C. quick cooking in a small quantity of water
    D. keeping sliced foods at room temperature

6. Of the following statements concerning food, the CORRECT one is:

    A. Vitamin pills are needed by everyone.
    B. Eggs are more digestible raw than cooked.
    C. Pork liver is less nutritious than beef liver.
    D. A diet high in protein is known to raise the basal metabolism.

7. Of the following, the CORRECT statement is

    A. Condensed milk is milk in which the water content has been reduced.
    B. Evaporated milk is milk in which the water content has been reduced.
    C. Homogenized milk is milk in which the liquid residue that results from churning butter has been added.
    D. Irradiated milk is pasteurized milk that has been exposed to ultra violet rays to add vitamin D.

8. During the digestive process, amino acids are produced *primarily* from

   A. fats
   B. carbohydrates
   C. vitamins
   D. proteins

9. The chemical element MOST often found to be deficient in both city and country diets is

   A. iron
   B. calcium
   C. iodine
   D. sodium

10. The sources of saturated fats are

    A. meats and cereals
    B. fish and vegetable oils
    C. vegatables and meats
    D. meats and dairy products

11. The intake of excessive vitamine D is HARMFUL to human beings because it may

    A. lead to pernicious anemia
    B. cause calcium deposits in the kidneys
    C. cause central nervous system irritability
    D. interfere with the ability to reproduce

12. Pernicious anemia is a form of anemia in which the blood does not have enough red cells and is usually treated with vitamin(s)

    A. C
    B. B_{12} and folic acid
    C. E and K
    D. A

13. If a mother wanted to protect her children from rickets, it would be essential to feed them foods which contained vitamin

    A. A
    B. B
    C. C
    D. D

14. The energy required for the body to maintain its internal life process is called

    A. basal metabolism
    B. metabolic rate
    C. nutritional requirement
    D. caloric balance

15. Tobacco is classified as a

    A. narcotic
    B. stimulant-sedative
    C. sympathomimetic
    D. hallucinogen

16. In the years since the publication of the Surgeon General's report on smoking,

    A. cigarette sales have fallen
    B. the number of girls who smoke has increased
    C. young people begin smoking at a later age
    D. filters have been developed that eliminate the danger

17. Emphysema, which can be caused by smoking, can be described as a disease in which the

    A. lung tissue loses its elasticity
    B. bronchial tubes are chronically inflamed

C. blood vessels supplying the lungs become narrow and roughened
D. diaphragm loses its elasticity

18. In the human body, nicotine

    A. produces a decreased heart rate and blood pressure
    B. improves the quality of one's physical performance
    C. causes a lasting condition of double vision
    D. causes a temporary constriction of the arteries of the arms and legs

18._____

19. Smoking cigarettes causes all of the following EXCEPT a(n)

    A. increase in the sensitivity of the organs of taste
    B. enlargement of the pupils of the eyes
    C. reduction in secretions in the oral cavity
    D. inhibition of gastric hunger contractions

19._____

20. Tobacco is

    A. habit forming
    B. addicting
    C. neither habit forming nor addicting
    D. associated with strong withdrawal sickness if a smoker tries to quit

20._____

21. A *positive* correlation has been observed between cigarette smoking and the incidence of

    A. arteriosclerosis   B. angina pectoris
    C. emphysema   D. motor ataxia

21._____

22. The ingredient in cigarettes that causes the so-called "cigarette cough" is

    A. nicotine   B. oxygen
    C. aldehydes   D. tar

22._____

23. Medical studies have shown that cigarette smoking

    A. causes a thickening of the membranes in the air passages
    B. increases the diffusibility of oxygen in the lungs among regular smokers
    C. decreases the heart rate of healthy men, both before and after exercise
    D. produces dilation of peripheral blood vessels

23._____

24. Nicotine is excreted from the body in the

    A. kidneys   B. liver
    C. lungs   D. sweat glands

24._____

25. Excessive exposure to the effects of X-rays may cause

    A. genetic changes in sex cells
    B. crippling diseases
    C. severe burns
    D. blindness

25._____

26. Teenagers suffering from an STD

    A. cannot be treated without the consent of their parents
    B. are sicker than adults
    C. can be treated without the consent of their parents
    D. cannot transmit the disease

27. When one is given an injection of dead or weakened germs, he is given

    A. gamma globulin   B. antitoxin
    C. a vaccine   D. a toxoid

28. All of the following are virus diseases EXCEPT

    A. poliomyelitis   B. influenza
    C. measles   D. typhoid fever

29. Aspirin is classified as a(n)

    A. analgesic   B. antihistamine
    C. sympathomimetic   D. anticoagulant

30. The MOST widely misused of all drugs is

    A. alcohol   B. marijuana
    C. heroin   D. cocaine

31. Early detection and treatment would have the greatest life saving potential in cancer of the

    A. rectum   B. skin
    C. lungs   D. breast

32. Approximately fifty percent of the total intake of strontium-90 is from

    A. milk and milk products B. vegetables
    C. fruits   D. cereal grains

33. Public utility plants located near rivers and using nuclear fuel are a source of _____ pollution.

    A. pathogenic   B. thermal
    C. detergent   D. chemical

34. Anxiety found in a child having a school phobia *invariably* originates in the child's fear of

    A. being enclosed
    B. being separated from his mother
    C. having to prove himself
    D. teachers

35. The individual who refuses to recognize a problem that he has is utilizing the defense mechanism known as

    A. regression   B. repression
    C. rationalization   D. projection

36. With regard to calcium and phosphorus in the diet, all of the following statements are correct EXCEPT:

    A. Large amounts of fat in the diet will result in poor absorption of calcium.
    B. Large doses of iron salts will lower phosphorus absorption.
    C. Large amounts of laxatives tend to produce poor absorption of calcium and phosphorus.
    D. It is necessary to have a much larger amount of phosphorus in the diet than that of calcium.

37. Bile is essential in the digestion of

    A. fats
    B. proteins
    C. carbohydrates
    D. minerals

38. The CORRECT statement is:

    A. Carbohydrates are emulsified by the bile.
    B. The digestion of proteins starts in the stomach and is continued in the small intestine.
    C. The digestion of starches begins in the small intestine and is continued in the large intestine.
    D. Minerals are merely dissovled and absorbed after digestive breakdown.

39. If a victim of poisoning is unconscious, the CORRECT first aid care to follow is to

    A. induce vomiting
    B. keep victim lying face down with head lower than hips
    C. dilute poison with water
    D. give milk or egg white to protect stomach lining

40. A wound in which there is a jagged, ragged tearing of the tissues is called a(n)

    A. laceration
    B. incised wound
    C. puncture wound
    D. abrasion

KEY (CORRECT ANSWERS)

1. B	11. C	21. C	31. D
2. D	12. B	22. D	32. D
3. C	13. D	23. A	33. D
4. D	14. A	24. C	34. B
5. C	15. C	25. A	35. B
6. D	16. A	26. C	36. D
7. B	17. A	27. C	37. A
8. D	18. D	28. D	38. D
9. A	19. B	29. A	39. B
10. D	20. A	30. A	40. A

TEST 2

DIRECTIONS: Each question or incomplete statement is followed by several suggested answers or completions. Select the one that BEST answers the question or completes the statement. *PRINT THE LETTER OF THE CORRECT ANSWER IN THE SPACE AT THE RIGHT.*

1. All of the following statements concerning the intake of alcohol in the body are correct EXCEPT: 1.____

    A. Although alcohol has a caloric content, it is expended instead of being stored in the body.
    B. A small percentage of the alcohol taken into the body is eliminated through the lungs.
    C. Alcohol produces a feeling of warmth with an actual lowering of body temperature.
    D. Digestive changes are necessary before alcohol can be absorbed from the stomach.

2. All of the following characteristics predispose a person to alcoholism EXCEPT having 2.____

    A. little tolerance for frustration
    B. low energy levels and strong impulse control
    C. strong feelings of alienation
    D. conflicts in family relationships

3. The time between the consuming of alcohol and its beginning to be absorbed into the bloodstream may be *as little as* _____ minutes. 3.____

    A. 2   B. 5   C. 8   D. 10

4. All of the following statements concerning alcohol and its effect on the body are correct EXCEPT: 4.____

    A. The constant presence of alcohol impairs the liver cells in their ability to store glycogen
    B. At high concentrations, alcohol causes the lessening of gastric juice secretion.
    C. Beriberi is one of the commonest deficiency diseases associated with alcoholism.
    D. Alcohol increases the enzyme action in the stomach.

5. The term "meninges" is associated LEAST with the 5.____

    A. callus   B. dura mater
    C. pia mater   D. arachnoid

6. The process of acquiring active immunity by having a specific disease and recovering, is an example of 6.____

    A. eliminating the source of infection
    B. upsetting the mode of transmission
    C. increasing the resistance to disease
    D. interfering with the mode of entry

7. All of the following are examples of antibodies EXCEPT 7.____

    A. precipitins   B. antitoxins
    C. agglutinins   D. vaccines

8. Of the following, the substance without addicting properties would be

   A. mescaline
   B. phenobarbital
   C. librium
   D. cocaine

9. When considered as a drug, the MOST accurate classification which describes alcohol is that it is a

   A. stimulant
   B. depressant
   C. hallucinogen
   D. tranquilizer

10. The MOST common signs and symptoms associated with the use of marijuana are

    A. thirst, drowsiness and passiveness
    B. pink eyes, increased pulse rate and hunger
    C. discomfort, anxiety and general ataxia
    D. increased libido, decreased blood pressure and pupil dilation

11. While under the influence of morphine, an addict will *usually*

    A. experience an abnormal dryness of the nose
    B. have contracted, pin point pupils of the eyes
    C. feel strong and superior and experience loss of fatigue
    D. be very talkative and will not listen to others

12. Of the following statements concerning drugs, the CORRECT one is:

    A. As a person's tolerance to barbiturates increases, his tolerance level to other drugs also increases.
    B. Many heroin addicts will use amphetamines when they cannot obtain heroin.
    C. Most experts consider barbiturate addiction more dangerous than heroin addiction.
    D. When skin popping, the user will most often inject directly into a vein.

13. Male testes are part of the

    A. adrenal glands
    B. accessory glands
    C. urethra
    D. endocrine system

14. A synonym for "afterbirth" is

    A. amnion
    B. umbilicus
    C. embryonic gut
    D. placenta

15. Fertilization *normally* takes place in the

    A. uterus
    B. fallopian tube
    C. vagina
    D. ovary

16. The hormone which affects male sexual development is called

    A. estrogen
    B. LH, luteinizing hormone
    C. testosterone
    D. progesterone

17. The menstrual cycle in a woman is *largely* controlled by the _____ gland(s).

    A. thyroid
    B. parathyroid
    C. adrenal
    D. pituitary

3 (#2)

18. In a male sterilization operation, the structures which are cut or tied off are the

   A. epididimi
   B. ureters
   C. seminal vesicles
   D. vas deferens

19. According to Federal and State Health and Safety Codes, workers must wear ear protection if noise levels exceed _____ decibels.

   A. 100   B. 110   C. 80   D. 90

20. The process of water purification in which chemicals are added to the water to assist in dissolving pollution materials is

   A. coagulation
   B. sedimentation
   C. disinfection
   D. aerobic

21. The pupil who fails to make the team and states "I do not like basketball anyway" is

   A. rationalizing
   B. showing off
   C. compensating
   D. conceptualizing

22. A person who suffers from a psychosomatic illness

   A. is seeking attention
   B. is subconsciously feigning symptoms
   C. has no physical problems
   D. has physical problems

23. A loss of contact with the surrounding world with a break or withdrawal from reality is characteristic of a(n)

   A. psychosis
   B. neurosis
   C. psychosomatic disorder
   D. ordinary maladjustment

24. Masturbation may be harmful because

   A. it is usually accompanied by fantasies
   B. it can reduce sexual gratification later on in marriage
   C. mental turmoil may result from guilt feelings
   D. it may result in premature ejaculation

25. The shifting of a weakness or the blame for a situation to some other person or thing is known as

   A. fantasy
   B. identification
   C. repression
   D. projection

26. All of the following associations regarding mental health are correct EXCEPT

   A. paranoia-sufferer - fails into a stupor
   B. mental retardation - low function of the intelligence capacity
   C. schizophrenia - fragmented personality
   D. catatonia - immobility and silence

27. Of the following, the CORRECT statement is:

   A. Emotional maturity comes with physical maturity.
   B. The emotionally mature person feels the need to "prove" himself.

C. Self understanding is not essential to achieving emotional maturity.
D. Emotional maturity enables one to adjust to environmental changes.

28. Extreme emotional upset will

    A. speed up digestion
    B. increase the heart rate
    C. decrease adrenalin secretions
    D. all of the above

28.____

29. The process of transforming food into a state suitable for conversion into body tissue is termed

    A. assimilation
    C. mitosis
    B. effusion
    D. resorption

29.____

30. Enzymes are *most closely* associated with

    A. proteins
    C. bile
    B. mineral salts
    D. cardiac sphincter

30.____

31. It is IMPORTANT for the first-aider to

    A. time artificial respiration to the victim's efforts at breathing
    B. give treatment for shock before commencing artificial respiration
    C. determine the cause of cessation of breathing before administering first aid
    D. administer artificial respiration in cases of gas poisoning, drug poisoning, electric shock and partial obstruction of breathing passages

31.____

32. Some of the symptoms of traumatic shock are

    A. perspiration, slow pulse, rapid breathing
    B. skin pallor, constricted pupils, shallow breathing, moist skin
    C. restlessness, nausea, weak but rapid pulse, dilated pupils
    D. shallow breathing, weak pulse, warm moist skin, eyes vacant

32.____

33. The MOST important emergencies are those which involve

    A. severe bleeding, stoppage of breathing, poisoning
    B. poisoning, broken bones, stoppage of breathing
    C. severe bleeding, stoppage of breathing, broken bones
    D. severe bleeding, unconciousness, poisoning

33.____

34. Mouth-to-mouth artificial respiration

    A. cannot be utilized when there are accompanying chest injuries
    B. requires less effort than manual methods of artificial respiration
    C. can be used only for children
    D. is ineffective in stoppage of breathing due to drug poisoning

34.____

35. If the first-aider notices that the victim's pupils are uneven in size, he should suspect

    A. electric shock
    C. drug overdose
    B. gas poisoning
    D. head injury

35.____

36. In cases of unconsciousness resulting from an epileptic seizure, the victim should be

   A. awakened immediately by using an ammonia ampule
   B. given artificial respiration
   C. allowed to sleep without disturbance
   D. thoroughly restrained from moving

37. In cases where a foreign body lodges in the throat, CORRECT first aid procedure is to

   A. encourage vomiting by placing fingers into the throat
   B. seat the victim and strike him firmly on the back between the shoulder blades (perform Heimlich maneuver)
   C. administer artificial respiration immediately
   D. allow the victim to attempt to cough

38. When treating a victim of simple fainting, the first aider should

   A. give the victim coffee to drink
   B. place the victim on his back in a recumbent position
   C. rub the victim's wrists
   D. hold a gauze pad sprinkled with ammonia over the victim's nostrils

39. In general, local first aid measures are UNNECESSARY in a rib fracture case if the

   A. pain is minimal
   B. swelling is hardly noticeable
   C. breathing causes discomfort
   D. deformity indicates the presence of a fracture

40. A compound fracture is one in which

   A. a bone is broken in two or more places
   B. the broken end of a bone pierces the skin
   C. a bone is both broken and out of place at a joint
   D. there is both a broken bone and a sprained muscle

KEY (CORRECT ANSWERS)

1. D	11. B	21. A	31. D
2. B	12. C	22. B	32. B
3. A	13. D	23. A	33. A
4. B	14. D	24. C	34. B
5. A	15. B	25. D	35. D
6. C	16. C	26. A	36. A
7. D	17. D	27. D	37. B
8. A	18. D	28. B	38. B
9. B	19. D	29. A	39. A
10. B	20. C	30. A	40. B

EXAMINATION SECTION
TEST 1

DIRECTIONS: Each question or incomplete statement is followed by several suggested answers or completions. Select the one that BEST answers the question or completes the statement. *PRINT THE LETTER OF THE CORRECT ANSWER IN THE SPACE AT THE RIGHT.*

1. According to Freudian theory, the _____ functions to encourage a person's tolerance of frustration.   1._____

    A. subconscious B. id
    C. ego   D. superego

2. Which of the following hormones controls the use of glucose by the body's cells?   2._____

    A. Cortisone   B. Insulin
    C. Adrenal steroids D. Thyroxine

3. A client who is receiving lithium carbonate should undergo regular monitoring of   3._____

    A. blood pressure B. blood level
    C. weight   D. urine

4. According to intrapsychic theory, the problem of separation anxiety is MOST likely to occur during the _____ stage.   4._____

    A. latency   B. oral   C. anal   D. phallic

5. A client with adrenal insufficiency is weak and dizzy upon arising in the morning. The MOST likely cause of this is   5._____

    A. lack of sodium
    B. increased intracavity fluid volume
    C. hypertension
    D. hypoglycemic reaction

6. The administration of Anectine prior to electroconvulsive therapy involves the major complication of   6._____

    A. loss of bowel control
    B. inhibition of breathing muscles
    C. memory loss
    D. the bite reflex

7. An infant with congenital hyperthyroidism is at risk for _____ if care is not given immediately.   7._____

    A. thyrotoxicosis B. acromegaly
    C. myxedema   D. mental retardation

8. For which of the following is lithium carbonate used as a control or modifier?   8._____

    A. Manic episode of bipolar disorder
    B. Acute agitation of schizophrenia

83

C. Agitated phase of paranoia
D. Depressive phase of major depression

9. Which of the following is the cause of acromegaly?

   A. Oversecretion of adrenal steroids
   B. Undersecretion of thyroid hormone
   C. Oversecretion of growth hormone
   D. Undersecretion of testosterone

10. At what approximate age does a person demonstrate the primary emergence of his or her personality?

    A. 6 months
    B. 18 months
    C. 2 years
    D. 8 years

11. Diabetic acidosis is caused by elevated _____ levels in the blood.

    A. lactic acid
    B. ketone
    C. albumin
    D. glucose

12. Which of the following behaviors is MOST likely to be demonstrated by an autistic child?

    A. Lack of response to external stimuli
    B. Sad facial expression
    C. Irrelevant smiling
    D. Rocking and flapping of hands

13. To evaluate the effectiveness of DDAVP in treating diabetes insipidus, which of the following should be monitored?

    A. Blood pressure
    B. Intake and output
    C. Pulse rate
    D. Serum glucose

14. Glucagon

    A. retards glycogenesis
    B. causes the release of insulin
    C. elevates blood sugar levels
    D. improves the storage of glucose

15. Of the following, the clearest evidence of mental illness is when a client

    A. does not seem to be able to complete tasks
    B. has difficulty relating to others
    C. has little interest in social activities or work
    D. encounters frequent periods of high anxiety

16. For a client with insulin-dependent diabetes mellitus, insulin needs will *decrease* when the client

    A. exercises
    B. is infected
    C. reaches middle age
    D. is emotionally stressed

17. The treatment for a client suffering from depression should focus on getting the client to

    A. express anger toward others
    B. admit an emotional problem
    C. articulate feelings of low self-esteem
    D. accept care and comfort willingly

18. A child who is about to undergo surgery to correct a congenital megacolon should be given a preoperative enema of

    A. barium
    B. isotonic saline
    C. tap water
    D. hypertonic phosphate

19. Which of the following is a common side effect associated with the use of Thorazine?

    A. Jaundice
    B. Melanocytosis
    C. Photosensitivity
    D. Excessive thirst

20. Piaget's theory of cognitive development states that at the age of six months, an infant should demonstrate

    A. a sense of time
    B. the ability to remember
    C. the onset of object permanence
    D. coordinated motor responses

21. Which of the following would MOST clearly reveal congenital hip dysplasia in a newborn infant?

    A. Different leg lengths
    B. Asymmetrical gluteal folds
    C. Limited adduction
    D. Skewed leg alignment

22. A client is diagnosed with an organic mental disorder. Which of the following nursing strategies would be MOST helpful to this client?

    A. Providing a diet high in carbohydrates
    B. Providing a variety of stimuli to keep the client's interest high
    C. Eliminating the need for choices
    D. Asking the client for input concerning the nursing care plan

23. Which of the following would be included in the early treatment of diabetic acidosis?

    A. IV fluids
    B. Kayexalate
    C. Potassium
    D. NPH insulin

24. Which level of consciousness BEST represents a person's feelings and attitudes?

    A. Conscious
    B. Unconscious
    C. Preconscious
    D. Foreconscious

25. What is the MOST common cause of diabetic ketoacidosis? 25.____
    A. Inadequate fluid intake
    B. Psychological stress
    C. Elevated insulin level
    D. Infection

KEY (CORRECT ANSWERS)

1. C
2. C
3. B
4. B
5. D

6. B
7. D
8. A
9. C
10. C

11. B
12. D
13. B
14. C
15. B

16. A
17. A
18. B
19. C
20. C

21. B
22. C
23. A
24. B
25. D

TEST 2

DIRECTIONS: Each question or incomplete statement is followed by several suggested answers or completions. Select the one that BEST answers the question or completes the statement. *PRINT THE LETTER OF THE CORRECT ANSWER IN THE SPACE AT THE RIGHT.*

1. A client with an anxiety disorder is likely to handle the anxiety in each of the following ways EXCEPT

    A. projecting it onto nonthreatening objects
    B. converting it into a physical symptom
    C. demonstrating regressive behavior
    D. acting out with antisocial behavior

    1._____

2. What type of diet is recommended for a client with Graves' disease?

    A. High roughage
    B. Low sodium
    C. Liquid
    D. High-calorie

    2._____

3. Which of the following is the cause of primary degenerative dementia?

    A. Anatomic brain changes
    B. Atrophy of the frontal lobes
    C. An extended history of malnutrition
    D. Excessive use of narcotics

    3._____

4. Which of the following blood gas results would indicate diabetic acidosis?

    A. Reduced HCO_3
    B. Elevated pH
    C. Reduced PO_2
    D. Elevated PCO_2

    4._____

5. The primary difference between a psychophysiologic disorder and a somatoform disorder is that a

    A. psychophysiologic disorder involves an actual change in tissues
    B. somatoform disorder is caused by emotions
    C. psychophysiologic disorder restricts the client's activities
    D. somatoform disorder is accompanied by a feeling of illness

    5._____

6. Which of the following is MOST likely to be a complication following the insertion of a ventriculoperitoneal shunt in a child with communicating hydrocephalus?

    A. Violent tremors
    B. Distended abdomen
    C. Yellowish discharge from shunt
    D. Fever

    6._____

7. Each of the following is a common physiological response to anxiety EXCEPT

    A. respiratory constriction
    B. dilated pupils
    C. hyperglycemia
    D. increased pulse rate

    7._____

8. It is MOST important for a nurse to monitor a client suffering from alcohol and cirrhosis for

   A. gastric pain
   B. blood in the stool
   C. dizziness
   D. constipation

9. To encourage a withdrawn and noncommunicative client to talk, the BEST nursing plan would include the attempt to

   A. ask the client to describe feelings
   B. ask simply-phrased questions that require yes or no answers
   C. join the client in an activity that the client enjoys
   D. concentrate on subjects that are nonthreatening

10. What is the function of glucose in a cell?

    A. Energy extraction
    B. Protein synthesis
    C. Cellular respiration
    D. Genetic coding

11. Which of the following treatments would be included in a plan for a client with severe and intractable depression and suicidal tendency?

    A. High doses of tranquilizers
    B. Electroconvulsive therapy
    C. Nondirective psychotherapy
    D. Thorazine

12. A *decrease* in the anterior pituitary secretion of ACTH would be caused by

    A. ketosis
    B. a *decrease* in the blood concentration of adrenal steroids
    C. an *increase* in the blood concentration of cortisol
    D. acidosis

13. A client is experiencing a phase of extreme elation and hyperactivity. Which of the following nursing interventions would BEST meet the client's nutritional needs?

    A. Assuming that the client will eat when hungry
    B. Firmly suggesting that the client sit and eat the meal that has been prepared
    C. Inducing an IV feeding to insure that the client is properly nourished
    D. Giving the client frequent high-calorie feedings that the client can feed to herself

14. Which of the following would be experienced by a client with acute cholecystitis accompanied by biliary colic?

    A. Melena
    B. Lipid intolerance
    C. Diarrhea
    D. Pain in lower left quadrant

15. Which of the following must be monitored especially closely following a hypophysectomy?

    A. Motor reflexes
    B. Urinary output
    C. Intracranial pressure
    D. Respiration

16. Which of the following would MOST accurately characterize the personality of a client with obsessive-compulsive personality disorder?

    A. Deep depression
    B. Indecisiveness and doubt
    C. Rapid mood swings
    D. Detailed delusions

17. Which of the following symptoms would MOST likely be revealed during an assessment of a client with Cushing's syndrome?

    A. Dehydration
    B. Migraine headaches
    C. Menorrhagia
    D. Hypertension

18. Most commonly, the behavior of a client with schizophrenia can be described as

    A. euphoric
    B. angry and hostile
    C. flat and apathetic
    D. depressed

19. Which of the following medications would be used to treat a child with cystic fibrosis?

    A. Antimetabolite
    B. Pancreatic enzymes
    C. Fat-soluble vitamins
    D. Aerosol mists

20. Which of the following would NOT be a helpful component of a nursing care plan for a severely depressed client?

    A. Short-term projects
    B. Client participation in activity planning
    C. Repetitive activities
    D. Simple instructions to be followed

21. A client with Addison's disease is experiencing hypotension. Most likely, this involves a disturbance in the production of

    A. mineralocorticoids
    B. proteins
    C. glucocorticoids
    D. insulin

22. Which of the following medications would be used to counter an overdose of narcotics?

    A. Methadone
    B. Thorazine
    C. Benzedrine
    D. Narcan

23. Prior to a serum glucose test, a client with Type II diabetes mellitus should

    A. have a clear liquid breakfast
    B. take prescribed medications
    C. void the bladder
    D. avoid food and fluids

24. Which of the following is the BEST description of a somatoform disorder? A(n)

    A. conscious defense against stress
    B. sublimation of stress
    C. psychological defense against anxiety
    D. unconscious means of controlling conflict

25. Which of the following tests is conducted to detect PKU in infant children?   25.____

    A. OCT   B. Phenistix test
    C. BUN   D. Guthrie blood test

KEY (CORRECT ANSWERS)

1. D   11. B
2. D   12. C
3. B   13. D
4. A   14. B
5. A   15. C

6. D   16. B
7. A   17. B
8. B   18. C
9. D   19. B
10. A   20. B

21. A
22. D
23. D
24. D
25. D

TEST 3

DIRECTIONS: Each question or incomplete statement is followed by several suggested answers or completions. Select the one that BEST answers the question or completes the statement. *PRINT THE LETTER OF THE CORRECT ANSWER IN THE SPACE AT THE RIGHT.*

1. A client recently admitted to an alcohol detoxification unit would probably exhibit each of the following EXCEPT   1.____

   A. hypertension
   B. nausea
   C. hyperactivity
   D. loss of appetite

2. Prior to an adrenalectomy, the client should   2.____

   A. increase fluid intake
   B. receive steroids
   C. have all medication withheld for 48 hours
   D. be placed on a high-protein diet

3. A client with an antisocial personality disorder   3.____

   A. learns quickly through experience and punishment
   B. is generally unable to defer gratification
   C. often masks his disorder by articulate communication
   D. suffers from a high level of anxiety

4. Which of the following is a defense mechanism that helps an individual channel unacceptable desires into socially approved behavior?   4.____

   A. Regression
   B. Denial
   C. Conversion
   D. Sublimation

5. Which of the following would NOT be a likely result of a laboratory test performed on a client suffering from diabetic ketoacidosis?   5.____

   A. Low CO_2
   B. Increased acidity
   C. High bicarbonate
   D. Increased blood sugar

6. Following an adrenalectomy, a client is MOST likely to exhibit the symptoms of   6.____

   A. sodium retention
   B. dehydration
   C. hypotension
   D. increased urinary output

7. It is MOST important for a nurse to _____ when attempting to resolve a crisis situation with a client.   7.____

   A. encourage socialization
   B. meet all of the client's dependency needs
   C. nurture the client's ego strengths
   D. introduce the client to a therapy group

8. Which of the following is NOT a typical indication of a hypoglycemic reaction to insulin?   8.____

   A. Paleness
   B. Excessive thirst
   C. Tremors
   D. Perspiration

9. A client is admitted to the hospital with a diagnosis of conversion disorder. The nurse should expect the client's attitude toward his physical symptoms to be one of

   A. hysteria
   B. indifference
   C. anger
   D. great sadness

10. Along with vitamin D, the regulatory agent that controls the overall calcium balance in the body is

    A. parathyroid hormone
    B. growth hormone
    C. thyroid hormone
    D. ACTH

11. A client is admitted to the hospital with Wernicke's encephalopathy caused by chronic alcoholism. The client's initial treatment would include

    A. an increase in fluid intake
    B. IM injection of thiamine
    C. administration of an anti-opiate
    D. administration of paraldehyde

12. Each of the following is a defect commonly associated with tetralogy of Fallot EXCEPT

    A. pulmonary artery stenosis
    B. mitral valve stenosis
    C. right ventricular hypertrophy
    D. overriding aorta

13. Which of the following statements, spoken to a nurse by a patient diagnosed with Alzheimer's disease, would indicate a need to accomplish Erikson's developmental task of ego integrity versus despair?

    A. I don't understand why I have to go through this.
    B. Please leave me alone.
    C. I can take care of myself.
    D. I am useless to everyone now.

14. The purpose of administering Mycifradin to a client with liver disease is to

    A. increase the urea digestive activity of enteric bacteria
    B. protect the liver from bacteria
    C. reduce ammonia-forming bacteria in the intestinal tract
    D. aid the digestion of complex proteins

15. Emotionally disturbed children

    A. seem unresponsive to their environment
    B. respond equally to all stimuli
    C. respond violently to most stimuli
    D. are immersed in their environment to the point of distraction

16. A client exhibiting cold intolerance may have

    A. increased levels of CO_2
    B. decreased blood pH

C. insufficient bile salts
D. decreased levels of T_3 and T_4

17. The part of the psyche that develops from internalizing the concepts of parents and other significant relations is the

    A. foreconscious
    B. id
    C. ego
    D. superego

18. Which of the following is NOT a typical sign of hypo-kalemia?

    A. Weakness
    B. Abdominal distention
    C. Edema
    D. Apathy

19. Which of the following might be experienced by a person who makes an abrupt withdrawal from habitual use of barbiturates?

    A. Gastric bleeding
    B. Cardiac arrhythmia
    C. Convulsions
    D. Ataxia

20. Which of the following would be observed in a toddler with cyanotic congenital heart disease?

    A. Orthopnea
    B. Blotchy skin
    C. Increased hematocrit
    D. Pitting edema

21. A delusional client is admitted for psychiatric treatment after harming a close relative. In talking about the incident, the client refers to herself in the third person. This is an example of the defense mechanism of

    A. conversion
    B. transference
    C. dissociation
    D. displacement

22. Which of the following is the clearest indication of diabetes insipidus?

    A. Elevated blood glucose
    B. Increased blood pressure
    C. Decreased urinary specific gravity
    D. Increased BUN

23. Which of the following is the MOST common cause of functional mental illness?

    A. Infection
    B. Chemical imbalance
    C. Social environment
    D. Genes

24. Which gland regulates the rate of oxygenation in the body's cells?

    A. Thyroid
    B. Adrenal
    C. Thalamus
    D. Pituitary

25. Which of the following is NOT thought to be a significant formative component of personality?

    A. Cultural setting
    B. Genetic background
    C. Psychologic development
    D. Biologic constitution

KEY (CORRECT ANSWERS)

1.	C	11.	B
2.	B	12.	B
3.	B	13.	D
4.	D	14.	C
5.	C	15.	A
6.	C	16.	D
7.	C	17.	D
8.	B	18.	C
9.	B	19.	C
10.	A	20.	C

21. C
22. B
23. C
24. A
25. B

TEST 4

DIRECTIONS: Each question or incomplete statement is followed by several suggested answers or completions. Select the one that BEST answers the question or completes the statement. *PRINT THE LETTER OF THE CORRECT ANSWER IN THE SPACE AT THE RIGHT.*

1. The preservation of sodium in the body's cells is accomplished by the hormone

   A. parathyroid hormone
   B. thyrocalcitonin
   C. aldosterone
   D. insulin

2. Which of the following behaviors would be LEAST likely to be demonstrated by a client with an organic mental disorder?

   A. An inclination to ignore the present circumstances while dwelling in the past
   B. A steadfast resistance to change
   C. The inability to focus on new interests
   D. A fixation on personal appearance and hygiene

3. Which of the following is a complication associated with hyperparathyroidism?

   A. Bone destruction
   B. Graves' disease
   C. Hypotension
   D. Tetany

4. Which of the following interventions should be undertaken to prevent thrombus formation in a client with sickle-cell anemia?

   A. Administer heparin or other anticoagulants
   B. Encourage exercise
   C. Maintain a high-roughage diet
   D. Increase oral fluid intake

5. A client with an obsessive-compulsive personality disorder will MOST likely react with _____ if he is interrupted in the performance of a ritual.

   A. hostility
   B. indifference
   C. confusion
   D. withdrawal

6. Which of the following would be experienced by a patient in a diabetic coma, but not by a patient in an HHNK coma?

   A. Kussmaul respirations
   B. Glycosuria
   C. Fluid loss
   D. Elevated blood glucose

7. Which of the following daily patterns tends to work best with clients who are depressed?

   A. Numerous sensory stimuli
   B. A simple daily schedule
   C. Removing the need for complicated decisions
   D. Multiple and varied activities

8. Glucocorticoids are secreted by the

   A. hypophysis cerebri
   B. adrenal glands
   C. thyroid
   D. pancreas

9. Prior to beginning lithium carbonate therapy, a client should undergo

   A. fluid and electrolyte evaluation
   B. renal evaluation
   C. psychomotor
   D. BUN evaluation

10. Which of the following is the result of an underproduction of thyroxin?

   A. Acromegaly   B. Cushing's disease
   C. Myxedema   D. Addison's disease

11. Which of the following is a common side effect of the major tranquilizers?

   A. Tremors   B. Diaphoresis
   C. Jaundice   D. Photosensitivity

12. Each of the following is likely to be revealed during the assessment of a client with hyperthyroidism EXCEPT

   A. weight loss   B. increased appetite
   C. constipation   D. nervousness

13. Severe emotional disturbances are often treated with tranquilizers to

   A. prevent complications
   B. make the client less dangerous to himself and others
   C. improve the client's mood
   D. make the client more receptive to psychotherapy

14. Which of the following symptoms would cause a nurse to stop giving Thorazine to a client?

   A. Uncoordinated movements   B. Jaundice
   C. Withdrawal   D. Tremors

15. What is the MOST likely cause of ascites in a patient with cirrhosis?

   A. Inhibited portal venous return
   B. Undersecretion of bile salts
   C. Gastric bleeding
   D. Overproduction of serum albumin

16. The defense mechanism used by clients who express anxiety through physical symptoms can BEST be described as

   A. psychosomatic   B. regressive
   C. psychoneurotic   D. dissociative

17. A 42-year-old client is admitted to the hospital with a diagnosis of Addison's disease. She is weak, hypotensive, and has low sodium and high potassium levels.
    The focus of the client's therapy should be

   A. lowering the level of eosiniphils
   B. restoring electrolyte balance
   C. increasing carbohydrate intake
   D. increasing lymph

18. A client who has been hospitalized for major depression has recently begun to receive Parnate. It is important that the nurse explain to the client that the use of this drug

    A. typically causes extreme photosensitivity
    B. may cause drowsiness
    C. increases the heart rate
    D. involves dietary restrictions

19. The MOST frequent cause of Cushing's syndrome is

    A. hyperplasia of pituitary
    B. hyperplasia of adrenal cortex
    C. decreased adrenocortical hormones
    D. insufficient production of ACTH

20. A group setting is particularly conducive to therapy because it

    A. takes the focus off the individual client
    B. forces clients to notice similarities with others
    C. establishes a learning environment
    D. encourages individual relationships

21. What is the purpose of installing a T-tube after a cholecystectomy?

    A. Draining bile from the cystic duct
    B. Protecting the common bile duct
    C. Preventing infection
    D. Providing a port for cholangiogram dye

22. A nurse notices that a socially agressive elderly client, who has been receiving Thorazine for several months, is sitting rigidly in a chair. What other adverse effects of the drug should the nurse watch for?

    A. Tremors   B. Slurred speech
    C. Excessive salivation D. Withdrawal

23. For what reason is an infant born with a cleft palate prone to infection?

    A. Mouth breathing
    B. Leakage of nasal mucus
    C. Poor nutrition from feeding disturbances
    D. Poor circulation in defective locus

24. Which of the following is a defense mechanism in which emotional conflicts are expressed through sensorimotor or somatic disability?

    A. Dissociation   B. Conversion
    C. Displacement   D. Regression

25. For the emergency treatment of ketoacidosis, what type of insulin should be administered? 25.____
    A. Zinc suspension
    B. NPH insulin
    C. Protamine zinc suspension
    D. Regular insulin injection

KEY (CORRECT ANSWERS)

1.	C	11.	A
2.	D	12.	C
3.	A	13.	D
4.	D	14.	B
5.	A	15.	A
6.	A	16.	C
7.	B	17.	B
8.	D	18.	D
9.	B	19.	B
10.	C	20.	C

21. B
22. A
23. A
24. B
25. D

MEDICAL SCIENCE

EXAMINATION SECTION
TEST 1

DIRECTIONS: Each question or incomplete statement is followed by several suggested answers or completions. Select the one that BEST answers the question or completes the statement. *PRINT THE LETTER OF THE CORRECT ANSWER IN THE SPACE AT THE RIGHT.*

1. The one of the following which is a kidney operation is a 1.____
    A. gastrectomy   B. nephrectomy   C. lobectomy
    D. craniotomy   E. hysterectomy

2. The one of the following which is the medical term for nearsightedness is 2.____
    A. myopia   B. strabismus   C. hyperopia
    D. nystagmus E. astigmatism

3. A patient with a Koch infection has 3.____
    A. gonorrhea   B. syphilis   C. cancer
    D. diabetes   E. tuberculosis

4. The one of the following which is the PRIMARY purpose of the Wasserman test taken during pregnancy is to 4.____

    A. prevent congenital symphilis
    B. find active cases of gonorrhea
    C. prevent infection of the husband
    D. prevent syphilis of the central nervous system
    E. prevent luetic heart disease

5. Diagnosing cancer in its early stages is important CHIEFLY because 5.____

    A. family members may be tested for hereditary predisposition
    B. chances of cure are greatest when treatment can begin early
    C. medication to prevent spread can be prescribed
    D. cancer can always be cured when treatment begins early
    E. the patient can be better isolated from contact with others

6. A cholecystectomy involves the removal of the 6.____
    A. thyroid   B. colon   C. liver
    D. gall bladder   E. spleen

7. A child has just recovered from acute rheumatic fever which has mildly affected his heart. The one of the following which is of GREATEST importance to him as a prophylactic measure is that 7.____

    A. his family be aware of the situation
    B. he attend a special class at school
    C. he have no stairs to climb
    D. he be on complete bed rest
    E. he take care to avoid colds

8. The one of the following conditions which is NOT mandatorily reportable to the Department of Health is

   A. smallpox B. cancer C. poliomyelitis
   D. syphilis E. tuberculosis

9. The one of the following which represents the GREATEST value of special classes for children with marked eye defects is that

   A. there is less mental competition with normal children
   B. Braille books are made available to them
   C. sight conservation is taught and practiced
   D. corrective eye exercises are emphasized
   E. they can adjust better in the group

10. The one of the following diseases for which a sedimentation rate test is of GREATEST value is

    A. hyperthyroidism B. rheumatic fever
    C. pneumonia D. toxemia
    E. diabetes

11. Syphilis is caused by an infection with

    A. spirochaeta pallida B. gram-negative diplocci
    C. tubercle bacilli D. streptococci
    E. staphlylocci

12. The one of the following tests which is a basis for, or a confirmation of, a diagnosis of diabetes is a

    A. complete blood count
    B. darkfield examination
    C. spinal fluid examination
    D. patch test
    E. glucose tolerance test

13. The one of the following diseases which is caused by a deficiency of vitamin D is

    A. rickets B. pellagra C. beriberi
    D. scurvy E. anemia

14. The one of the following diseases which has been MOST prevalent in the United States in the last five years is

    A. heart disease B. typhoid C. poliomyelitis
    D. tuberculosis E. cancer

15. In establishing a diagnosis of pulmonary tuberculosis, the one of the following which is MOST valuable to the doctor is

    A. the Mantoux test B. Roentgen study
    C. gastric lavago D. a thermometer
    E. fluoroscopic study

16. The one of the following which is the MOST common cause of death from heart disease in the age group of one week to five years is

    A. hypertension
    B. angina pectoris
    C. syphilitic heart disease
    D. congenital heart disease
    E. rheumatic heart disease

17. According to our present knowledge of the effects of certain diseases during the first three months of pregnancy, the one of the following diseases which would have the MOST harmful effect on the unborn fetus is

    A. German measles
    B. gonorrhea
    C. heart disease
    D. lobar pneumonia
    E. thrombophlebitis

18. According to the American Heart Association's classification, a 24-year-old female patient classified as Functional, Class IA would be

    A. on complete bed rest
    B. warned against pregnancies
    C. allowed normal activity
    D. on a convalescent status
    E. restrained from any stair climbing

19. The one of the following diseases which is caused by a birth injury is

    A. cerebral palsy
    B. meningitis
    C. hydrocele
    D. congenital syphilis
    E. epilepsy

20. In helping a patient who has arteriosclerotic heart disease to plan for his future, the one of the following phases on which you would specifically seek information from the patient's doctor is the

    A. emotional basis of the illness
    B. etiology of the disease process
    C. functioning capacity of the patient
    D. awareness of hereditary predisposition
    E. anatomical changes which have occurred

21. The one of the following eye conditions which is MOST commonly found in the premature infant is

    A. strabismus
    B. myopia
    C. phylctenular keratitis
    D. retrolental fibroplasia
    E. glaucoma

22. The one of the following cases in which eclampsia is MOST likely to occur is

    A. diabetes
    B. shock therapy
    C. syphilitic infection
    D. measles
    E. pregnancy

23. A delusion is a

    A. disharmony of mind and body
    B. fantastic image formed during sleep

C. false judgment of objective things
D. cessation of thought
E. distorted perception or image

24. The one of the following which is the MOST common form of treatment employed by psychiatrists in treating patients with mental disorders is

    A. hypnotism
    B. hydrotherapy
    C. electroshock
    D. insulin shock
    E. psychotherapy

25. A masochistic person is one who

    A. is very melancholy
    B. has delusions of grandeur about himself
    C. derives pleasure from being cruelly treated
    D. believes in a fatalistic philosophy
    E. derives pleasure from hurting another

26. Surgery is ESPECIALLY difficult during the oedipal period because of the

    A. father attachment
    B. mental age
    C. castration anxieties
    D. rejection complex
    E. separation from siblings

27. A psychometric test is one which attempts to measure

    A. social adjustment
    B. emotional maturity
    C. physical activity
    D. personality development
    E. intellectual capacity

28. The one of the following conditions which falls into the classification of a psychosis rather than psychoneurosis is

    A. anxiety hysteria
    B. schizophrenia
    C. neurasthenia
    D. conversion hysteria
    E. compulsion neurosis

29. The one of the following which BEST describes psychosomatic medicine is

    A. the understanding and treatment of both mind and body in illness
    B. the treatment of disease by psychiatric methods only
    C. the separation of mind and body in medical treatment
    D. the psychological testing of all individuals
    E. a system of socialized medical planning

30. The one of the following conditions for which shock treatment is FREQUENTLY used is

    A. alcoholism
    B. Parkinson's syndrome
    C. multiple sclerosis
    D. schizophrenia
    E. diabetes

31. The incidence of any particular disease is called the _____ rate.

    A. mortality
    B. morbidity
    C. endemic
    D. death
    E. differential

32. The one of the following which is the PRIMARY purpose of the mass chest x-ray surveys is to   32.____

    A. find active cases of tuberculosis
    B. give early treatment for tuberculosis
    C. educate the public
    D. lower the death rate among the aged
    E. carry out a research project

33. When a child develops whooping cough after having been closely exposed to the disease, the cause is said to be   33.____

    A. endogenous   B. exogenous   C. endemic
    D. endoglobular   E. ectatic

34. The one of the following diseases for which the necessary medication will be given free by the Department of Health is   34.____

    A. poliomyelitis   B. pneumonia   C. cancer
    D. syphilis   E. epilepsy

35. The branch of medical science which deals with the conditions of the older age group is called   35.____

    A. pediatrics   B. dietetics   C. gerontology
    D. orthopedics   E. cardiology

KEY (CORRECT ANSWERS)

1.	B	16.	D
2.	A	17.	A
3.	E	18.	C
4.	A	19.	A
5.	B	20.	C
6.	D	21.	D
7.	E	22.	E
8.	B	23.	C
9.	C	24.	E
10.	B	25.	C
11.	A	26.	C
12.	E	27.	E
13.	A	28.	B
14.	A	29.	A
15.	B	30.	D

31. B
32. A
33. B
34. D
35. C

TEST 2

DIRECTIONS: Each question or incomplete statement is followed by several suggested answers or completions. Select the one that BEST answers the question or completes the statement. *PRINT THE LETTER OF THE CORRECT ANSWER IN THE SPACE AT THE RIGHT.*

1. Eclampsia is MOST likely to occur in the course of

   A. pregnancy
   B. poliomyelitis
   C. German measles
   D. scarlet fever

2. The one of the following diseases which is characterized by an overabundance of white cells in the body is

   A. hemophilia
   B. polycythemia
   C. anemia
   D. leucemia

3. The GREATEST single factor in improving the prognosis in diabetes in children is

   A. improvement in standards of living
   B. the discovery of insulin
   C. greater emphasis on prenatal care
   D. improved surgical techniques

4. The one of the following which FREQUENTLY causes a baby to be cyanotic at birth is

   A. a neurological disorder
   B. congenital heart disease
   C. gonorrhea
   D. tuberculosis

5. In establishing a diagnosis of *grand mal*, the one of the following which would be MOST helpful to the doctor is an(the)

   A. electrocardiogram
   B. encephalogram
   C. basal metabolism rate
   D. blood pressure reading

6. Oophorectomy is a surgical procedure involving removal of the

   A. kidney
   B. brain lobe
   C. ovary
   D. thyroid gland

7. The one of the following laboratory procedures which is used SPECIFICALLY in diagnosing cancer is a

   A. glucose tolerance test
   B. dark-field examination
   C. blood test
   D. Papanicolaou smear

8. Cerebral palsy is known as _____ disease.

   A. Pott's B. Little's C. Addison's D. Grave's

9. An electroencephalogram is used in establishing a diagnosis of

   A. rheumatic heart disease
   B. cholecystitis
   C. Hodgkin's disease
   D. epilepsy

104

10. The one of the following conditions which is NOT caused by the dysfunction of endocrine glands is

    A. myxedema
    B. duodenal ulcer
    C. cretinism
    D. Addison's disease

11. A diagnostic procedure used in determining the presence of syphilis is a

    A. patch test
    B. dark-field examination
    C. sputum test
    D. gastric analysis

12. An eye condition necessitating the use of glasses which COMMONLY appears with the advent of middle age is

    A. myopia
    B. strabismus
    C. presbyopia
    D. fibroplasia

13. The one of the following laboratory tests which is performed to determine or confirm the presence of central nervous system syphilis is a

    A. glucose tolerance test
    B. sedimentation test
    C. colloidal gold test
    D. Papanicolaou smear

14. A COMMON surgical procedure used in the treatment of duodenal ulcer is

    A. nephrectomy
    B. cholecystectomy
    C. lobectomy
    D. subtotal gastrectomy

15. The one of the following tests which is used to determine the presence of dysfunction of the thyroid gland is

    A. a sputum test
    B. an electroencephalogram
    C. gastric analysis
    D. a basal metabolism test

16. The MOST effective antibiotic in present-day treatment of syphilis is

    A. penicillin
    B. streptomycin
    C. terramycin
    D. aureomycin

17. The one of the following which is COMMONLY used to determine the presence of a brain tumor is

    A. a cardiogram
    B. urinalysis
    C. a glucose tolerance test
    D. a ventriculogram

18. Under the Sanitary Code, it is necessary to report the positive results of certain tests or specimen examinations to the Department of Health within 24 hours.
    The one of the following which does NOT have to be reported is

    A. a positive Zondek-Aschheim test
    B. the presence of Klebs-Loeffler bacilli
    C. the presence of bacillus typhosus
    D. a positive Kline-Young test

19. A curette is a

    A. healing drug
    B. curved scalpel
    C. long hypodermic needle
    D. scraping instrument

20. A myocardial infarct would occur in the
    A. heart   B. kidneys   C. lungs   D. spleen

Questions 21-25.

DIRECTIONS: For Questions 21 through 25, Column I lists body organs and Column II lists names of surgical procedures. For each body organ listed in Column I, select the surgical procedure in Column II which involves the organ, and write the letter which precedes the surgical procedure in the answer blank corresponding to the number of the question.

COLUMN I

21. Brain
22. Gall bladder
23. Larynx
24. Reproductive organs
25. Stomach

COLUMN II

A. Cholecystectomy
B. Enucleation
C. Gastrectomy
D. Lobotomy
E. Nephrectomy
F. Orchidectomy
G. Tracheotomy

KEY (CORRECT ANSWERS)

1. A
2. D
3. B
4. B
5. B
6. C
7. D
8. B
9. D
10. B
11. B
12. C
13. C
14. D
15. D
16. A
17. D
18. A
19. D
20. A
21. D
22. A
23. G
24. F
25. C

EXAMINATION SECTION
TEST 1

DIRECTIONS: Each question or incomplete statement is followed by several suggested answers or completions. Select the one that BEST answers the question or completes the statement. *PRINT THE LETTER OF THE CORRECT ANSWER IN THE SPACE AT THE RIGHT.*

1. The one of the following diseases which is the LEADING cause of death in the 10-to-15 year age group is 1.____
    A. cancer B. tuberculosis C. poliomyelitis
    D. diabetes E. rheumatic fever

2. The one of the following which would MOST likely be a result of untreated syphilis is 2.____
    A. paresis B. phlebitis C. carcinoma
    D. silicosis E. angina pectoris

3. The one of the following which is MOST likely to be used in establishing a diagnosis of epilepsy is a(n) 3.____
    A. electrocardiogram B. spinal x-ray
    C. fluoroscopic examination D. electroencephalogram
    E. psychometric examination

4. The pathology of diabetes involves the FAILURE of the body to produce an adequate supply of 4.____
    A. sugar B. carbohydrates C. insulin
    D. salt E. bile

5. The one of the following statements that is TRUE about diabetes is that 5.____
    A. it can generally be cured if medical orders are followed
    B. it can generally be kept under control but not cured
    C. it is an infectious disease
    D. blindness is an inevitable result of it
    E. controlled diabetes is a progressively disabling disease

6. Scurvy is caused by a deficiency of vitamin 6.____
    A. A B. B C. C D. E E. K

7. Vitamin D deficiency is common because 7.____
    A. it can only be injected
    B. it is generally associated with poorly tasting foods
    C. only physicians can administer it
    D. it is not found naturally in many foods

8. The one of the following vitamins that is used as an aid in coagulating blood is vitamin 8.____
    A. A B. B C. C D. E E. K

9. The one of the following statements that is TRUE of Duchenne muscular dystrophy is that
   A. it is transmitted to the male children through the mother
   B. the male is the carrier of the disease
   C. the brain is primarily affected because of a lack of blood supply
   D. it is caused by a nutritional deficiency in the antepartum period
   E. only female children are susceptible to the disease

10. If a patient is repeatedly admitted to the hospital because of a series of mishaps in which he has suffered broken bones, the one of the following that is MOST likely to be true is that he is
    A. a rigid person   B. a diabetic   C. malingering
    D. accident prone   E. psychotic

11. The one of the following groups of illnesses that is known to be caused by bacteria is
    A. mental diseases   B. acute infectious diseases
    C. nutritional diseases   D. degenerative diseases
    E. cancerous tumors

12. The one of the following with which Hodgkin's Disease is COMMONLY associated is
    A. neurasthenia   B. meningitis   C. poliomyelitis
    D. cancer   E. tuberculosis

13. The one of the following diseases in which the determination of the sedimentation rate is IMPORTANT for diagnostic purposes is
    A. rheumatic heart disease   B. congenital heart disease
    C. hypertensive heart disease   D. diabetes
    E. gonorrhea

14. The one of the following disease classifications that would INCLUDE spinal meningitis is
    A. cancer or tumor   B. nutritional disease
    C. acute infectious disease   D. focal or local infection
    E. acute poisoning or intoxication

15. The one of the following diseases that may cause visual impairment and blindness is
    A. ringworm   B. osteomyelitis
    C. poliomyelitis   D. gall bladder disease
    E. diabetes

16. The one of the following that is NOT an anesthetic is
    A. cholesterol   B. nitrous oxide   C. sodium pentothal
    D. procaine   E. ethyl chloride

17. The one of the following that BEST describes the restrictions to be applied to Mr. K., a cardiac patient classified, according to the standards of the American Heart Association, as functional, Class IVD, is
    A. limited activity
    B. complete bed rest
    C. four hours rest daily
    D. prohibition of stair climbing, alcohol or tobacco
    E. convalescent status

17.____

18. Over time, geriatrics has become an increasingly important branch of medicine CHIEFLY due to
    A. greater specialization within the medical profession
    B. the discovery of penicillin and aureomycin
    C. advances in medical education
    D. increases in hospitalization
    E. the increase in the span of life

18.____

19. The one of the following which is MOST likely to be an occupational disease is
    A. cancer
    B. cerebral hemorrhage
    C. septicemia
    D. asthma
    E. nephritis

19.____

20. The one of the following that is a NUTRITIONAL disease is
    A. tuberculosis
    B. scurvy
    C. hepatitis
    D. lymphoma
    E. scabies

20.____

21. Morbidity rate refers to the
    A. incidence of an illness
    B. ratio of births to deaths
    C. bacterial count
    D. degree of disability caused by an illness
    E. death rate

21.____

22. A pediatrician is a doctor who specializes in the treatment of
    A. children
    B. foot diseases
    C. disabling illnesses
    D. orthopedic diseases
    E. the aged

22.____

23. A sadistic person is one who
    A. receives gratification through suffering pain
    B. secures a great deal of satisfaction from his own body
    C. receives gratification from inflicting pain on others
    D. turns all feelings towards others back into his own personality
    E. seeks solace through deep mental depression

23.____

24. The one of the following which is said to be the masculine counterpart of the *Electra Complex* is the _____ complex.
    A. sexual perversion
    B. frustration
    C. Oedipus
    D. reanimation
    E. repression

24.____

25. The one of the following conditions for which a patient would be admitted to a state mental hospital is
    A. schizophrenia
    B. muscular dystrophy
    C. pathological lying
    D. congenital syphilis
    E. psychoneurosis

    25.____

26. The one of the following statements which BEST describes the difference between a hallucination and a delusion is that
    A. hallucinations occur only at night
    B. delusions occur only with menopause
    C. delusions are primarily provoked by sexual function
    D. a hallucination has a basis in beliefs or ideas
    E. a delusion has a basis in beliefs or ideas

    26.____

27. Finger sucking in early childhood has long been a subject of discussion among psychiatrists.
    The one of the following statements that is GENERALLY accepted as true is that
    A. finger sucking denotes pending neuroses and the parents need psychiatric consultation
    B. finger sucking is a normal activity of early childhood and should not be interfered with
    C. finger sucking alters the child's facial contours and should be heavily discouraged
    D. finger sucking by a child over nine months old is due to emotional upset and needs treatment
    E. the physician should discuss possible remedial measures such as guards on fingers

    27.____

28. The one of the following who is said to be the *Father of Medicine* is
    A. Hippocrates
    B. Pasteur
    C. Galen
    D. Sydenham
    E. Plato

    28.____

29. The one of the following who is credited with the improvement of conditions in mental hospitals and the founding of new ones in the United States is
    A. Andrew Jackson
    B. Dorothea Dix
    C. William Knowlton
    D. Robert Stack
    E. Rene Laennec

    29.____

30. The one of the following doctors whose name is COMMONLY associated with much of the early growth and subsequent progress of medical social work is Dr.
    A. Sigmund Freud
    B. Richard C. Cabot
    C. Elizabeth Blackwell
    D. Carmyn Lombardo
    E. Thomas Parran

    30.____

KEY (CORRECT ANSWERS)

1.	A	11.	B	21.	A
2.	A	12.	D	22.	A
3.	D	13.	A	23.	C
4.	C	14.	C	24.	C
5.	B	15.	E	25.	A
6.	C	16.	A	26.	E
7.	D	17.	B	27.	B
8.	E	18.	E	28.	A
9.	A	19.	D	29.	B
10.	D	20.	B	30.	B

EXAMINATION SECTION
TEST 1

DIRECTIONS: Each question or incomplete statement is followed by several suggested answers or completions. Select the one that BEST answers the question or completes the statement. *PRINT THE LETTER OF THE CORRECT ANSWER IN THE SPACE AT THE RIGHT.*

1. The psychologist whose name is MOST often associated with the theory that the experience of birth has a profound influence on personality development and that an individual who has a slow, prolonged birth is likely to have a personality which fights, struggles and plunges is

    A. Horney
    B. Freud
    C. Sullivan
    D. Rank

    1.____

2. Which of the following is the MOST correct statement concerning puberty and physical maturity?

    A. Boys and girls who experience early puberty will achieve physical maturity and cease growing later than will the late maturers.
    B. Boys and girls who experience early puberty will achieve physical maturity and cease growing sooner than will the late maturers.
    C. Boys and girls who experience early puberty will achieve physical maturity and cease growing at approximately the same time as the late maturers.
    D. None of the above

    2.____

3. The MOST prominent difficulties of the middle years of childhood revolve around

    A. relations with peer groups
    B. parent-child relationships
    C. schooling and the ability to learn
    D. physical development

    3.____

4. In the normal population, the range of achievement of children of the same age in grades 5 and 6 is approximately from

    A. 1 to 2 years
    B. 2 to 4 years
    C. 3 to 5 years
    D. 5 to 8 years

    4.____

5. The MOST accurate statement concerning anxiety, of the following, is that anxiety is

    A. needed for the socialization process
    B. not needed for the socialization process
    C. less produced by "mental" punishment than by physical punishment
    D. of negligible effect in producing neurosis

    5.____

6. Of the following, the area of greatest similarity among children is in their

    A. inherited traits
    B. rates of development
    C. sequences of development
    D. patterns of growth dimensions

    6.____

7. Of the following, which is the MOST significant factor in determining the choice of friends among children between the ages of six and ten?
   - A. Mutual interests
   - B. Similar personality traits
   - C. Conveniently close location
   - D. Social and economic standing of parents

8. Lewin, in defining his structural concepts of psychology, represented them
   - A. topologically
   - B. metrically
   - C. geometrically
   - D. orthographically

9. As part of the socialization process, the phenomenon of ambivalence is at its highest intensity during the
   - A. toddler years
   - B. preschool years
   - C. early school years
   - D. intermediate school years

10. The child's need to be a "goody-goody" and his willingness to conform are MOST frequently observed during the
    - A. phallic period
    - B. latency period
    - C. prepubertal period
    - D. adolescent period

11. Joe Flirp is a great health education teacher, to a large extent, because the boys model themselves after him. The foregoing illustrates the psychological mechanism of
    - A. sublimation
    - B. displacement
    - C. regression
    - D. identification

12. "You're much too authoritarian," said the principal to the teacher. "And I won't stand for that in my school." The principal is demonstrating the psychological mechanism of
    - A. sublimation
    - B. conversion
    - C. projection
    - D. identification

13. Margaret Snorble, unhappy because of her lack of friendship, devoted all her energy to studying. She became the number one student in her grade. Margaret is demonstrating the psychological mechanism of
    - A. sublimation
    - B. conversion
    - C. introjection
    - D. fantasy

14. Ben was ill now and then. However, each time after a short rest, he quickly became well. This tendency or process is known as
    - A. redintegration
    - B. regression
    - C. homeostasis
    - D. somatistation

15. Joanie asked for apple pie and was told that there was none left. "Oh, well," said she, "give me peach pie. I like it better anyway." Joanie is demonstrating the psychological mechanism of
    - A. regression
    - B. displacement
    - C. rationalization
    - D. sublimation

16. The principal had just left after telling Miss Jones she had to improve the quality of her lesson plans. Tears came to her eyes; she stamped her foot several times, pounded on the desk and then broke into uncontrolled sobbing. Miss Jones' behavior is an example of the psychological mechanism of

    A. introjection
    B. projection
    C. sublimation
    D. regression

17. Of the following statements concerning praise and punishment, which is LEAST in accord with modern psychological principles?

    A. When a child is bad, spank him.
    B. When a child is bad, say, "If you're not good, I won't love you any more."
    C. When a child is good, give him something to show your approval.
    D. When a child is good, say, "That's O.K. Let's try to do better next time."

18. Which one of the following is NOT characteristic of the development of a group?

    A. Emergence of collective goals
    B. Solidification of individual roles within the group structure
    C. Growth of group norms for behavior
    D. Development of a group atmosphere or social climate

19. The status of an individual in a group is determined, for the MOST part, by

    A. the possession of those qualities the group deems important
    B. his socio-economic level
    C. his status in other groups of which he is a member
    D. the amount of time and energy he is willing to devote to the purposes of the group

20. In comparison with other members of a group, the leader tends to

    A. hold himself in higher esteem
    B. be less spontaneous
    C. be more desirous of being of service to others
    D. be more willing to accept a low level of performance from members of the group

21. The individual who emerges as the leader of a group is usually

    A. the person who, in the judgment of the group, can best meet the demands of the particular problem
    B. superior to the other members of the group in a wide variety of abilities
    C. chosen on the basis of personal qualities rather than ability
    D. the same person, no matter in what activities the group participates

22. The degree of cohesiveness which has been established in a group is MOST likely to be lowered by

    A. unfavorable evaluation of the group by outsiders
    B. favorable evaluation of the group by outsiders
    C. decreasing the amount of interaction in the group
    D. increasing the degree of interaction in the group

23. Research has shown that neighborhood gangs tend to be more cohesive than groups of the same age functioning as clubs in more formal youth agencies. This would suggest that

    A. the club is potentially longer-lived than the gang
    B. young people join clubs only if they are not accepted by the gang
    C. clubs will not be able to function adequately in a given neighborhood until some way is found to destroy gangs already in existence
    D. the activities of the gang meet the needs of its members better than those of the club program do

24. Studies of the cohesiveness of small groups have indicated that the more cohesive a group, the

    A. more willing will the group be to defend itself against external criticism
    B. less likely is it that the group will permit internal disagreement with its objective or goals
    C. less perceptive is the group of its own solidarity
    D. more susceptible is the group to disruption caused by loss of a leader

25. According to Sullivan, anxiety serves as a defense against the danger of

    A. conditioned fears
    B. self-discovery
    C. destructive people on the outside
    D. interpersonal destructiveness

26. The system of classifying people into those who move towards, against, and away from people was devised by

    A. Alexander   B. Fromm
    C. Fenichel   D. Horney

27. Scientific investigators generally agree that the development of human behavior begins

    A. at the time of conception
    B. during the prenatal period
    C. at birth
    D. at the time of initial social interaction

28. Of the following, the MOST frequent reason why two 11-year old boys stop "being friends" is

    A. lack of agreement concerning activities to be undertaken
    B. lack of recent contact
    C. a clash of personalities
    D. parental disapproval

29. Of the following, the MOST important determinant of leadership in pre-adolescent children is the child's

    A. self-confidence   B. sex
    C. physical attractiveness   D. socio-economic status

5 (#1)

30. Of the following, the one MOST likely to be associated with poor emotional development in a sixth-grade girl is

   A. lack of interest in boys
   B. striving for perfection in all her school work
   C. desire to please her parents in everything she does
   D. a strong interest in arithmetic, with only passive interest in other school subjects

30._____

31. The author of FOUNDATIONS OF READING INSTRUCTION is

   A. Paul Witty   B. Emmett A. Betts
   C. David H. Russell   D. Helen M. Robinson

31._____

32. The Dolch 220-word basic vocabulary consists of words that

   A. are most commonly used in fifteen basic readers on first and second grade levels
   B. are most commonly used in compositions by primary-grade children
   C. must be recognized as "sight words" because they do not follow regular phonetic principles
   D. make up fifty percent of reading matter used in the elementary schools

32._____

33. The MOST rapid rate of growth among children between the ages of 2 and 8 is found at age

   A. 2   B. 4   C. 6   D. 8

33._____

34. Studies of the relationship between sex and reading disability of elementary school pupils generally reveal that among pupils with reading disabilities the number of

   A. girls exceeds the number of boys
   B. boys and girls is about equal
   C. boys is slightly greater than the number of girls
   D. boys is about 3 times the number of girls

34._____

35. Research reports agree that the reading interests of groups of children

   A. begin to be different for boys and girls during the primary grades
   B. change consistently as children grow older
   C. center on animal stories during pre-adolescent years
   D. show no difference between boys and girls until junion high school years

35._____

36. The MOST accurate statement to make regarding the cause of reading disability is that research shows that most reading difficulties are primarily due to

   A. low intelligence
   B. familial discord
   C. insufficient motivation to read
   D. a complex of interrelated factors

36._____

37. Fernald's name is associated with a teaching procedure by which a child learns words by means of a

   A. look-and-say technique   B. visual motor approach
   C. tracing-and-writing procedure D. letter sound blending approach

37._____

38. A diagnostic report of a child's reading states that he has no word analysis techniques. This diagnosis is equivalent to saying that he

    A. has a poor meaningful vocabulary
    B. cannot understand what he reads
    C. cannot sound out words
    D. cannot adjust his rate

39. Where mixed dominance is identified as a possible causal factor for a child who makes many reversal errors, it would be BEST for the teacher to

    A. stress left to right direction in reading
    B. change the child's hand preference
    C. change the child's eye preference
    D. stress an oral approach in reading

40. The mother of a first-grade child is concerned about her child's reading. It appears that the child can read only the words in her primer, but cannot sound out any words not in her book. Of the following, the BEST explanation to the mother would be that

    A. it is all right because the children are not taught phonics today
    B. it is all right because the child will learn to sound words
    C. it is serious and the child will get special help soon
    D. it is all right since children are taught to read whole words first, then the sounds

41. As a means of changing the current behavior pattern of an adolescent, which of the following forces will generally prove to be MOST potent? Disapproval of the behavior pattern by

    A. the adolescent's parents
    B. his classroom teacher
    C. a group of his peers
    D. an adult he admires

42. Of the following, the characteristic that is MOST important in determining an individual's status in a group of pre-adolescent girls is her

    A. school achievement
    B. socio-economic status
    C. ability to make friends
    D. intelligence

43. If the results of studies of boys' clubs are applicable to the school situation, one may expect the greatest amount of aggressive behavior to be noted in classes where the classroom climate may be described as

    A. permissive
    B. laissez-faire
    C. democratic
    D. autocratic

44. Which of the following authors would you be LEAST likely to recommend for information about child care?

    A. Sidonie Gruenberg
    B. Jean Piaget
    C. Ernest Harms
    D. Benjamin Spock

7 (#1)

45. Of the following, which one is NOT an authority in reading? 45.____

   A. Gates B. Russell
   C. Harris D. Bullis

46. Studies have shown that the ratio of reading disability among boys as compared to girls is: 46.____

   A. 4 to 1 B. 3 to 1 C. 2 to 1 D. equal

47. Which of the following terms refers to the maintenance of stability in the physiological functioning of the organism? 47.____

   A. functional autonomy B. canalization
   C. homeostasis D. maturation

48. A recent comprehensive survey of child-rearing patterns in America found mothers of the working class when compared in their toilet-training practices with mothers of the middle class to be 48.____

   A. more permissive B. more indifferent
   C. more severe D. more accepting

49. Studies of the relationship of body build and character traits have in general been found to be 49.____

   A. positively correlated
   B. negatively correlated
   C. statistically significantly correlated
   D. inconclusive

50. The theory that psychical compensation for a feeling of physical or social inferiority is responsible for the development of a psychoneurosis is attributed to 50.____

   A. Adler B. Horney
   C. Freud D. Sullivan

KEY (CORRECT ANSWERS)

1. D	11. D	21. A	31. B	41. C
2. B	12. C	22. C	32. D	42. C
3. C	13. A	23. D	33. A	43. D
4. D	14. C	24. A	34. D	44. B
5. A	15. C	25. B	35. B	45. D
6. C	16. D	26. D	36. D	46. B
7. C	17. B	27. B	37. C	47. C
8. A	18. B	28. B	38. C	48. C
9. B	19. A	29. A	39. A	49. D
10. B	20. A	30. B	40. D	50. A

TEST 2

DIRECTIONS: Each question or incomplete statement is followed by several suggested answers or completions. Select the one that BEST answers the question or completes the statement. *PRINT THE LETTER OF THE CORRECT ANSWER IN THE SPACE AT THE RIGHT.*

1. Of the following, the MOST important consideration in distinguishing anxiety from fear is the

    A. intensity of the emotion
    B. extent of relation to subjective as distinguished from objective conditions
    C. actuality of danger
    D. strength of the personality organization of the one who is affected

    1.___

2. Wishes of children of elementary school age deal mainly with

    A. improvement of their own inner strength, character, or intelligence
    B. improvement of their personal appearance
    C. possessions, pleasant experiences, privileges, opportunities for enjoyment
    D. exploitation of family relationships

    2.___

3. The psychological climate of the home which influences adjustment of the child is MOST closely related to the

    A. number of children in the home
    B. educational level of the parents
    C. occupational level of the father
    D. attitudes of the parents

    3.___

4. With reference to emotional stability, intellectually gifted children as a group compared to average children are

    A. generally inferior   B. the same
    C. generally superior   D. unpredictably related

    4.___

5. Piaget distinguishes between two kinds of thought, logical and autistic. It is his thesis that the child's way of thinking is

    A. basically autistic
    B. either logical or autistic
    C. basically logical
    D. situated between the logical and the autistic

    5.___

6. According to research findings, the MOST effective way to help a child deal with a specific fear, such as a fear of dogs, is to

    A. have the parents and others who are close to the child set an example of fearlessness
    B. explain matters to him in terms he can understand readily
    C. help him by degrees to come actively and directly to grips with the situation
    D. try to effect "positive reconditioning" by presenting the feared stimulus with an attractive one

    6.___

7. A fundamental principle of the psychoanalytic school which has been accepted by most schools of psychology is the

   A. development of the collective unconscious
   B. theory of the existence of a dynamic unconscious
   C. development of an oedipus complex situation
   D. relationship between early psychosexual development and later adult behavior

8. In comparing the rate of biological growth for boys and girls between the ages of 5-7 and 7-10, the latter period shows

   A. a slightly more accelerated rate than the former
   B. a slightly less accelerated rate than the former
   C. a markedly more accelerated rate than the former
   D. a rate equal to the former period

9. The concept of "stages" in describing human development is LEAST applicable to

   A. Freud's psychoanalytic theory
   B. Piaget's cognitive theory
   C. Skinner's behavior theory
   D. Erikson's personality theory

10. The principal effect of nursery school attendance is upon the child's

    A. social development
    B. intellectual development
    C. perceptual development
    D. motor development

11. Which of the following terms is MOST clearly associated with stubborn reading disability?

    A. Apraxia   B. Dysplasia   C. Dyslexia   D. Aphasia

12. The boy who is encouraged or required to be more independent at an earlier age tends to develop a(n)

    A. low threshold for frustration
    B. inability to work well with others
    C. reluctance to accept adult authority
    D. strong need to achieve

13. Pioneering studies in eliminating children's fears were conducted by Mary Cover Jones. The methods used, which are consistent with present-day learning theory, included all but ONE of the following:

    A. Direct conditioning
    B. Social imitation
    C. Feeding responses
    D. Systematic desensitization

14. In contrast to upward mobile adolescents, downward mobile adolescents are

    A. less ambivalent in self-concept
    B. less interested in job security
    C. more confident in social relationships
    D. more dependent on their parents

15. In which of the following situations would a classroom atmosphere of competitiveness be LEAST detrimental to the cultivation of interpersonal relationships? Classmates are

   A. unfamiliar with one another, but equal in abilities
   B. familiar with one another and equal in abilities
   C. unfamiliar with one another and greatly disparate in abilities
   D. familiar with one another and greatly disparate in abilities

16. On group intelligence tests, Cyril Burt found the highest correlations between

   A. identical twins reared apart
   B. siblings reared together
   C. parents and own children living together
   D. identical twins reared together

17. An adolescent boy would like to have a girlfriend. As an example of sublimation, he might

   A. proclaim himself a "woman-hater"
   B. withdraw from all interpersonal relationships
   C. convince himself that girls are really crazy about him
   D. begin to write romantic poetry

18. Jim studies all night before an examination in an attempt to learn the entire course. This is an example of

   A. distributed practice
   B. massed practice
   C. practice effect
   D. spread of effect

19. The best-controlled studies of the influence of genetic factors on human behavior are found in investigations of

   A. newborn babies
   B. identical twins
   C. fraternal twins
   D. siblings

20. Terman's follow-up studies on a group of gifted children as compared to children of average intelligence revealed them to have

   A. better adjustment as shown on personality and character tests
   B. greater physical problems
   C. lower incomes
   D. more uneven academic achievement

21. Which one of the following is the MOST important determinant of leadership among pre-adolescent boys?

   A. Intellectual ability
   B. Physical size and strength
   C. Popularity with girls
   D. Sensitivity to the needs of others

22. Billy wants to be admired, but he is too clumsy to achieve this goal through sports. Therefore, although not a bright pupil, he studies long hours and earns very high grades. This may be cited as an example of

    A. compensation
    B. projection
    C. rationalization
    D. reaction formation

23. Of the following, the MOST important factor making for the development of friendship among young children is

    A. similarity in interests
    B. similarity in social class
    C. geographic proximity
    D. friendship among parents

24. Harlow's work on mothering in monkeys suggests that the affective bond between the infant and the mother is based on

    A. feeding
    B. grooming
    C. tactile contact
    D. primitive vocalization

25. The CORRECT order of Piaget's developmental stages is

    A. concrete operations, preoperational, sensorimotor, formal operational
    B. concrete operations, sensorimotor, preoperational, formal operational
    C. sensorimotor, concrete operations, preoperational, formal operational
    D. sensorimotor, preoperational, concrete operations, formal operational

26. Piaget's process which states that children invent increasingly more and better schemata for adapting to their environment is known as

    A. assimilation
    B. equilibrium
    C. accommodation
    D. conservation

27. Which of the following is NOT considered by Erikson to be a developmental task of adolescence?

    A. Development of a sense of shared identity with another
    B. Development of sexual identity
    C. Ability to see one's life in perspective
    D. Experimentation with different roles

28. A six-year-old child who is able to solve a conservation problem would be classified under which of the following stages described by Piaget?

    A. Sensorimotor
    B. Formal operations
    C. Preoperational
    D. Concrete operations

29. During adolescence, girls *generally* surpass boys in

    A. scientific ability
    B. mathematical ability
    C. ability to perform verbal tasks
    D. gross motor skills

30. The CORRECT order of Freud's stages of psychosexual development is:

    A. Oral, latency, anal, phallic, genital
    B. Oral, anal, phallic, latency, genital
    C. Phallic, oral, anal, latency, genital
    D. Latency, oral, genital, anal, phallic

31. According to Erikson, a MAJOR developmental conflict a child faces in the elementary school age period is the conflict between

    A. initiative and guilt
    B. identity and identity diffusion
    C. industry and inferiority
    D. trust and mistrust

32. According to Piaget, in the preoperational stage children

    A. begin to classify and order activities internally
    B. begin to integrate sensory and motor activities
    C. gain the ability to think logically about a problem
    D. are unable to transcend the here and now and are dependent on immediate perception

33. A pupil is able to reason simultaneously about whole and part and is able to classify according to two or three properties. According to Piaget, the pupil is in the _____ stage.

    A. sensory-motor
    B. formal operations
    C. preoperational
    D. concrete operations

34. According to Kohlberg, moral development proceeds through a sequence of stages that are

    A. dependent on the individual's personality and the way in which society reacts to that personality
    B. strongly influenced by individual differences in educational experience and religious training
    C. characterized by increasing symmetry, conventionality, and objectivity
    D. universal and invariant from one culture to another

35. The technique in which a particular form or sequence of behavior is established by reinforcing successively closer approximations to that behavior is called

    A. discriminative responding
    B. shaping
    C. classical conditioning
    D. fading

36. The HIGHEST need in Maslow's hierarchy of human needs is

    A. safety
    B. love
    C. self-actualization
    D. integration

37. According to Piaget, a child's thinking becomes completely general and capable of dealing with the hypothetical during the _____ stage.

    A. sensorimotor
    B. concrete operations
    C. preoperational
    D. formal operations

38. MOST child development specialists believe that a child's peer groups begin to replace the family as a socializing agent

    A. after the age of 5 or 6
    B. between the age of 2 or 3
    C. near the beginning of adolescence
    D. toward the end of adolescence

39. According to Erik Erikson, a key developmental task for the early elementary school years involves

    A. establishing a personal identity
    B. building confidence, resourcefulness, and enthusiasm
    C. surviving a psychosocial moratorium
    D. handling developmental discontinuity

40. Peter maintains that "everyone else in my class thinks I'm a crook." The mechanism of adjustment Peter is probably utilizing is usually referred to as

    A. projection
    B. rationalization
    C. compensation
    D. identification

41. Of the following, the BEST means of helping a child develop tolerance for tension is to

    A. protect the child from experiencing frustration
    B. make the child face reality through frequent experience of failure
    C. make sure that the child is uniformly successful
    D. help the child achieve some success and face some failure

42. Phil always develops a headache when he is called upon to complete a difficult task. Phil's headache is a(n)

    A. hysteroid reaction
    B. compensatory reaction
    C. reaction formation
    D. paranoid reaction

43. Which of the following is characteristic of the person who overcompensates?

    A. Projection
    B. Repression
    C. Self-repudiation
    D. Rationalization

44. A child who has been rejected by his parents tries to "show off" at every opportunity. Such a child is usually

    A. unaware of the nature of his frustration
    B. not capable of reacting more effectively
    C. reacting objectively to his stress situation
    D. deliberately trying to show his parents his need for affection

45. CHILD-CENTERED GROUP GUIDANCE OF PARENTS as described by Slavson deals with

    A. the understanding of the behavior and specific acts
    B. of children and ways of dealing with them appropriately
    C. free-associative catharsis which uncovers anxiety-inducing memories, acts and situations
    D. diminution of guilt on the part of the parents
    E. intellectually recognizing and emotionally accepting latent, covert and repressed impulses and strivings in children

46. Which of the following statements BEST expresses the central theme in Bruno Bettelheim's book, LOVE IS NOT ENOUGH? The disturbed child needs to identify with a person who

    A. accepts his feelings
    B. clearly structures his environment
    C. permits regression
    D. is maternal and "giving"

47. The leisure time activities of the typical pre-adolescent boys' group are mainly given over to

    A. a succession of activities suited to a changing number of players
    B. games governed by a highly organized series of rules
    C. aimless circulation over a relatively large area looking for something to do
    D. just "hanging around with the boys"

48. The normal age range of reading ability between the best and the poorest reader in a typical sixth grade is about

    A. 2 years   B. 3 years
    C. 5 years   D. 7 years

49. Of the following books, the one NOT written by A.T. Jersild is

    A. IN SEARCH OF SELF
    B. CHILDREN'S FEARS
    C. LOVE IS NOT ENOUGH
    D. WHEN TEACHERS FACE THEMSELVES

50. Studies in child development at Yale University were done primarily under the direction of

    A. Lawrence K. Frank   B. Samuel R. Slavson
    C. Arnold Gesell   D. Albert Deutsch

KEY (CORRECT ANSWERS)

1. B	11. C	21. B	31. C	41. D
2. C	12. D	22. A	32. A	42. A
3. D	13. D	23. C	33. B	43. C
4. C	14. D	24. C	34. B	44. A
5. D	15. B	25. D	35. B	45. A
6. C	16. D	26. B	36. C	46. A
7. B	17. D	27. C	37. D	47. A
8. B	18. B	28. D	38. D	48. D
9. C	19. B	29. C	39. A	49. C
10. A	20. A	30. B	40. A	50. C

EXAMINATION SECTION
TEST 1

DIRECTIONS: Each question or incomplete statement is followed by several suggested answers or completions. Select the one that BEST answers the question or completes the statement. *PRINT THE LETTER OF THE CORRECT ANSWER IN THE SPACE AT THE RIGHT.*

1. In Freud's theory, the aspect of personality that operates according to the pleasure principle is called the
    A. id
    B. ego
    C. superego
    D. unconditioned stimulus

    1._____

2. The soundness with which a test measures what it is intended to measure is referred to as its
    A. validity
    B. reliability
    C. positive correlation
    D. statistical significance

    2._____

3. When two treatments combine to have an effect that is greater than the sum of the individual treatment effects, we say that there is a _____ effect.
    A. main
    B. synergistic
    C. teratogen
    D. developmental systems

    3._____

4. According to psychologist Kurt Lewin, *There is nothing so practical as a good*
    A. fact
    B. theory
    C. assumption
    D. 5-cent cigar

    4._____

5. A researcher designs a study in which he will give candy to one group of children for breakfast, and eggs and cereal to a second group. He then plans to test the children's physical endurance during gym class at 9:30 in the morning.
   Regarding this study, we can say that the type of food is the
    A. control variable
    B. dependent variable
    C. independent variable
    D. sample

    5._____

6. In Pavlov's classic experiments with dogs, the bell was the
    A. unconditioned stimulus
    B. conditioned stimulus
    C. unconditioned response
    D. conditioned response

    6._____

7. The practice of rooming-in allows the
    A. father to stay in the hospital room overnight
    B. hospital to double-up on rooms to save costs
    C. mother to stay at home to have the baby
    D. baby to be with the mother whenever the mother wishes

    7._____

8. Which of the following is a statement fundamental to social learning theory?
    A. Many behaviors are learned gradually through shaping.
    B. Many behaviors are learned quickly through observation and imitation (modelling).
    C. The frequency of a desired behavior is affected by rewards contingent on the behavior.
    D. Knowledge is constructed as a result of interaction between the individual and the environment.

    8._____

9. The belief that racial mixing results in inferior offspring is contradicted by the idea of

   A. paradigms
   B. critical periods
   C. hybrid vigor
   D. natural selection

10. Betty Rubin's newborn snuggles near his mom's breast and turns his head several times to find a good nursing position. Just then the phone rings loudly and he startles, throws his arms out and loses his comfortable position. Which two reflexes are illustrated in order of appearance?

    A. Babinski and Moro
    B. Rooting and Moro
    C. Rooting and Babinski
    D. Moro and Babinski

11. When looking at theories and applying them, they are NOT

    A. things that evolve over time
    B. facts
    C. systematic and organized assumptions
    D. affected by the theorist's social context

12. One reason for having a control group in an experimental study is to

    A. keep the children in the experimental group from controlling the outcome
    B. check to see if events external to the study made the experimental group score high or low
    C. see what happens to children who are initially different from the control group
    D. make the experiment a case study

13. A limited time period when rapid development takes place in an organ, a part of the body, or a behavior is referred to as a(n)

    A. age of viability
    B. developmental pull
    C. critical period
    D. pseudodevelopmental phase

14. Mrs. Jann says her new baby wants to learn things just because they are interesting. Who would agree with her?

    A. Freud   B. Skinner   C. Watson   D. Piaget

15. Every gene is a sequence of

    A. somatic cells
    B. trophoblasts
    C. DMA
    D. chorionics

16. An individual's tendency to discount information that is not consistent with what he or she already believes is an example of

    A. negation bias
    B. confirmatory bias
    C. blind procedure
    D. construct validity

17. During the first half of the 20th century, there were a number of movements designed to improve humankind by eliminating, sterilizing, or forbidding marriage to individuals perceived to be inferior. These are classified as

    A. ego-defense
    B. classical conditioning
    C. social interactionist
    D. eugenics

18. Reflexes such as rooting, Babinski, Moro, and tonic neck

   A. develop slowly during the neonatal and infancy periods
   B. replace the voluntary movements made by infants at birth
   C. begin to appear after neonates are able to maintain a normal body temperature
   D. are typically replaced by voluntary behaviors during the first year of life

19. Piaget indicated that babies know about the world through their interactions with objects. He called this

   A. object reality
   B. object permanence
   C. sensorimotor intelligence
   D. state interaction

20. Which of the following statements is based on a *behavioral* view of child development?

   A. Children seek stimulation.
   B. You may play with your toys after you have cleaned up your room.
   C. Children need to work out their emotional conflicts through dramatic play.
   D. Leave her alone; she'll grow out of it.

21. Alcohol and cigarette smoke are examples of environmental agents that adversely affect prenatal development. They are called

   A. anoxias   B. perinatals
   C. surrogates   D. teratogens

22. Which of the following is an important focus in the development systems approach to child development?

   A. Mutual interaction throughout many levels of organization
   B. Neurological maturation
   C. Equilibration
   D. Progression from one stage to the next

23. Which of the following is NOT an example of a social biological effect?
    A

   A. child's exposure to high levels of lead resulting in a lowered IQ
   B. child born with fetal alcohol syndrome
   C. child who develops a fear of dogs after being bitten
   D. man living near Chernobyl whose sperm have chromosomal damage

24. A child who is learning soccer skills might be guided through the zone of proximal development by

   A. having the child practice with a more skilled peer
   B. receiving a reinforcement for each skill level mastered
   C. exposure to unconditioned stimuli
   D. shaping successive approximations to the target behavior

25. Do infants who sleep separately from their mothers grow up to be more independent than those who sleep with their mothers?

    A. Yes
    B. No
    C. There is no research on this
    D. There is no definitive answer according to research done

---

KEY (CORRECT ANSWERS)

1. A
2. A
3. B
4. B
5. C

6. B
7. D
8. B
9. C
10. B

11. B
12. B
13. C
14. D
15. C

16. B
17. D
18. D
19. C
20. B

21. D
22. A
23. C
24. A
25. D

TEST 2

DIRECTIONS: Each question or incomplete statement is followed by several suggested answers or completions. Select the one that BEST answers the question or completes the statement. *PRINT THE LETTER OF THE CORRECT ANSWER IN THE SPACE AT THE RIGHT.*

1. Depth perception is

   A. formed from concepts
   B. learned by habituation
   C. innate
   D. modeled from parents

   1.____

2. Grammatical errors are common in the language of preschoolers. Which of the following is appropriate advice for how to handle grammatical errors?

   A. Use a direct approach by saying *No,* then telling them how they should say the sentence
   B. With each error, ask a question about what the child said, using the correct use of the word in the question
   C. Say, *Please try saying that sentence again*
   D. Listen for content and use the correct grammar in conversational responses to the child

   2.____

3. The Chess and Thomas longitudinal study of easy, difficult, and slow-to-warm-up children suggests that the _____ is critical for successful child rearing.

   A. goodness-of-fit between child temperament and parental interaction styles
   B. genetic temperament of the child matters more than the initial parenting style
   C. initial parenting style matters more than the early temperament of the child
   D. child's genetics and peer group

   3.____

4. Preschooler Seth Thomas is counting a dozen blocks on the table. He touches them all, some twice, and ends up with a count of 15. What kind of counting error is he making?

   A. Coordination
   B. Hierarchical
   C. Partitioning
   D. Tagging

   4.____

5. Which of the following is NOT a good example of functional autonomy?

   A. Brushing your teeth
   B. Good manners
   C. Bulimia
   D. Breathing

   5.____

6. Which of the following is most likely to promote locomotor development in 4-month-old infants?

   A. Placing them in a stomach-down prone position on the floor
   B. Laying them on their backs and encouraging spontaneous leg exercises
   C. Providing lots of pillows to permit climbing and more upright positioning
   D. Stimulating after 6 months since development isn't facilitated until then

   6.____

7. The degree to which a 9-month-old exhibits stranger anxiety can be reduced by

   A. the mother being in constant contact with her baby
   B. the child's inability to crawl or walk away
   C. social referencing
   D. social games

   7.____

8. According to a research study, when mothers brought their babies in for a doctor's examination, it was found that the group of mothers who stood closest to their babies had more early contact with their children. It is difficult to argue that this means that these mothers had bonded better with their children because the outcome measure lacks _____ validity.

   A. predictive
   B. face
   C. external
   D. internal

9. Which of the following are characteristics of infant-directed or child-directed speech (CDS)?

   A. More narrow pitch range
   B. Less contrast between high and low pitches
   C. Longer pauses between words
   D. All of the above

10. According to analysis of Maccoby's study on infants' babbling, does babbling relate to or predict later intelligence?

    A. Yes, for boys only
    B. Yes, for girls only
    C. Yes, for both boys and girls
    D. No; when boys and girls are separated, there is no relation

11. Which of the following is the most noticeable change in appearance during the preschool years?

    A. Protruding stomach
    B. Rapid growth of legs and trunk
    C. Fast growth in height
    D. Weight gained faster than during year one

12. During the preschool years, there are many changes in motor development. Which of the following is NOT an accurate statement about motor development changes?

    A. Fine motor development of the fingers allows marked improvement in coloring, cutting, and pasting.
    B. Because their center of gravity moves up, they are more coordinated in climbing and jumping.
    C. Jumping ability improves markedly in part due to thrusting their arms forward rather than *winging* their arms in a jump.
    D. In climbing ladders and jungle gyms, there is a change from marked-time climbing to alternating feet.

13. Which of the following was found to be a productive way to overcome attachment difficulties between mothers and babies during the first year of life?

    A. Trying to get the baby to imitate the mother's actions
    B. Soliciting the baby's attention when he looked away
    C. Teaching the mother to choose appropriate responses to the baby's signals
    D. Teaching the mother to plan a regular schedule of activities in order to establish a routine with the infant

14. In number conservation tasks, most preschoolers judge which row has more objects by

    A. the length of the row
    B. counting the objects in the display
    C. making another row that is identical to the first and counting objects as they make the second row
    D. compensation

15. By 6 years of age, when most children enter first grade, their vocabularies range from about _____ words.

    A. 3,000-6,000
    B. 7,000-9,000
    C. 10,000-14,000
    D. 15,000-20,000

16. Baby Shemirah now has the ability to imagine actions in her head. Piaget would say that this ability allows a strong concept of

    A. object permanence
    B. imagination
    C. habituation
    D. fixation

17. A significantly slower than average rate of growth that is due to feeding and caregiving problems rather than to disease or heredity is termed

    A. encropresis
    B. failure-to-thrive
    C. slow-growth syndrome
    D. maturational lag

18. Two-month-old baby Watson looks longer at his own mother than he does at the occasional sitter, visiting grandma, or the bookmobile delivery woman. This recognition is based upon his mother's

    A. facial features
    B. hairline
    C. eye contact
    D. voice cues

19. At age 11 months, Missy started saying *da-da* rather than her usual *dadadada*. According to developmental linguists, she is now

    A. overextending
    B. babbling
    C. modifying
    D. using a protoword

20. Peter and his younger sister Sally were playing *house,* Peter told Sally to set the table while he cooked the turkey, showing her how to count the forks and napkins. Then he asked her to think of a good desert.
    Peter is _____ his sister's pretend play abilities.

    A. categorizing
    B. scaffolding
    C. modeling
    D. decentrizing

21. Jill can't take another point of view and tells you what the child sitting on the other side of the mountain can see. Piaget would say that she is

    A. hierarchical
    B. self-centered
    C. identity-bound
    D. egocentric

22. Many 3-year-old children were quite frightened by the dinosaur movie, JURASSIC PARK. The reason is that younger children

    A. can't centrate on film
    B. can't distinguish appearance from reality
    C. have highly tuned emotional systems
    D. have too much imagination

23. Which of the following is supported by research on infant and toddler development?

    A. The weight of the brain's cortex is unaffected by environmental factors.
    B. It is fairly easy to separate the effects of malnourishment and stimulation deprivation.
    C. About 10% of the adult's brain weight develops during the first two years.
    D. A stimulating environment can produce more growth of brain cells.

24. Selma is 3 years old. Her dad has read TEDDY BEAR, TEDDY BEAR to her many times. Now Selma can *read* it aloud with inflection, even though she isn't actually reading the words. Selma is a(n) _____ reader.

    A. beginning   B. coded
    C. emergent   D. syllabic

25. Which of the following is true concerning hearing problems in infants?

    A. It is difficult for infants to learn sign language.
    B. When deaf children learn sign language, they learn it at a slower rate than hearing children learn oral language.
    C. If infants make vocal sounds, they must be able to hear them.
    D. Infants learning sign language babble in sign just as hearing infants babble orally.

KEY (CORRECT ANSWERS)

1. C
2. D
3. A
4. C
5. D

6. A
7. C
8. B
9. C
10. B

11. B
12. B
13. C
14. A
15. C

16. A
17. B
18. B
19. D
20. B

21. D
22. B
23. D
24. C
25. D

TEST 3

DIRECTIONS: Each question or incomplete statement is followed by several suggested answers or completions. Select the one that BEST answers the question or completes the statement. *PRINT THE LETTER OF THE CORRECT ANSWER IN THE SPACE AT THE RIGHT.*

1. Kohlberg called the first level of moral development *preconventional*. At this level, children make moral decisions

   A. based on what is expected of them by society
   B. based on a simple set of philosophical principles
   C. on the basis of self-interest
   D. on the basis of living up to what close family members expect of them

2. The ability to attend to the form rather than the meaning of language is called

   A. phonological awareness
   B. metalinguistic awareness
   C. multisyllabic interpretations
   D. word boundary interpretations

3. Emotions can have positive or negative natures. This is called the

   A. target   B. valence   C. surrogate   D. polarity

4. Which of the following illustrates the secular growth trend?

   A. April is an Olympic champion in running and hasn't begun her menstrual period, even at age 15.
   B. June is very uncomfortable with her transition to adulthood based mainly on her individual perceptions.
   C. August is beginning her menstrual period at age 11, and her great-grandmother, who didn't begin until 15, is quite concerned.
   D. October is not faring very well in academics or social situations and her doctor wants her checked for secondary characteristics.

5. Carl has not seen the word *unbending* before, but he knows what *bending* means. Since he also understands *un*, he will be able to figure out what *unbending* means by

   A. understanding the word from its grammatical structure
   B. inferring word meaning from morphological knowledge
   C. learning from the suffix information
   D. getting the meaning from context

6. When Maria finally realizes that she will always be a girl, even if she cuts her hair or changes her clothes, we say she has achieved

   A. gender identity   B. gender constancy
   C. gender typing   D. sex-role structure

7. Why does Piaget label the thinking of school-age children as *concrete operational*?

   A. As long as they can see what they are talking about, or are familiar with it, they can think logically.
   B. While they cannot think abstractly, they can cement abstract ideas together if they make sense.
   C. Since the structure is basic or concrete, the thinking process can only be basic.
   D. They can juggle variables and contemplate possibilities about situations that exist only in their minds.

8. In the 3-kinds-of-memory-store model, which memory is our *working memory*?

   A. Sensory
   B. Long-term
   C. Short-term
   D. Intermediate

9. Carrie, a third grade girl, according to the research on beliefs and expectations is most likely to

   A. respond to failure by increasing her efforts
   B. believe that when she fails, she can expect more reinforcement from her teacher
   C. attribute failure to a lack of ability
   D. attribute her poor performance to nonintellectual aspects of her work

10. Race was examined as a risk factor in Sameroff's study because

    A. research has demonstrated that children from different races vary in their risk-taking behavior
    B. race is related to many negative outcomes in our society, even if it does not cause them
    C. minority children mature earlier, which puts them at risk
    D. experiments have demonstrated a causal relationship between race and cognitive performance

11. In regard to socialization and moral development, _____ is the process whereby adult values are adopted as the child's own, and _____ explains why the child adopts, the characteristics of the same-sex parent.

    A. social responsiveness; proximity seeking
    B. proximity seeking; social responsiveness
    C. identification; internalization
    D. internalization; identification

12. Cleo's dad decided to ignore Cleo's whining about not wanting to go to bed. Eventually she stopped whining. One night she smiled as she was putting on her pajamas, and her dad said, *My, I do like to see those nice bedtime smiles.* Cleo became happier about bedtime.
    Her clever dad first used a(n) _____ procedure, then a(n) _____ procedure.

    A. social cognition; reinforcement
    B. extinction; reinforcement
    C. extinction; exhortation
    D. social cognition; exhortation

13. Sternberg's triarchic theory of intelligence differentiates between which three aspects of mental ability?   13.____

    A. Verbal, quantitative, analytical
    B. Analytical, creative, practical
    C. Logical-mathematical, bodily-kinesthetic, interpersonal
    D. Memory, convergent, divergent

14. _____ are the primary engines of development,   14.____

    A. Chaos and individualism   B. Continuity and change
    C. Proximal processes   D. Peer groups

15. What is the level of intelligence for most ADHD children?   15.____

    A. Above normal   B. Normal
    C. Below normal   D. No data available

16. Which of the following best describes brain growth during the school-age years?   16.____

    A. Brain weight equals adult levels by age 6.
    B. Brain myelination is complete by age 7.
    C. Brain lateralization begins at age 6.
    D. The head grows quickly during the school-age years.

17. Sally is going through tremendous physical changes and is increasing in height and weight very quickly. However, she has not yet reached menarche. What term do we give to this period of development?   17.____

    A. Puberty   B. Juvenescence
    C. Pubescence   D. Presexagesimal

18. Changes that occurred in diary recordings from the late 19th century to the early 20th century were from   18.____
    I. no explicit sexual content in entries in the 19th century to entries discussing heterosexual and homosexual behaviors in the 20th century
    II. strong family loyalty apparent in entries in the 19th century to disregard for parents and thoughts of running away in the 20th century
    III. entries planning to make alterations in one's character in the 19th century to plans to make alterations in one's outer appearances in the 20th century

    The CORRECT answer is:

    A. I only   B. II only   C. I, III   D. I, II, III

19. Over the course of this century, the ratio of youths to adults has   19.____

    A. steadily increased
    B. steadily decreased
    C. both decreased and increased
    D. mirrored the secular growth trend

20. Which of the following is a secondary sex characteristic?   20.____

    A. Ovulation   B. Menstruation
    C. Axillary hair   D. Muscle development

21. Some data shows that little girls don't imitate Batman and Power Rangers nearly as much as little boys do. According to Bandura, this occurs because

    A. girls are innately less aggressive
    B. boys have more imagination
    C. girls don't perceive themselves as similar to the models
    D. boys don't want to be perceived as *sissies*

22. Sue's preschool teacher said to her, *You're spending so much time on those drawings, and they are so colorful! Won't they look niee on the art wall!* Sue sees herself as an artist, and returns to the painting area every day. Her teacher has used

    A. verbal prompting   B. response cost
    C. positive attribution   D. social cognizing

23. Studies of children who have been exposed to violence show all but one of the following:

    A. Exposure to violence decreases children's future orientation
    B. Real news on television helps children to understand that violence is not a major threat
    C. Children's confidence is declining for believing that adults can protect them from violence
    D. Children are becoming desensitive to violence

24. What does current research point to as the primary problem in dyslexia?

    A. Language processing   B. Vision problems
    C. Visual-motor problems   D. Low intelligence

25. Arnold Sameroff's study of the accumulation of risk factors shows that

    A. each accumulation of an additional risk factor in a child's environment was related to an equal decrease in the child's later IQ
    B. categorical programs are likely to be the most successful at dealing with the accumulation of risk factors
    C. some risk factors put a child at much greater risk for a decreased IQ than others
    D. children with one or two risk factors had only slightly lower later IQs than those with no risk factors

KEY (CORRECT ANSWERS)

1. C
2. B
3. B
4. C
5. B

6. B
7. A
8. C
9. C
10. B

11. D
12. B
13. B
14. C
15. B

16. A
17. C
18. C
19. C
20. C

21. C
22. C
23. B
24. A
25. D

EXAMINATION SECTION
TEST 1

DIRECTIONS: Each question or incomplete statement is followed by several suggested answers or completions. Select the one that BEST answers the question or completes the statement. *PRINT THE LETTER OF THE CORRECT ANSWER IN THE SPACE AT THE RIGHT.*

1. Methadone is a synthetic substitute for
    - A. demerol
    - B. morphine
    - C. laudanum
    - D. pentothal

2. A family of synthetic drugs made from coal tar is the
    - A. opiates
    - B. cocaines
    - C. bromides
    - D. barbiturates

3. A drug which does NOT cause physical addiction or withdrawal symptoms but is regulated by the government as a narcotic is
    - A. codeine
    - B. morphine
    - C. cocaine
    - D. heroin

4. The term *tracks* is associated with the users of
    - A. L.S.D.
    - B. red devils
    - C. methadone
    - D. heroin

5. Of the following drugs, the one that is a stimulant is
    - A. alcohol
    - B. amphetamines
    - C. barbiturates
    - D. opiates

6. Amytal, Seconal and Nembutal are prescription drugs classified as
    - A. barbiturates
    - B. hallucinogens
    - C. opiates
    - D. amphetamines

7. A drug which is classed legally as a narcotic while medically it is NOT is
    - A. opium
    - B. cocaine
    - C. heroin
    - D. codeine

8. Of the following regarding barbiturates, the INCORRECT statement is:
    - A. More people die as a result of acute intoxication from barbiturates than from any other drug poisoning
    - B. Taking barbiturates along with alcoholic beverages may prove to be fatal
    - C. The medicinal use of barbiturates has been prescribed for sedation, sleep-producing, epilepsy, and high blood pressure
    - D. Barbiturates are not depressants

9. The CORRECT association related to the special language of drug users is
    - A. candy–hallucinogens
    - B. cartwheels–tranquilizers
    - C. bennies–barbiturates
    - D. co-pilots–amphetamines

10. As related to treatment and rehabilitation of drug abuse, the CORRECT association is

   A. detoxification–substituting a less harmful drug
   B. maintenance–peer group support
   C. encounter therapy–in-patient hospitalization
   D. therapeutic community–halfway house using former addicts

11. Methaqualone is used medically as a

   A. safe substitute for barbiturates
   B. non-addicting anti-convulsant
   C. prescription for sleeplessness
   D. prevention of skeletal abnormalities in human fetuses

12. All of the following statements concerning the intake of alcohol in the body are correct EXCEPT:

   A. Although alcohol has a caloric content, it is expended instead of being stored in the body.
   B. A small percentage of the alcohol taken into the body is eliminated through the lungs.
   C. Alcohol produces a feeling of warmth with an actual lowering of body temperature.
   D. Digestive changes are necessary before alcohol can be absorbed from the stomach.

13. All of the following characteristics predispose a person to alcoholism EXCEPT having

   A. little tolerance for frustration
   B. low energy levels and strong impulse control
   C. strong feelings of alienation
   D. conflicts in family relationships

14. The MOST effective approach for a teacher to use in an alcohol education unit is to

   A. stress the evils of alcoholism
   B. emphasize the importance of the freedom of the individual to make responsible choices
   C. present facts about alcohol to the students
   D. use the scare approach to discourage students from using alcohol

15. In developing a program of treatment of the alcoholic, the LEAST important consideration is

   A. hospitalization until completion of the treatment
   B. detoxification
   C. physical rehabilitation including nutritional assistance
   D. maintenance of abstinence

16. One of the EARLIEST effects of alcohol on the body is

   A. reduced heart action
   B. loss of equilibrium
   C. decrease in judgment and self-control
   D. blurred and double vision

17. It is CORRECT to state that the *immediate* effect of alcohol on the body is to

    A. constrict surface blood vessels
    B. decrease the rate of the heartbeat
    C. increase blood pressure
    D. decrease body temperature

18. Of the following concerning alcohol, the CORRECT statement is:

    A. Alcohol acts principally on the central nervous system
    B. As a rule, black coffee will do away with intoxication
    C. There are no individual differences among people which relate to alcoholism
    D. About 50% of the alcohol consumed is eliminated unchanged through the kidneys and lungs

19. As alcohol is oxidized in the body tissues, the energy it contains is

    A. used up in muscular activity
    B. used in accelerated activity of the nervous system
    C. stored in the body
    D. given off as heat

20. Of the following, the substance with addicting properties would be

    A. mescaline   B. phenobarbital
    C. librium   D. cocaine

21. When considered as a drug, the MOST accurate classification which describes alcohol is that it is a

    A. stimulant   B. depressant
    C. hallucinogen   D. tranquilizer

22. The MOST common signs and symptoms associated with the use of marijuana are

    A. thirst, drowsiness, and passiveness
    B. pink eyes, increased pulse rate, and hunger
    C. discomfort, anxiety. and general ataxia
    D. increased libido, decreased blood pressure, and pupil dilation

23. While under the influence of morphine, an addict will *usually*

    A. experience an abnormal dryness of the nose
    B. have contracted, pinpoint pupils of the eyes
    C. feel strong and superior and experience loss of fatigue
    D. be very talkative and will not listen to others

24. Of the following statements concerning drugs, the CORRECT one is:

    A. As a person's tolerance to barbiturates increases, his tolerance level to other drugs also increases.
    B. Many heroin addicts will use amphetamines when they cannot obtain heroin.
    C. Most experts consider barbiturate addiction more dangerous than heroin addiction.
    D. When skin popping, the user will most often inject directly into a vein.

25. The time between the consuming of alcohol and its beginning to be absorbed into the bloodstream may be *as little as* _____ minutes.

   A. 2   B. 5   C. 8   D. 10

26. All of the following statements concerning alcohol and its effect on the body are correct EXCEPT:

   A. The constant presence of alcohol impairs the liver cells in their ability to store glycogen
   B. At high concentrations, alcohol causes the lessening of gastric juice secretion
   C. Beriberi is one of the commonest deficiency diseases associated with alcoholism
   D. Alcohol increases the enzyme action in the stomach

27. The MOST severe withdrawal reactions result from addiction to

   A. cocaine   B. heroin
   C. barbiturates   D. mescaline

28. The difference between marijuana and heroin is that

   A. marijuana has no proven medical use
   B. heroin is more addictive
   C. pure heroin is better to use than pure marijuana
   D. the emotions are more directly affected by marijuana than by heroin

29. With regard to marijuana, the CORRECT statement is:

   A. More severe penalties will decrease the problem.
   B. Marijuana use usually leads to heroin use.
   C. Marijuana is harmless.
   D. Driving under the influence of marijuana is hazardous.

30. Of the following statements, it is TRUE to say that marijuana

   A. is an aphrodisiac
   B. is addictive
   C. interferes with the thought processes
   D. causes violence and crime

31. The MOST widely misused of all drugs is

   A. alcohol   B. marijuana
   C. heroin   D. cocaine

32. All of the following concerning heroin are correct EXCEPT it

   A. is an antispasmodic
   B. is a derivative of opium
   C. is considered a hypnotic rather than a narcotic
   D. has mild, pain relieving powers

33. All of the following associations are correct EXCEPT

    A. narcotic–novocaine
    B. barbiturate–luminal
    C. stimulant–amphetamine
    D. sedative–benzedrine

34. Alcohol supplies to the body

    A. minerals
    B. protein
    C. calories
    D. none of these

35. All of the following statements concerning alcohol are correct EXCEPT:

    A. The effects of alcohol upon the brain are not felt until the alcohol begins to get into the bloodstream.
    B. While alcohol is absorbed quickly by the body, it is eliminated slowly.
    C. The metabolism of alcohol in the body is speeded up by increased activity.
    D. The stomach cannot change alcohol.

KEY (CORRECT ANSWERS)

1. B	11. C	21. B
2. C	12. D	22. B
3. C	13. B	23. B
4. D	14. B	24. C
5. B	15. A	25. A
6. A	16. C	26. B
7. B	17. D	27. C
8. D	18. A	28. B
9. D	19. D	29. D
10. B	20. C	30. C
	31. A	
	32. C	
	33. D	
	34. C	
	35. C	

EXAMINATION SECTION
TEST 1

DIRECTIONS: Each question or incomplete statement is followed by several suggested answers or completions. Select the one that BEST answers the question or completes the statement. *PRINT THE LETTER OF THE CORRECT ANSWER IN THE SPACE AT THE RIGHT.*

1. The fact is that alcohol

    A. stimulates driving alertness when sleep is needed
    B. is a depressant
    C. has no caloric value
    D. affects all persons in the same degree

    1._____

2. The fallacy is that alcohol

    A. slows reaction time
    B. has no mineral value
    C. is an anesthetic
    D. cures a cold

    2._____

3. The CORRECT regimen for an alcoholic is to

    A. drink less gradually
    B. drink just before meals
    C. stop drinking alcohol beverages completely
    D. drink only at home

    3._____

4. In the brain, excessive alcohol acts as a(n)

    A. stimulant
    B. anaesthetic
    C. readily available fuel
    D. vitamin-carrier

    4._____

5. The trend toward alcoholism is MOST often

    A. a symptom of personality maladjustment
    B. caused by heredity
    C. associated with the sex of the individual
    D. associated with the individual's occupation

    5._____

6. Excessive intake of alcoholic beverages over a period of time

    A. hampers the production of gastric juice
    B. reduces nervous anxiety
    C. increases mental alertness
    D. dilates the blood vessels

    6._____

7. Today, the nature of general clinical treatment of alcoholism is

   A. group psychotherapy
   B. incarceration
   C. tapering off and substitution
   D. physiotherapy

8. An ounce of alcohol (95%) has an APPROXIMATE caloric value of

   A. 200   B. 300   C. 400   D. 500

9. *Alcoholics Anonymous* was organized by

   A. alcoholic addicts
   B. the federal government
   C. private organizations
   D. the American Medical Association

10. It is believed that atabuse

    A. sensitizes humans against alcohol
    B. forms an unstable compound with alcohol
    C. stimulates the gag reflex
    D. promotes elimination of alcohol from the body

11. Excessive alcohol intake ultimately

    A. stimulates body reactions
    B. accelerates mental alertness
    C. depresses
    D. lowers body resistance to infections

12. The malnutrition associated with alcoholism USUALLY results from

    A. impaired digestion
    B. disturbed metabolism
    C. excessive craving for proteins
    D. reduction in diet essentials

13. Excessive use of alcohol is indulged in because it is believed to

    A. quiet the nerves
    B. stimulate brain action
    C. relieve emotional tension
    D. overcome social inadequacy

14. Alcohol FIRST affects

    A. judgment   B. memory
    C. muscular coordination D. control of speech

15. To the nervous system, alcohol acts as a

    A. stimulant B. depressant
    C. gratifier D. agitator

16. Characteristic symptoms of chronic alcoholism include

    A. damage to brain tissue
    B. increase in weight
    C. exsiccosis
    D. periods of depression

17. The anesthetizing action of alcohol FIRST affects the exercise of

    A. muscular coordination B. control of speech
    C. judgment D. memory

18. Acute intoxication may properly be labeled a psychosis because it involves

    A. severe loss of contact with reality
    B. emotional inadequacies
    C. intellectual limitations
    D. bodily as well as mental disease

19. The treatment of alcoholic pellagra is a balanced diet AND

    A. penicillin injections
    B. oral antibiotics
    C. thiamin injections
    D. amytal injections

20. *Cured* alcoholics

    A. can control the amount they drink
    B. cannot ever *drink normally*
    C. need moral help to drink within *normal limits*
    D. can drink some alcohol as long as they eat with it

21. Alcohol is MOST often used excessively in order to

    A. induce sleep
    B. stimulate brain action
    C. overcome social inadequacy
    D. furnish temporary release from tensions

22. To cure drug addiction, the A.M.A. believes that the BEST procedure is to

    A. maintain stable dosages in addicts
    B. furnish narcotics at no cost
    C. establish withdrawal clinics
    D. give constant control in a drug–free environment

23. Of the following, the MOST dangerous of the narcotic poisons is   23.____
    A. codeine   B. opium   C. heroin   D. marijuana

24. Statistics indicate that MOST youngsters start the drug habit with   24.____
    A. marijuana   B. heroin   C. cocaine   D. morphine

25. Alcohol is a   25.____
    A. stimulant   B. narcotic   C. depressant   D. none of these

KEY (CORRECT ANSWERS)

1. B		11. C
2. D		12. D
3. C		13. C
4. B		14. A
5. A		15. B
6. A		16. D
7. A		17. C
8. A		18. A
9. A		19. C
10. A		20. B

21. D
22. D
23. C
24. A
25. C

TEST 2

DIRECTIONS: Each question or incomplete statement is followed by several suggested answers or completions. Select the one that BEST answers the question or completes the statement. *PRINT THE LETTER OF THE CORRECT ANSWER IN THE SPACE AT THE RIGHT.*

1. In general, of the following, the MOST effective cure of addiction to drugs is

    A. sustained medical treatment
    B. change of occupation
    C. voluntary tapering off of the use of drugs
    D. conquering the habit by will power

    1._____

2. The method used to train teenagers in the control of narcotic habits in a school on Ward's Island is the

    A. penal colony
    B. strict regulatory
    C. clinical examination control
    D. permissive

    2._____

3. A drug which is a substitute for morphine in the treatment of drug addiction is

    A. codeine   B. demerol   C. pantapon   D. methadone

    3._____

4. An hypnotic drug which does NOT initiate drug addiction is

    A. dormison
    B. sodium amytal
    C. sodium phenobarbital
    D. seconal

    4._____

5. The MOST harmful drug derived from opium is

    A. heroin   B. morphine   C. cocaine   D. codeine

    5._____

6. The MOST recent statistics indicate that, of the following, the leading cause of accidental deaths from poisoning is

    A. morphine
    B. narcotine
    C. barbituates
    D. lead

    6._____

7. Marijuana is made from

    A. opium
    B. codeine
    C. hemp leaves
    D. cocoa

    7._____

8. To a drug addict, reefer or joint mean

    A. cigarettes
    B. powders
    C. capsules
    D. pills

    8._____

9. *Goofballs* used by drug addicts contained

    A. chloral
    B. hyposcyamine
    C. stramonium
    D. barbituric acid

    9._____

10. Recent statistics indicate that MOST youngsters start the drug habit with

    A. marijuana   B. heroin   C. cocaine   D. morphine

    10._____

11. Recent information regarding cocaine indicates that it

   A. is purely recreational
   B. is highly addictive
   C. is helpful in reducing stress and hypertension
   D. should be used only prescribed by a physician

12. A habit-forming drug is

   A. sulfathiozole   B. quinidine
   C. demerol   D. potassium acetate

13. Usually, the FIRST step to drugs by a youngster is a

   A. deck   B. snort   C. reefer   D. cap

14. Preventing unlawful trade in narcotics is assigned to

   A. Drug Authority
   B. Bureau of Narcotics
   C. Bureau of Customs
   D. United Nations Commission on Narcotic Drugs

15. *Tolerance* in drug addiction means the amount that

   A. quiets the nerves
   B. produces unconsciousness
   C. can be taken without character changes
   D. produces the desired effect

16. Marijuana is obtained from the

   A. hemp plant   B. thorn apple
   C. cocoa shrub   D. nightshade plant

17. According to the authorities, relationship between the incidence of cancer and smoking is

   A. controversial   B. negative
   C. positive   D. incidental

18. The responsibility for preventing unlawful domestic trade in narcotics rests with the

   A. United Nations Commission on Narcotics
   B. Bureau of Customs, U.S. Treasury Department
   C. Drug Enforcement Agency (DEA), U.S. Treasury Department
   D. United States Drug Authority, Legal Division

19. In addicts, drug withdrawal symptoms include vomiting and changes in

   A. A. pupils of the eyes
   B. muscular control
   C. color of the skin
   D. color of the whites of the eyeballs

20. If a teacher discovers a pupil who is taking drugs, she should report it to the   20._____

    A. dean or assistant principal
    B. police
    C. principal of the school
    D. pupil's parents

21. In addicts, a moderate drug abstinence syndrome is characterized by   21._____

    A. fever, increased blood pressure, insominia, acute restlessness, and rapid breathing
    B. depression, excessive perspiration, and yawning
    C. inertia, body tremors, and fits of sneezing
    D. diarrhea, chills, and depression

22. Opium is derived from   22._____

    A. hemp fiber   B. nightshade plant
    C. poppy   D. ragweed

23. A *mainliner* is a drug addict who uses the drug for   23._____

    A. intra-muscular injection
    B. snorting
    C. smoking
    D. intra-venal injection

24. Prolonged administration of narcotics is MOST likely to result in   24._____

    A. addiction
    B. reduced physical resistance
    C. increased aggressiveness
    D. need for a change in prescription

25. A plant from which peyote is obtained is the   25._____

    A. nightshade plant   B. fox glove
    C. gentian   D. mescal catcus

26. *Half-way house* is the name of a(n)   26._____

    A. dual purpose house providing facilities for living as well as conducting a business
    B. nursing home for terminal care of cancer patients
    C. rehabilitation center for ex-drug addicts and patients released from mental hospitals
    D. nursing home for senile aged persons

27. To avoid detection, the heroin addict injects the

   A. nasal mucosa and the gums
   B. gums and the vagina
   C. nasal mucosa and the vagina
   D. conjunctiva

27._____

28. A highly dangerous and addictive synthetic narcotic is

   A. amidol
   B. amidone
   C. cobalamine
   D. pyridoxine

28._____

29. During the 1993-1997 term of President Clinton, drug use by young people

   A. remained steady
   B. increased by one million
   C. declined
   D. cannot be statistically determined

29._____

30. A POSITIVE effect of decriminalizing drug use by medical administration would be

   A. fewer addicts
   B. increased medical costs
   C. less drug-related crime
   D. making drug use more acceptable

30._____

KEY (CORRECT ANSWERS)

1.	A	11.	B	21.	A
2.	D	12.	C	22.	C
3.	D	13.	C	23.	D
4.	A	14.	B	24.	A
5.	A	15.	D	25.	D
6.	C	16.	A	26.	C
7.	C	17.	C	27.	B
8.	A	18.	C	28.	B
9.	D	19.	A	29.	B
10.	A	20.	C	30.	C

EXAMINATION SECTION
TEST 1

DIRECTIONS: Each question or incomplete statement is followed by several suggested answers or completions. Select the one that BEST answers the question or completes the statement. *PRINT THE LETTER OF THE CORRECT ANSWER IN THE SPACE AT THE RIGHT.*

1. Marked improvement in a child's ability to draw a man over a brief period of time is MOST likely to be related to

    A. better social adjustment
    B. maturational effect
    C. the overcoming of a reading disability
    D. recovery from an illness

1._____

2. Phenylketonuria, which is associated with intellectual disability, is a disorder of

    A. the reticuloendothelia system
    B. metabolism
    C. cerebral damage
    D. gyral defect

2._____

3. A patient asserts, *I can't stand the agony I suffer when I go against my mother's wishes.* The therapist replies, *You really like to punish that momma inside of you for your dependency, don't you?*
    This response can be viewed as an example of

    A. reassurance   B. interpretation
    C. support   D. reflection of feeling

3._____

4. A shy young first grade boy becomes extremely attached to his teacher. He brings her presents, asks her to help him with his clothing a great deal, and wants to sit near her all the time.
    He is MOST likely manifesting the mental mechanism of

    A. introjection   B. sublimation
    C. reaction-formation   D. transference

4._____

5. The peculiarities of language behavior in the schizophrenic arise from his extreme need of a feeling of

    A. personal security   B. self-denial
    C. isolation   D. disarticulation

5._____

6. The theory that psychical compensation for a feeling of physical or social inferiority is responsible for the development of a psychoneurosis is attributed to

    A. Adler   B. Horney   C. Freud   D. Sullivan

6._____

7. Which of the following terms refers to the maintenance of stability in the physiological functioning of the organism?

   A. Functional autonomy
   B. Canalization
   C. Homeostasis
   D. Maturation

8. Extensive studies of the personality and behavior of intellectually gifted children generally reveal that they

   A. are physically better developed on the whole than average children
   B. are more likely to be emotionally disturbed than average children
   C. are more prone to divorce in later life than average children
   D. more often come from homes in which emotional disturbance is present

9. Expert opinion of professional workers with the physically handicapped indicates that a list of behavior characteristics would be headed generally by feelings of

   A. aggression   B. hostility   C. inferiority   D. courage

10. Children with pykno-epilepsy suffer from _____ convulsions.

    A. diencephalic
    B. visceral
    C. psychic equivalent
    D. no

11. Children with albinism and aniridia may read MOST comfortably with levels of illumination that, in relation to average levels of illumination, are

    A. upper   B. middle   C. lower   D. uneven

12. Phenylpyruvic amentia has been traced to which of the following?

    A. Nutritional deficiency in the prenatal environment
    B. A single recessive gene
    C. Pathological nidation
    D. Effects of radiation

13. Age of mother has been found to be MOST closely associated with the incidence of which of the following?

    A. Cerebral palsy
    B. Cerebral angiomatosis
    C. Down syndrome
    D. Hydrocephaly

14. The so-called visual area of the cerebral cortex is located in the _____ lobe.

    A. frontal
    B. parietal
    C. occipital
    D. temporal

15. Hypothyroidism is due to _____ in childhood.

    A. thyroid insufficiency
    B. pituitary insufficiency
    C. thyroid excess
    D. pituitary excess

16. The inability to express oneself in words in spite of an adequate understanding and imaginal representation is called

    A. agraphia   B. aphemia   C. agnosia   D. aphexia

17. Clara Thompson saw psychoanalysis as a method of therapy primarily designed to 17._____
    A. give the individual new insights into his past experiences
    B. help the individual master his difficulties in living
    C. have the individual re-enact his relationships with his parents
    D. strengthen the individual's ego defenses

18. According to Freud, the source of the large majority of the dreams recorded during analysis is 18._____
    A. a recent and psychologically significant event which is directly represented in the dream
    B. several recent and significant events which are combined by the dream into a single whole
    C. one or more recent and significant events which are represented in the dream-content by allusion to a contemporary but indifferent event
    D. a subjectively significant experience which is constantly represented in the dream by allusion to a recent but indifferent impression

19. When an individual permits unpleasant impulses or thoughts access to consciousness but does not permit their normal elaboration in associative connections and in affect, the psychoanalytic adjustment mechanism involved is 19._____
    A. rationalization   B. conversion
    C. isolation   D. introjection

20. In psychoanalytic thinking, repression can BEST be thought of as a(n) 20._____
    A. attempt in projection
    B. special type of introjection
    C. reflection of acceptance of Id impulses
    D. temporal form of regression

KEY (CORRECT ANSWERS)

1. A
2. B
3. B
4. D
5. A

6. A
7. C
8. A
9. C
10. D

11. C
12. B
13. C
14. C
15. A

16. B
17. B
18. D
19. C
20. D

TEST 2

DIRECTIONS: Each question or incomplete statement is followed by several suggested answers or completions. Select the one that BEST answers the question or completes the statement. *PRINT THE LETTER OF THE CORRECT ANSWER IN THE SPACE AT THE RIGHT.*

1. The behavior pattern considered to be deviate by clinicians is

    A. infractions of the moral code
    B. generosity
    C. recessive personality
    D. resistance to authority

2. A symptom of dementia praecox is

    A. tick paralysis
    B. negativism
    C. extroversion
    D. eremophobia

3. According to classic psychoanalytic thinking, the disorder MOST responsive to psycho-analytic therapy is

    A. compulsive neurosis
    B. hysteria
    C. narcissistic neurosis
    D. obsessive neurosis

4. For the therapist, the MOST common meaning of resistance is that it is a(n)

    A. index of lack of suitability for treatment
    B. defensive attempt on the part of the patient
    C. reflection of superior therapeutic promise
    D. relatively rare phenomenon in psychotherapy

5. In a normal distribution, the percentage of children whose IQ's fall between 90 and 110 is APPROXIMATELY

    A. 40   B. 50   C. 60   D. 70

6. The pioneer in mental diseases who was the first to make a distinction between emotional disorder and intellectual disability was

    A. Kraepelin   B. Seguin   C. Esquirol   D. Galton

7. In psychoanalytic thinking, the term superego generally embraces the

    A. necessary social prohibitions as well as the higher cultural strivings and ideals
    B. unconscious strivings of the person as well as the ego-ideal
    C. unconscious reproaches of the person as well as the id strivings
    D. unconscious ego and its defense mechanism as well as the ego-ideal

8. A major contribution of Fromm to psychoanalysis can be considered to be his

    A. attempt to formulate the dynamics of orality and the concept of original sin
    B. belief that man has innate social feeling and a drive for perfection
    C. effort to relate the psychological forces operating in man to the society within which he lives
    D. effort to integrate the concept of psychosexual development with Rankian principles

9. José, a ten-year-old, has a hyperthyroid condition. It is MOST likely that his behavior will be characterized by

   A. shyness, withdrawal, and reticence
   B. negativism, aggressiveness, and uncooperativeness
   C. placidity, passivity, and psychomotor delays
   D. restlessness, irritability, and excessive activity

10. The etiology of intellectual disability which is attributed to mechanical damage to the fetus would be classified as

    A. exogenous   B. endogenous
    C. heterogenous   D. none of the above

11. The majority of children of intellectually disabled parents will have IQ's that in relation to the IQ's of their parents are

    A. somewhat lower
    B. somewhat higher
    C. lower for boys and higher for girls
    D. lower for girls and higher for boys

12. Stuttering and stammering are MOST likely to develop between the ages of _____ years.

    A. 2 and 5   B. 6 and 9
    C. 10 and 13   D. 14 and 18

13. Most cases of stuttering are PRIMARILY the result of

    A. changed handedness   B. hereditary factors
    C. physiological defects   D. emotional problems

14. Anorexia is a condition which manifests itself in a loss of

    A. vision   B. appetite
    C. motor control   D. smell

15. Most differences in play activities and interests between boys and girls in the elementary school years can PROBABLY be attributed to

    A. inherent biological differences
    B. inherent emotional differences
    C. instinctual influences
    D. cultural influences

16. The rate and pattern of early motor development of children depend MAINLY upon

    A. experience   B. acculturation
    C. maturation   D. training

17. Of the following, the BEST index of the anatomical age of young children is

    A. brain weight   B. ossification
    C. basal metabolism   D. dentition

18. When children of very superior mental ability are compared in size and weight with children of the same age whose mental ability is average, the former children are found to be

   A. above average
   B. average
   C. below average
   D. either above or below average, depending on the age level

18.____

19. The average child speaks his first word at _____ months.

   A. 6   B. 9   C. 12   D. 15

19.____

20. In Pavlov's classical study of conditioning, the unconditioned stimulus was the

   A. food   B. bell
   C. salivation   D. electric shock

20.____

21. Contemporary reinforcement learning theory suggests that the MOST effective learning takes place when correct responses are _____ and incorrect responses _____.

   A. rewarded; ignored   B. rewarded; punished
   C. ignored; punished   D. none of the above

21.____

22. According to the literature, girls tend to develop physiologically and socially about

   A. the same as boys
   B. one to two years more slowly than boys
   C. one to two years more quickly than boys
   D. none of the above

22.____

23. The mother of a newborn infant is told by her physician that she will have to have corrective surgery performed within the next 2 years. It is expected that the operation in addition to her convalescence will keep her away from her baby approximately one month. The period during which the separation would be LEAST advisable from the standpoint of the child's emotional development is between the ages of _____ months.

   A. 1 and 6   B. 8 and 16
   C. 16 and 20   D. 20 and 24

23.____

24. Of the following, the term to which empathy is LEAST related is

   A. sublimation   B. identification
   C. introjection   D. projection

24.____

KEY (CORRECT ANSWERS)

1.	C	11.	B
2.	B	12.	A
3.	B	13.	D
4.	B	14.	B
5.	B	15.	D
6.	C	16.	C
7.	A	17.	B
8.	C	18.	A
9.	D	19.	C
10.	A	20.	A

21. A
22. C
23. B
24. A

———

EXAMINATION SECTION
TEST 1

DIRECTIONS: Each question or incomplete statement is followed by several suggested answers or completions. Select the one that BEST answers the question or completes the statement. *PRINT THE LETTER OF THE CORRECT ANSWER IN THE SPACE AT THE RIGHT.*

1. Epilepsy is MAINLY associated with

    A. brain injury
    B. migraine
    C. dysrhythmia
    D. aggressivity

2. A disturbance of language perception and expression is called

    A. aphasia B. amnesia C. amentia D. alexia

3. Alcoholism is MOST commonly connected with

    A. dysrhythmia
    B. neurosis
    C. psychopathy
    D. overt homosexuality

4. The polygraph is MOST useful for diagnosing

    A. epilepsy
    B. aggressivity
    C. deception
    D. brain damage

5. The electroencephalogram is MOST useful for diagnosing

    A. brain tumor
    B. epilepsy
    C. brain injury
    D. mental deficiency

6. Shock therapy was recommended for

    A. paranoid schizophrenics
    B. depressed psychotics
    C. severe psychoneurotics
    D. psychopaths

7. Prefrontal lobotomy had been recommended for

    A. aggressive psychotics
    B. apathetic psychotics
    C. paranoid psychotics
    D. psychopaths

8. Most authorities believe that mental deficiency is _____ hereditary.

    A. never B. always C. sometimes D. rarely

9. Recent experiments utilizing glutamic acid in an attempt to raise the intellectual level of retarded children have resulted in

    A. inconclusive findings
    B. a marked temporary rise in intellectual level
    C. a marked permanent rise in intellectual level
    D. a slight temporary decline in intellectual level

10. An individual's Rorschach protocol may be MOST profitably interpreted in the light of his

    A. behavior while being tested
    B. case history
    C. other test results
    D. presenting problems

11. If a child is mentally retarded, his academic potential can be explained MOST readily to his parent in terms of the status of other children

    A. in his class
    B. of similar CA
    C. of similar MA
    D. of similar IQ

12. It is MOST probable that a school-age child characterized, on the basis of psychological tests, as a mental defective might, in fact, be

    A. epileptic
    B. deaf
    C. mute
    D. schizophrenic

13. The classroom behavior MOST characteristic of the brain injured child includes

    A. distractibility, hyperactivity, and lack of inhibition
    B. listlessness, withdrawal, and compulsiveness
    C. aggressiveness, fearfulness, and egocentrism
    D. perseveration, fatigue, and apathy

14. A child's MOST rapid rate of mental growth generally occurs

    A. during the first few months of life
    B. between the ages of 3-6
    C. between the ages of 6-12
    D. during early adolescence

15. A psychopath may be distinguished by the fact that he commits antisocial acts

    A. consistently
    B. without customary reaction to guilt
    C. without awareness of what he is doing
    D. violently

16. Of the following techniques, the one which is considered to be characteristic of non-directive or client-centered therapy is

    A. encouraging transference
    B. reflection of feeling
    C. free association
    D. permissive questioning

17. Psychoanalytic writers consider the MOST important aspect of an analyst's training to be his

    A. training in psychoanalytic concepts
    B. training in medicine
    C. training in analysis
    D. general psychological training

18. In the transference situation, it is MOST probable that there will be _____ feeling(s) between analyst and patient.

    A. positive
    B. negative
    C. neutral
    D. positive and negative

19. The sequelae of encephalitis

    A. are now preventable in virtually every case of the disease
    B. may become evident long after an acute attack of the disease
    C. respond readily to treatment when detected
    D. are physical and emotional but rarely mental

20. The mental mechanism most strongly EMPHASIZED in psychoanalytic formulations of schizophrenia is

    A. repression
    B. conversion
    C. projection
    D. regression

21. Paranoia differs from the paranoid type of schizophrenia in

    A. the occurrence of delusions in one and not the other
    B. the fact that the paranoid patient does not act on the basis of his delusions
    C. the amount of *psychopathic tainting* in the family history
    D. that the delusions are more systematized

22. According to the Freudian psychoanalysts, the personality changes in general paresis are due to

    A. oedipus complex
    B. infantile sex urges
    C. sublimations
    D. changes in narcissism

23. A patient who touched his chin when asked to touch his nose would be MOST likely to be suffering from

    A. motor apraxia
    B. motor ataxia
    C. sensory apraxia
    D. agnosia

24. Shock treatment for schizophrenia, especially by the use of metrazol, was introduced at first because of the theory that

    A. shock arouses special physiological defense mechanisms by way of the *alarm reaction*
    B. shock stimulates the autonomic nervous sytem and thus facilitates homeostasis
    C. convulsions protect epileptics against developing schizophrenic symptoms
    D. shock as a form of punishment gratifies the patient's masochistic tendencies

25. From his survey of experimental evidence on the effect of infant care on later personality, Orlansky was led to the conclusion that such factors as breastfeeding and toilet-training

    A. are of no significance for later personality
    B. are significant determiners of personality
    C. are relevant to personality only insofar as they indicate the mother's attitude, which is the effective factor
    D. may help determine personality but constitutional and post-infantile factors should receive major emphasis

KEY (CORRECT ANSWERS)

1.	C	11.	C
2.	A	12.	D
3.	B	13.	A
4.	C	14.	A
5.	B	15.	B
6.	B	16.	B
7.	A	17.	C
8.	C	18.	D
9.	A	19.	B
10.	B	20.	D

21. D
22. D
23. A
24. C
25. D

TEST 2

DIRECTIONS: Each question or incomplete statement is followed by several suggested answers or completions. Select the one that BEST answers the question or completes the statement. *PRINT THE LETTER OF THE CORRECT ANSWER IN THE SPACE AT THE RIGHT.*

1. A part of the nervous system NOT known to have any connection with emotional behavior is referred to as the

    A. parasympathetic nervous system
    B. basal ganglia
    C. frontal lobes of cerebral cortex
    D. temporal lobes of cerebral cortex

    1._____

2. A phobia is _____ anxiety.

    A. less specific than
    B. more specific than
    C. synonymous with an
    D. less acute than

    2._____

3. The division of the autonomic nervous system that coordinates bodily changes in fear and anger is

    A. sacral
    B. sympathetic
    C. emergency
    D. cranial

    3._____

4. The effect of familiarity in the case of inter-racial attitudes is

    A. dependent upon the nature of the contact
    B. a tendency to breed contempt
    C. greater understanding and acceptance
    D. of little importance one way or the other

    4._____

5. Negativism is MOST typical of children at the age of _____ year(s).

    A. one   B. three   C. six   D. nine

    5._____

6. Children's groups about the age of two typically show

    A. much cooperation
    B. sex segregation
    C. parallel activity
    D. none of the above

    6._____

7. In which of the following functions does development depend MOST completely upon maturation?

    A. Roller skating
    B. Swimming
    C. Singing
    D. Walking

    7._____

8. In the first months of an infant's life, the baby's reflex responses are

    A. almost the only reactions the baby shows
    B. virtually absent from behavior
    C. more accurate than later in life
    D. less conspicuous than generalized mass reactions

    8._____

9. Play and reading interests of boys and girls will be found to be most DIFFERENT at the age of _____ years.

   A. three   B. six   C. twelve   D. eighteen

10. The unsociability often reported for very bright children is MOST likely to be due to

    A. their biological makeup
    B. their complete absorption in intellectual pursuits
    C. their lack of personal attractiveness
    D. the absence of suitable companions

11. If we measure a number of individuals upon a variety of complex mental functions, we will find that the different functions show _____ relationship.

    A. a negative
    B. no
    C. a fairly high degree of positive
    D. practically a perfect positive

12. Of the following general statements about deterioration in mental patients, which is the MOST questionable at present?

    A. More recently acquired forms of reaction are lost before those formed earlier in life.
    B. Generalization and abstraction in psychoses is qualitatively the same as that in the young child.
    C. Deterioration in many cases regarded as hopeless appears to be reversible.
    D. The responses of a deteriorated person show generally a definite patterning which tends to mask his defects.

13. Concerning the course of intellectual deterioration in the mental disorders, it is CORRECT to state that

    A. defect in the ability to generalize is more characteristic of schizophrenia than of other psychotic states
    B. concept formation deteriorates more slowly in schizophrenia than in senile psychosis
    C. decreased speed and persistence in mental activity are characteristic of epilepsy
    D. senile patients suffer more impairment in the recall of long past events than in recent memory

14. According to mental test comparisons of cooperative patients in the various disease groups, the group which shows the LEAST intellectual impairment is

    A. paranoid schizophrenia   B. psychopathic personality
    C. hebephrenic schizophrenia   D. hysteria

15. Schizophrenic speech is BEST characterized by

    A. loose, approximate use of words and reaction to superficial similarities among ideas and objects
    B. loose, approximate use of words and failure to make use of similarities or analogies

C. unusual amount of stammering and reaction to superficial similarities among ideas and objects
D. unusual amount of stammering and failure to make use of similarities or analogies

16. It is the central, distinguishing feature of the depressive phase of manic-depressive psychosis that the patient   16._____

    A. is keenly aware of lacking a motive for existence
    B. attaches his depression to some irrelevant or imaginary cause
    C. is excessively disturbed over some recent trouble
    D. is overactive, restless, and even agitated

17. In which of the following abilities do dull and gifted children tend to differ most markedly?   17._____

    A. Arithmetical computation
    B. Drawing
    C. Reading comprehension
    D. Spelling

18. The schizophrenic patient is said to exhibit loss of affect. This amounts to   18._____

    A. decreased attention to one's personal feeling tone
    B. lack of emotional reaction toward abstract ideas
    C. increased affectivity to ideas and decreased affectivity concerning persons and events
    D. increased affectiveness in environment but less to abstractions

19. Ability to establish a conditioned response in the eyelid has been found to be a point of differentiation between   19._____

    A. idiopathic epilepsy and hysterical seizures
    B. malingering and traumatic neurosis
    C. senile dementia and cerebral arteriosclerosis
    D. hysterical and organic blindness

20. The MAIN distinction between normal grief and reactive neurosis is in the   20._____

    A. feelings of inadequacy and unreality
    B. lack of basis in real occurrence
    C. duration and intensity of the emotional display
    D. intellectual retardation

21. Kretschmer's dysplastic type applies to those with   21._____

    A. compact, round, fleshy habitus
    B. strong, solid, muscular build
    C. slender bodies, long bones, little muscular strength
    D. conspicuous disharmony due to abnormal functioning of the endocrine glands

22. Which of the following is NOT characteristic of anxiety neurosis? 22.____

    A. Increase of irritable tension
    B. Vague somatic complaints
    C. Hypersensitivity to external stimuli
    D. Temporary muscular paralysis of the limbs

23. Involutional melancholia is usually characterized by a 23.____

    A. marked motor agitation   B. motor depression
    C. flight of ideas   D. loss of affect

24. From our knowledge about hallucinatory phenomena, it can be stated reliably that 24.____

    A. hallucinations occur in association with a dreamlike state
    B. hallucinations and imagery are similar processes differing only in intensity
    C. mescal-induced hallucinations are not similar to schizophrenic hallucinations
    D. organized hallucinations can be produced by direct stimulation of the brain surface

25. Which of the following is NOT a form of epilepsy? 25.____

    A. Grand mal   B. Pyknolepsy
    C. Jacksonian   D. Parkinsonian

KEY (CORRECT ANSWERS)

1. B   11. C
2. B   12. B
3. D   13. A
4. A   14. A
5. B   15. A

6. C   16. A
7. D   17. C
8. D   18. C
9. C   19. D
10. D   20. C

21. D
22. D
23. A
24. D
25. D

EXAMINATION SECTION
TEST 1

DIRECTIONS: Each question or incomplete statement is followed by several suggested answers or completions. Select the one that BEST answers the question or completes the statement. *PRINT THE LETTER OF THE CORRECT ANSWER IN THE SPACE AT THE RIGHT.*

1. Which of the following findings is MOST consistent with early alcohol withdrawal?
    A. Heart rate of 50-60 beats per minute
    B. Heart rate of 120-140 beats per minute
    C. Blood pressure of 90/60 mmHg
    D. Blood pressure of 140/80 mmHg

   1.____

2. Which of the following patients would have the HIGHEST risk for suicide?
    A. Patient who talks about wanting to die
    B. Patient who plans a violent death and has the means to do so
    C. Patient who appears depressed, frequently thinks about dying, and gives away all personal possessions
    D. Patient who says they may do something if life does not improve soon

   2.____

3. Which medical condition is commonly associated with patients with bulimia nervosa?
    A. Diabetes   B. HIV   C. Cancer   D. Hepatitis C

   3.____

4. What action would be considered as a primary nursing intervention for a victim of child abuse?
    A. Teach the victim coping skills
    B. Ensure the safety of the victim
    C. Analyze the family dynamics
    D. Assess the scope of the problem

   4.____

5. Somatoform disorder is defined as
    A. management consisting of a specific medical treatment
    B. expression of conflicts through bodily symptoms
    C. a voluntary expression of psychological conflicts
    D. physical symptoms explained by organic causes

   5.____

6. What is a proper plan for treating a school-age child with attention deficit hyperactivity disorder?
    A. Ignore the child's hyperactivity
    B. Child should be removed from the classroom when disruptive
    C. Child should have as much structure as possible
    D. Encourage the child to play to release excess energy

   6.____

7. Which characteristic is common for a child with conduct disorder?
   A. Ritualistic behaviors
   B. Preference for inanimate objects
   C. Severe violations of age-related normal behavior
   D. Easily distracted

8. School phobia is commonly relieved by
   A. allowing the parent to be with the child in the classroom
   B. immediately returning the child to school with a family member
   C. telling the student why attendance at school is important
   D. allowing the child to enter the school before the other children

9. If a child has an I.Q. of 45, what classification of mental retardation does this value represent?
   A. Mild   B. Moderate   C. Severe   D. Profound

10. Which characteristics are common for a child with autistic disorder?
    A. Aggression, stealing, lying
    B. Easily distracted, impulsive, and hyperactive
    C. Intolerant to change, disturbed relatedness, stereotypes
    D. Angry, argumentative, and disobedient

11. Which of the following would NOT be an acceptable therapeutic approach for caring for an autistic child?
    A. Providing safety measures
    B. Rearranging the environment to motivate the child
    C. Engaging a diversion when acting out
    D. Providing an atmosphere of acceptance

12. According to Piaget's Cognitive Stages of Development, a 5-year-old child is in what stage of development?
    A. Sensorimotor stage   B. Concrete operations
    C. Pre-operational   D. Formal operation

13. What is indicated if a patient states they have to increase their level of alcohol intake to achieve the desired effect?
    A. Tolerance   B. Withdrawal
    C. Intoxication   D. Weight gain

14. If an alcoholic patient is experiencing tremors, irritability, hypertension, and fever, what condition will soon follow?
    A. Esophageal varices   B. Korsakoff's syndrome
    C. Wernicke's syndrome   D. Delirium tremens

15. What would be the proper treatment for a patient in delirium tremens?
    A. Adequate fluids and high nutrient foods
    B. Placed in a quiet, dimly lit room
    C. Administration of Librium
    D. Monitoring vital signs every hour

16. If a patient presents with hallucinations, agitation, and an irritated nasal septum, which illicit drug did the patient MOST likely ingest?
    A. Marijuana
    B. Cocaine
    C. Heroin
    D. Methamphetamine

    16.____

17. What would be the appropriate medication for a patient who presents with needle tracks in the arm, in a stupor, and with a pinpoint pupil?
    A. Narcan   B. Methadone   C. Naltrexone   D. Disulfiram

    17.____

18. If an elderly patient presents with increasing forgetfulness, decreasing daily function, and using a toothbrush to comb his hair, which of the following conditions is being exhibited by this patient?
    A. Aphasia   B. Amnesia   C. Apraxia   D. Agnosia

    18.____

19. What would be a PRIMARY treatment intervention for a patient with moderate stage dementia?
    A. Providing a safe and secure environment
    B. Providing adequate nutrition and hydration
    C. Encouraging memories to decrease isolation
    D. Encouraging to independently care for themselves

    19.____

20. Through which characteristic is dementia different from delirium?
    A. Dementia promotes slurred speech
    B. Dementia has a gradual onset
    C. Dementia includes clouding of the consciousness
    D. Dementia includes a sensory perceptual change

    20.____

21. What would be the BEST advice you could give to a patient who feels the need to starve themselves?
    A. Exercise until the need to starve passes
    B. Allow the patient to starve to relieve anxiety
    C. Tell the patient's family immediately
    D. Tell the patient to approach a nurse and talk out their feelings

    21.____

22. Which characteristic is a sign of improvement for patients with anorexia nervosa?
    A. Weight loss
    B. Weight gain
    C. Eating meals in the dining room
    D. Participation in group activities

    22.____

23. What is the MAJOR difference between anorexia nervosa and bulimia nervosa?
    Bulimic patients
    A. will have periods of binge eating and purging
    B. will have lesser anxiety
    C. will have peculiar food handling patterns
    D. have poor self-esteem

    23.____

24. A caregiver can build a therapeutic relationship with a bulimic patient by performing all of the following actions EXCEPT
    A. discussing their eating behavior
    B. establishing an atmosphere of trust
    C. helping patients identify feelings associated with binging and purging
    D. educating the patient about the condition of bulimia nervosa

25. Which condition would be characterized by an intense fear of riding in an elevator?
    A. Arachnophobia
    B. Agoraphobia
    C. Xenophobia
    D. Claustrophobia

KEY (CORRECT ANSWERS)

1.	B		11.	B
2.	B		12.	C
3.	A		13.	A
4.	C		14.	D
5.	B		15.	D
6.	C		16.	B
7.	C		17.	A
8.	B		18.	D
9.	B		19.	A
10.	C		20.	B

21.	D
22.	B
23.	A
24.	A
25.	D

TEST 2

DIRECTIONS: Each question or incomplete statement is followed by several suggested answers or completions. Select the one that BEST answers the question or completes the statement. *PRINT THE LETTER OF THE CORRECT ANSWER IN THE SPACE AT THE RIGHT.*

1. What should be the INITIAL treatment action for a patient with claustrophobia?
    A. Accept the patient's fear without opinion or criticism
    B. Assist the patient to find the cause of the fear
    C. Allow the patient to talk about their fear as much as possible
    D. Establish a trusting relationship

    1.____

2. Which is evidence of a caregiver developing a countertransference reaction?
    A. Confronting the patient about discrepancies in their behavior
    B. Revealing personal information to the patient
    C. Focusing on the feelings of the patient
    D. Ignoring the patient's wants and needs

    2.____

3. In attempting to be accomplished when conducting desensitization, the patient
    A. stops using illicit drugs
    B. stops abusing alcohol
    C. overcomes disabling fear
    D. admits to all wrongdoings

    3.____

4. Which of the following should you advise patients who are prescribed to take valium?
    A. Increase fluid intake
    B. Decrease fluid intake
    C. Avoid caffeinated beverages
    D. Avoid alcoholic beverages

    4.____

5. How does malingering differ from somatoform disorder?
    A. Malingering is stress that is expressed through physical symptoms
    B. Malingering is gratification from the environment
    C. Malingering has evidence from an organic basis
    D. Malingering is a deliberate effort to handle upsetting events

    5.____

6. What is the MOST successful form of therapy for a somatoform disorder?
    A. Prescription medications
    B. Stress management
    C. Psychotherapy
    D. Milieu therapy

    6.____

7. What method would you use to treat a psychiatric patient who speaks a foreign language?
    A. Use pictures to communicate
    B. Speak in universal phrases
    C. Simply use nonverbal communication
    D. Employ the services of an interpreter

    7.____

8. The _____ theory attempts to explain obsessive compulsive behaviors related to unconscious conflicts between id impulses and the superego.
   A. cognitive
   B. psychoanalytic
   C. behavioral
   D. interpersonal

9. _____ the patient's obsessive compulsive disorder is the MOST successful behavior when caring for a patient with obsessive-compulsive disorder?
   A. Rejecting   B. Preventing   C. Accepting   D. Challenging

10. Which of the following characteristics would NOT be a factor for a patient having diminished sexual arousal?
    A. Medications
    B. Health status
    C. Education and work history
    D. Relationship with spouse

11. Getting the patient to _____ is the ultimate goal of treating a patient with somatoform disorder.
    A. take the prescribed medications
    B. recognize the signs and symptoms of physical illness
    C. cope with physical illness
    D. express anxiety verbally rather than through physical symptoms

12. What is MOST important when counseling a family whose teenage son has just been diagnosed with schizophrenia?
    A. The distressing symptoms of schizophrenia can respond to medications.
    B. Symptoms of this disease imbalance the brain.
    C. Genetic history is a factor for developing schizophrenia.
    D. Schizophrenia can affect every aspect of a patient's functioning.

13. A patient who states they only abuse alcohol and cocaine to deal with a stressful marriage and stressful job is exhibiting which defense mechanism?
    A. Displacement
    B. Rationalization
    C. Sublimation
    D. Projection

14. A pregnant female continues to use heroin throughout her pregnancy. Which of the following conditions would this child be at risk for developing?
    A. Heroin dependence
    B. Mental retardation
    C. Schizophrenia
    D. Anorexia nervosa

15. What is the MOST important medical intervention when caring for a victim of sexual assault?
    A. Preserving an unbroken chain of evidence
    B. Preserving the patient's privacy
    C. Determining the identity of the attacker
    D. Assessing for sexually transmitted diseases

16. Which of the following is NOT a factor for a victim of family violence to safely remain in the home?
    A. Ability of patient to relocate
    B. Socioeconomic status of the family
    C. Availability of community shelters
    D. A non-abusive family member to intervene on behalf of the victim

16._____

17. Inability to _____ would be a sign of early onset of Alzheimer's disease.
    A. balance a checkbook
    B. take care of self
    C. relate to family members
    D. remember own name

17._____

18. Which neurotransmitter is responsible for the development of Alzheimer's disease?
    A. Serotonin
    B. Dopamine
    C. Epinephrine
    D. Acetylcholine

18._____

19. What products should be avoided by patients who are taking lithium carbonate to stabilize moods?
    A. Caffeine   B. Diuretics   C. Antacids   D. Antibiotics

19._____

20. Which of the following situations would NOT increase stress on a healthy family system?
    A. Birth of a child
    B. Parental arguments
    C. Child going away to college
    D. Death of a grandparent

20._____

21. Patients who take monoamine oxidase inhibitors as antidepressants should avoid
    A. dairy and green vegetables
    B. red meat and poultry
    C. aged cheese and red wine
    D. flour, grains, and rice

21._____

22. What should a caregiver assess prior to administering thorazine to an agitated patient?
    A. Pulse rate
    B. Blood pressure
    C. Blood urea nitrogen level
    D. Liver enzymes

22._____

23. A patient who is prescribed benzodiazepine oxazepam should avoid excessive consumption of
    A. shellfish   B. coffee   C. sugar   D. salt

23._____

24. What is the PRIMARY purpose of Alcoholics Anonymous?
    A. Teach positive coping mechanisms
    B. Alleviate stress
    C. Help members maintain sobriety
    D. Provide fellowship among members

24._____

25. What would be the initial treatment intervention if a patient experiences a panic attack in your presence?
    A. Remain with patient and promote a safe environment
    B. Reduce external stimuli
    C. Encourage physical activity
    D. Teach coping mechanisms

25.____

KEY (CORRECT ANSWERS)

1. A
2. B
3. C
4. D
5. D

6. B
7. D
8. B
9. C
10. C

11. D
12. A
13. B
14. A
15. A

16. B
17. A
18. D
19. B
20. B

21. C
22. B
23. B
24. C
25. A

EXAMINATION SECTION
TEST 1

DIRECTIONS: Each question or incomplete statement is followed by several suggested answers or completions. Select the one that BEST answers the question or completes the statement. *PRINT THE LETTER OF THE CORRECT ANSWER IN THE SPACE AT THE RIGHT.*

1. Which of the following factors contributes MOST to the difficulty people experience in adjusting to retirement? 1.____

    A. Missing the work environment
    B. Death of a spouse
    C. Reduced income
    D. Declining health

2. Which of the following BEST illustrates *social* death? 2.____

    A. Talking about a dying person who is capable of hearing
    B. Bringing a dying person to a nursing home
    C. Helping a dying person to share his/her thoughts that are intimate
    D. Treating a dying person as a child

3. Which of the following groups tends to have the GREATEST fear of death? 3.____

    A. Sporadically religious people
    B. Atheists
    C. Strongly religious people
    D. Converts

4. Acceptance is the last stage in the dying process.
Which one of the following sequences lists the first four stages in the CORRECT order? 4.____

    A. Anger, denial, depression, bargaining
    B. Anger, bargaining, denial, depression
    C. Denial, depression, anger, bargaining
    D. Denial, anger, bargaining, depression

5. Which one of the following is NOT a basic dimension of adult independence? 5.____

    A. Cultural   B. Economic
    C. Social   D. Physical

6. Approximately what percent of senior citizens are living in their own households? 6.____

    A. 80%   B. 90%   C. 60%   D. 70%

7. _____ is the process of getting over another person's death. 7.____

    A. Ageism   B. Disengagement
    C. Bereavement   D. Dependency

8. The degree of independence in old age is attributed to several key factors. Which one of the following is NOT considered to be a key factor?

    A. Finances
    B. Mobility
    C. Housing
    D. Religion

9. According to Barbara Anderson and Margaret Clark's book entitled CULTURE AND AGING, adaptation to aging is defined by various adaptive tasks.
    In their study of a San Francisco community, they found that the task to which more than half of the maladapted could NOT adjust was to

    A. substitute sources of need satisfaction
    B. accept the aging process
    C. revise criteria for self-evaluation
    D. integrate values and life goals

10. Approximately what percent of senior citizens have serious alcohol-related problems?

    A. 35%   B. 25%   C. 15%   D. 5%

11. Which of the following BEST describes the expression *dying trajectory*?
    The length of time between

    A. initial and terminal diagnoses
    B. a terminal diagnosis and death
    C. an initial diagnosis and recovery
    D. a healthy state and death

12. S.C.O.R.E. is an organization which helps owners of small businesses who are having management problems.
    What does the acronym S.C.O.R.E. stand for?

    A. Service Committee of Retired Educators
    B. Senior Council of Retired Engineers
    C. Senior Conference of Retired Employers
    D. Service Corps of Retired Executives

13. Approximately what percent of senior citizens have NEVER married?

    A. 3%   B. 10%   C. 17%   D. 25%

14. Which of the following meets all the conditions for a primary group formation?

    A. Hospital   B. Church   C. Family   D. School

15. The family life cycle, as defined by sociologists, contains several stages.
    Which of the following is NOT one of those stages?

    A. Marriage
    B. Bearing children
    C. Divorce
    D. Staying together until one spouse dies

16. Author Alan Kerckhoff was able to determine three norm value clusters associated with a family.
    Which of the following sequences describes these clusters in CORRECT order from least bonding to greatest bonding among family members?

    A. Modified, extended, nucleated
    B. Nucleated, modified, extended
    C. Modified, nucleated, extended
    D. Nucleated, extended, modified

17. Of all the senior citizens who get married each year, approximately what percent of these are first-time marriages?

    A. 5%   B. 10%   C. 15%   D. 20%

18. The two MOST important factors affecting marriage for older people are income and

    A. geographical location   B. gender ratio
    C. church affiliation   D. community involvement

19. Homogamy means the tendency for people of _____ backgrounds to _____.

    A. different; marry
    B. similar; divorce
    C. different; convert to the same religion
    D. similar; marry

20. Approximately how many older men are there for each 100 older women?

    A. 45   B. 60   C. 75   D. 90

21. Which of the following groups of older people has the HIGHEST mortality and suicide rates?

    A. Divorced   B. Married
    C. Never married   D. Widowed

22. Approximately what percent of senior citizens are great-grandparents?

    A. 30%   B. 40%   C. 50%   D. 60%

23. Approximately what percent of senior citizens have AT LEAST one living sibling?

    A. 30%   B. 45%   C. 65%   D. 80%

24. According to most sociologists, what is the accepted number of years which separates one generation from the next?

    A. 15   B. 20   C. 25   D. 30

25. The average number of children in a *completed* family is

    A. 1.6   B. 2.1   C. 2.6   D. 3.1

4 (#1)

KEY (CORRECT ANSWERS)

1. C
2. A
3. A
4. D
5. A

6. B
7. C
8. D
9. A
10. C

11. B
12. D
13. B
14. C
15. C

16. B
17. A
18. B
19. D
20. C

21. A
22. B
23. D
24. B
25. C

TEST 2

DIRECTIONS: Each question or incomplete statement is followed by several suggested answers or completions. Select the one that BEST answers the question or completes the statement. *PRINT THE LETTER OF THE CORRECT ANSWER IN THE SPACE AT THE RIGHT.*

1. Approximately what percent of the world population are senior citizens (aged 65 or over)? 1.____

    A. 3% B. 6% C. 9% D. 12%

2. Before the mid-1800's, the LARGEST compensating factor for the high annual death rate was the 2.____

    A. number of illnesses
    B. number of births
    C. population density
    D. limit of available medicine

3. Approximately what percent of the United States population are senior citizens? 3.____

    A. 25% B. 21% C. 17% D. 13%

4. When annual death rates fall from high unstable levels to low steady ones, this change is called an 4.____

    A. edacious transition
    B. effusive transfer
    C. epidemiologic transition
    D. endemic transfer

5. Which country has the SECOND largest elderly population? 5.____

    A. United States
    B. Great Britain
    C. India
    D. China

6. Which of the following is a characteristic of a rectilinear age structure? 6.____

    A. Middle-age mortality increases
    B. Birth rate decreases
    C. Middle-age and old-age mortality are inversely related
    D. Early and middle-age mortality is low

7. The countries _____ and _____ are closer to population equilibrium than are other developed nations. 7.____

    A. Sweden; Switzerland
    B. France; Switzerland
    C. France; Germany
    D. Germany; Sweden

8. Sociologists follow a general guideline that past the age of 30 the risk of death doubles every _____ years. 8.____

    A. 16 B. 12 C. 8 D. 4

9. In countries which are classified as *low-mortality*, cancer and _____ disease account for about 75% of all deaths for people aged 65 and older. 9.____

    A. lung
    B. cardiovascular
    C. kidney
    D. intestinal

10. What is the concept of *pleiotropy*, as proposed by biologist George Williams in a paper on senescence?

    A. Individual genes are involved in multiple processes.
    B. Some genes create harmful physiological effects.
    C. Certain genes dominate other genes.
    D. Most genes are geared toward the fitness of the body.

11. The London biologist T.B.L. Kirkwood proposed the theory of *antagonistic pleiotropy* to explain senescence.
    According to his theory, senescence occurs directly as a result of which of the following?

    A. Evolution   B. Gene abnormality
    C. Fat tissue   D. Sexual reproduction

12. In studies on (non-human) primates, which method has been shown to slow down the aging process?

    A. Dietary restriction   B. Active sexual activity
    C. Climate control   D. Human contact

13. The French researcher Jean-Marie Robine and his colleagues have demonstrated that women in Western societies can expect to spend up to _____ % of their lives disabled.

    A. 35   B. 25   C. 15   D. 5

14. Which two social problems are recognized by gerontologists as the MOST difficult that an aging population will face in future years?

    A. Funding health care and social isolation
    B. Age-based entitlement programs and funding health care
    C. Social isolation and age-based entitlement programs
    D. Caring for relatives and fear of dying

15. The acronym O.B.S. describes the behavior deficiencies associated with senility. What do the initials O.B.S. mean?

    A. Oblique Behavior Syndrome
    B. Oblique Brain Syndrome
    C. Organic Brain Syndrome
    D. Organic Behavior Syndrome

16. One theory on aging is referred to as the *reservoir theory*. Which of the following accurately describes this theory?
    Each person('s)

    A. accumulates a given amount of energy in the first year of life
    B. body will eventually wear out, part by part
    C. ends life with a specific amount of vitality unused
    D. begins life with a limited amount of energy

17. Most research on aging involves cross-sectional studies. These studies involve comparing what elements?

   A. A particular group at different time periods
   B. Two or more age groups
   C. Two or more ethnic groups
   D. A particular segment of a population

18. According to the United States Bureau of the Census, which one of the following minority groups has the HIGHEST percent in the over-65 category?

   A. Black
   B. Chinese
   C. American Indian
   D. Japanese

19. In the year 1900, what percent of the United States population was aged 65 or older?

   A. 12%   B. 9%   C. 6%   D. 3%

20. What is recognized as the major source of income for MOST retired people?

   A. Medicare
   B. Annuities
   C. Social Security
   D. Insurance benefits

21. Gerontologists agree that the MAJOR source of stress for elderly people is

   A. fatigue
   B. illness
   C. helplessness
   D. insecurity

22. In the stages related to the process of dying, which of the following is considered the *middle* stage?

   A. Bargaining
   B. Depression
   C. Anger
   D. Denial

23. The average life expectancy in this century has

   A. increased
   B. decreased
   C. stayed the same
   D. only increased in females

24. As a general rule,

   A. men outlive women
   B. women outlive men
   C. both sexes have the same life expectancy
   D. there is no average life expectancy for either sex

25. In the next 15 years, the population of senior citizens is expected to

   A. slowly decrease
   B. remain constant
   C. dramatically increase
   D. have greater longevity

4 (#2)

KEY (CORRECT ANSWERS)

1. B
2. B
3. D
4. C
5. C

6. D
7. A
8. C
9. B
10. A

11. D
12. A
13. B
14. B
15. C

16. D
17. B
18. B
19. D
20. C

21. C
22. A
23. A
24. B
25. C

HERE'S TO YOUR HEALTH
HEALTHY PEOPLE 2010

Contents

Introduction 1

A Systematic Approach to Health Improvement 7
    Healthy People 2010 Goals 8
    Objectives 17
    Determinants of Health 18
    Health Status 21

Leading Health Indicators 24
    Physical Activity 26
    Overweight and Obesity 28
    Tobacco Use 30
    Substance Abuse 32
    Responsible Sexual Behavior 34
    Mental Health 36
    Injury and Violence 38
    Environmental Quality 40
    Immunization 42
    Access to Health Care 44

Appendix:
    Short Titles for Healthy People 2010 Objectives

Introduction

Healthy People 2010 presents a comprehensive, nationwide health promotion and disease prevention agenda. It is designed to serve as a roadmap for improving the health of all people in the United States during the first decade of the 21st century.

Like the preceding Healthy People 2000 initiative—which was driven by an ambitious, yet achievable, 10-year strategy for improving the Nation's health by the end of the 20th century—Healthy People 2010 is committed to a single, overarching purpose: promoting health and preventing illness, disability, and premature death.

The History Behind the Healthy People 2010 Initiative

Healthy People 2010 builds on initiatives pursued over the past two decades. In 1979, *Healthy People: The Surgeon General's Report on Health Promotion and Disease Prevention* provided national goals for reducing premature deaths and preserving independence for older adults. In 1980, another report, *Promoting Health/Preventing Disease: Objectives for the Nation*, set forth 226 targeted health objectives for the Nation to achieve over the next 10 years.

Healthy People 2000: National Health Promotion and Disease Prevention Objectives, released in 1990, identified health improvement goals and objectives to be reached by the year 2000. The Healthy People 2010 initiative continues in this tradition as an instrument to improve health for the first decade of the 21st century.

Healthy People 2010 is grounded in science, built through public consensus, and designed to measure progress.

The Development of Healthy People 2010 Goals and Objectives

Healthy People 2010 represents the ideas and expertise of a diverse range of individuals and organizations concerned about the Nation's health. The Healthy People Consortium—an alliance of more than 350 national organizations and 250 State public health, mental health, substance abuse, and environmental agencies—conducted three national meetings on the development of Healthy People 2010. In addition, many individuals and organizations gave testimony about health priorities at five Healthy People 2010 regional meetings held in late 1998.

On two occasions—in 1997 and in 1998—the American public was given the opportunity to share its thoughts and ideas. More than 11,000 comments on draft materials were received by mail or via the Internet from individuals in every State, the District of Columbia, and Puerto Rico. All the comments received during the development of Healthy People 2010 can be viewed on the Healthy People Web site: http://www.health.gov/healthypeople/.

The final Healthy People 2010 objectives were developed by teams of experts from a variety of Federal agencies under the direction of Health and Human Services Secretary Donna Shalala, Assistant Secretary for Health and Surgeon General David Satcher, and former Assistant Secretaries for Health. The process was coordinated by the Office of Disease Prevention and Health Promotion, U.S. Department of Health and Human Services.

The Goals of Healthy People 2010

Healthy People 2010 is designed to achieve two overarching goals:

- Increase quality and years of healthy life.
- Eliminate health disparities.

These two goals are supported by specific objectives in 28 focus areas (see page 17). Each objective was developed with a target to be achieved by the year 2010. A full explanation of the two goals can be found in the next section of this document: "A Systematic Approach to Health Improvement."

The Relationship Between Individual and Community Health

Over the years, it has become clear that individual health is closely linked to community health—the health of the community and environment in which individuals live, work, and play. Likewise, community health is profoundly affected by the collective beliefs, attitudes, and behaviors of everyone who lives in the community.

Indeed, the underlying premise of Healthy People 2010 is that the health of the individual is almost inseparable from the health of the larger community and that the health of every community in every State and territory determines the overall health status of the Nation. That is why the vision for Healthy People 2010 is "Healthy People in Healthy Communities."

> **Community health is profoundly affected by the collective beliefs, attitudes, and behaviors of everyone who lives in the community.**

How Healthy People 2010 Will Improve the Nation's Health

One of the most compelling and encouraging lessons learned from the Healthy People 2000 initiative is that we, as a Nation, can make dramatic progress in improving the Nation's health in a relatively short period of time. For example, during the past decade, we achieved significant reductions in infant mortality. Childhood vaccinations are at the highest levels ever recorded in the United States. Fewer teenagers are becoming parents. Overall, alcohol, tobacco, and illicit drug use is leveling off. Death rates for coronary heart disease and stroke have declined. Significant advances have been made in the diagnosis and treatment of cancer and in reducing unintentional injuries.

But we still have a long way to go. Diabetes and other chronic conditions continue to present a serious obstacle to public health. Violence and abusive behavior continue to ravage homes and communities across the country. Mental disorders continue to go undiagnosed and untreated. Obesity in adults has increased 50 percent over the past two decades. Nearly 40 percent of adults engage in no leisure time physical activity. Smoking among adolescents has increased in the past decade. And HIV/AIDS remains a serious health problem, now disproportionately affecting women and communities of color.

Healthy People 2010 will be the guiding instrument for addressing these and emerging health issues, reversing unfavorable trends, and expanding past achievements in health.

The Key Role of Community Partnerships

Community partnerships, particularly when they reach out to nontraditional partners, can be among the most effective tools for improving health in communities.

Partnerships are effective tools for improving health in communities.

For the past two decades, Healthy People has been used as a strategic management tool for the Federal Government, States, communities, and many other public- and private-sector partners. Virtually all States, the District of Columbia, and Guam have developed their own Healthy People plans modeled after the national plan. Most States have tailored the national objectives to their specific needs.

Businesses; local governments; and civic, professional, and religious organizations also have been inspired by Healthy People to print immunization reminders, set up hotlines, change cafeteria menus, begin community recycling, establish worksite fitness programs, assess school health education curriculums, sponsor health fairs, and engage in myriad other activities.

Everyone Can Help Achieve the Healthy People 2010 Objectives

Addressing the challenge of health improvement is a shared responsibility that requires the active participation and leadership of the Federal Government, States, local governments, policymakers, health care providers, professionals, business executives, educators, community leaders, and the American public itself. Although administrative responsibility for the Healthy People 2010 initiative rests in the U.S. Department of Health and Human Services, representatives of all these diverse groups shared their experience, expertise, and ideas in developing the Healthy People 2010 goals and objectives.

Healthy People 2010, however, is just the beginning. The biggest challenges still stand before us, and we all have a role in building a healthier Nation.

Regardless of your age, gender, education level, income, race, ethnicity, cultural customs, language, religious beliefs, disability, sexual orientation, geographic location, or occupation, Healthy People 2010 is designed to be a valuable resource in determining how you can participate most effectively in improving the Nation's health. Perhaps you will recognize the need to be a more active participant in decisions affecting your own health or the health of your children or loved ones. Perhaps you will assume a leadership role in promoting healthier behaviors in your neighborhood or community. Or perhaps you will use your influence and social stature to advocate for and implement policies and programs that can improve dramatically the health of dozens, hundreds, thousands, or even millions of people.

Whatever your role, this document is designed to help you determine what *you* can do—in your home, community, business, or State—to help improve the Nation's health.

Other Information Is Available About Healthy People 2010

Healthy People 2010: Understanding and Improving Health is the first of three parts in the Healthy People 2010 series. The second part, *Healthy People 2010*, contains detailed descriptions of 467 objectives to improve health. These objectives are organized into 28 specific focus areas. The third part, *Tracking Healthy People 2010*, provides a comprehensive review of the statistical measures that will be used to evaluate progress.

Healthy People 2010 contains 467 objectives to improve health, organized into 28 focus areas.

Healthy People in Healthy Communities

A Systematic Approach to Health Improvement

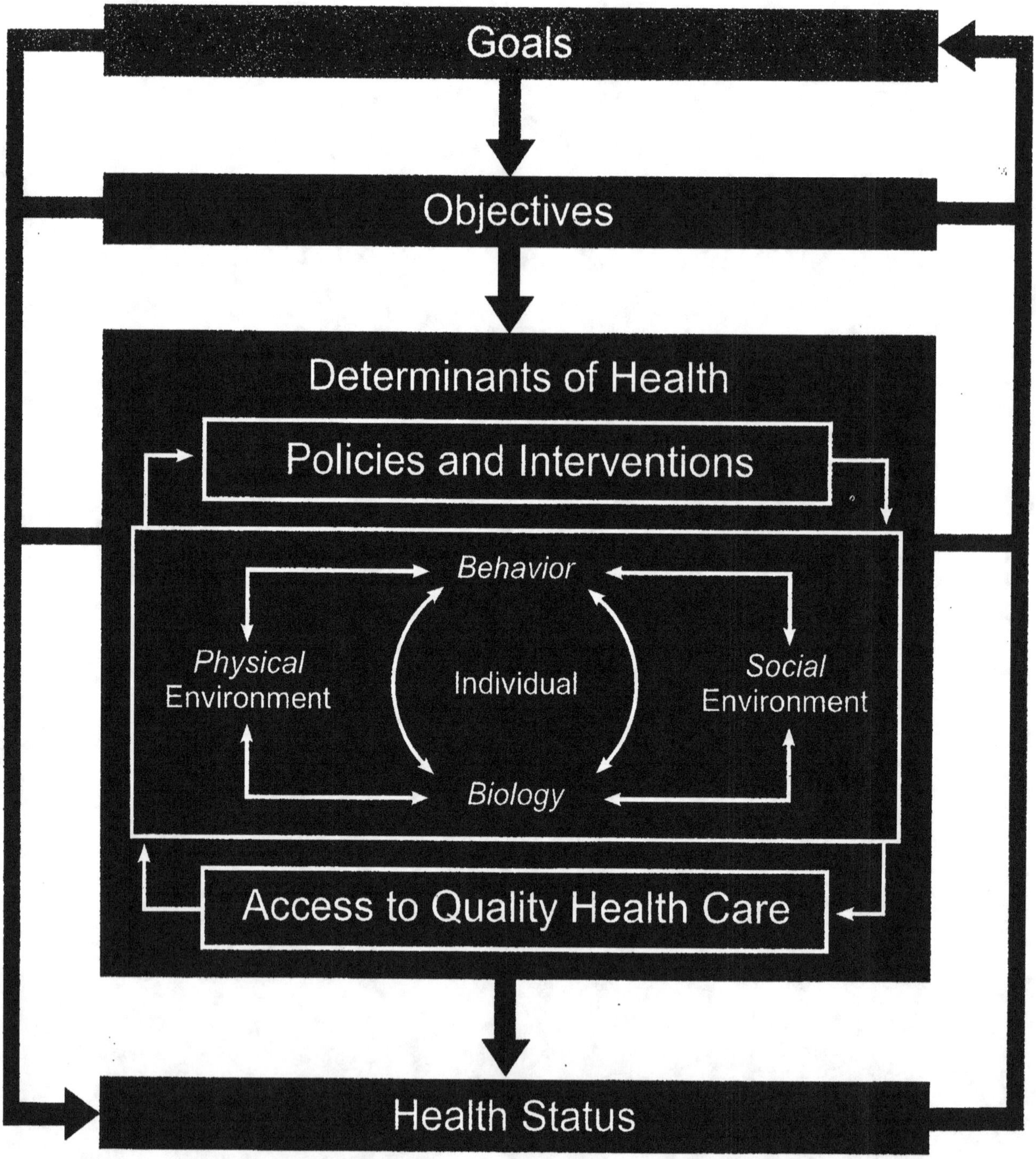

A Systematic Approach to Health Improvement

Healthy People 2010 is about improving health—the health of each individual, the health of communities, and the health of the Nation. However, the Healthy People 2010 goals and objectives cannot by themselves improve the health status of the Nation. Instead, they need to be recognized as part of a larger, systematic approach to health improvement.

This systematic approach to health improvement is composed of four key elements:

- Goals
- Objectives
- Determinants of health
- Health status

Whether this systematic approach is used to improve health on a national level, as in Healthy People 2010, or to organize community action on a particular health issue, such as promoting smoking cessation, the components remain the same. The goals provide a general focus and direction. The goals, in turn, serve as a guide for developing a set of objectives that will measure actual progress within a specified amount of time. The objectives focus on the determinants of health, which encompass the combined effects of individual and community physical and social environments and the policies and interventions used to promote health, prevent disease, and ensure access to quality health care. The ultimate measure of success in any health improvement effort is the health status of the target population.

Successful community partnerships use a systematic approach to health improvement.

Healthy People 2010 is built on this systematic approach to health improvement.

Healthy People 2010 Goals

Goal 1: Increase Quality and Years of Healthy Life

The first goal of Healthy People 2010 is to help individuals of all ages increase life expectancy *and* improve their quality of life.

Life Expectancy

Life expectancy is the average number of years people born in a given year are expected to live based on a set of age-specific death rates. At the beginning of the 20th century, life expectancy at birth was 47.3 years. Fortunately, life expectancy has increased dramatically over the past 100 years (see figure 1). Today, the average life expectancy at birth is nearly 77 years.

Life expectancy for persons at every age group also has increased during the past century. Based on today's age-specific death rates, individuals aged 65 years can be expected to live an average of 18 more years, for a total of 83 years. Those aged 75 years can be expected to live an average of 11 more years, for a total of 86 years.

Differences in life expectancy between populations, however, suggest a substantial need and opportunity for improvement. At least 18 countries with populations of 1 million or more have life expectancies greater than the United States for both men and women (see figure 2).

Figure 1. Past and projected female and male life expectancy at birth, United States, 1900—2050.

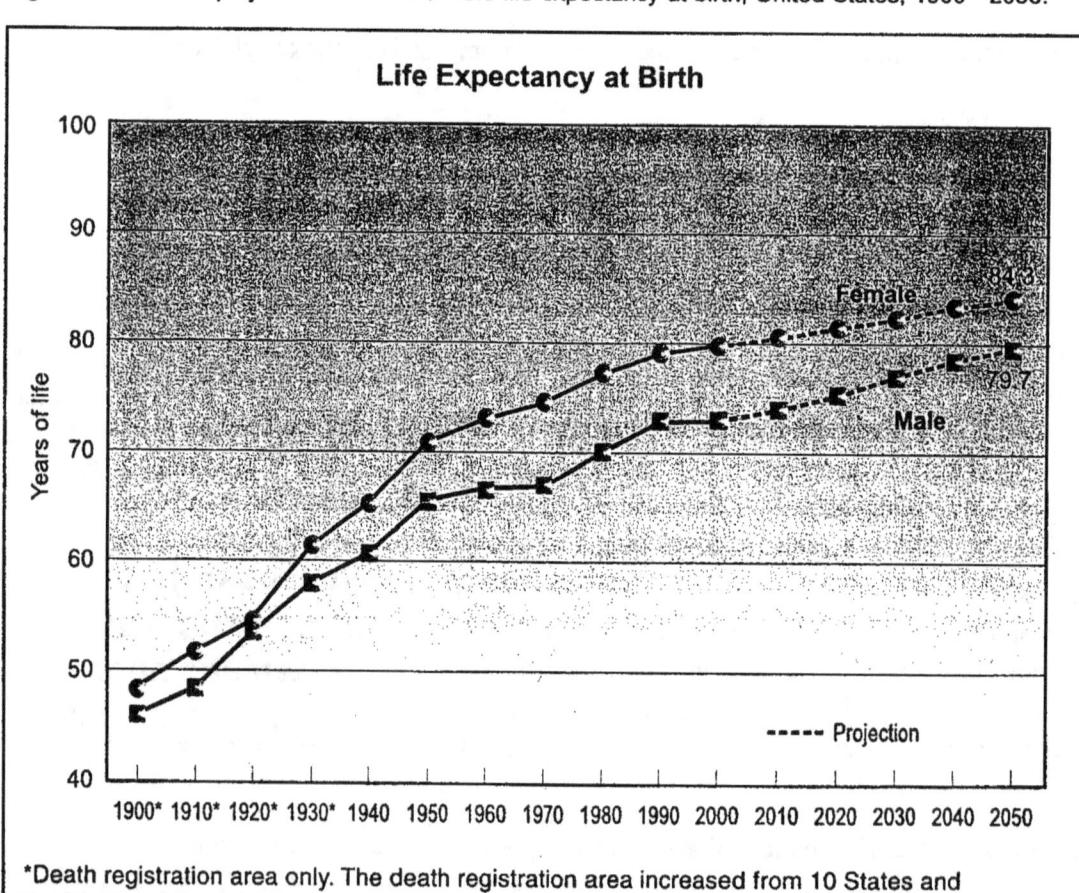

*Death registration area only. The death registration area increased from 10 States and the District of Columbia in 1900 to the entire United States in 1933.

Source: U.S. Department of Commerce, Bureau of the Census.

Healthy People 2010 Goals

Figure 2. Life expectancy at birth by gender and ranked by selected countries, 1995.

Life Expectancy by Country

Female		Male	
Country	Years of Life Expectancy	Country	Years of Life Expectancy
Japan	82.9	Japan	76.4
France	82.6	Sweden	76.2
Switzerland	81.9	Israel	75.3
Sweden	81.6	Canada	75.2
Spain	81.5	Switzerland	75.1
Canada	81.2	Greece	75.1
Australia	80.9	Australia	75.0
Italy	80.8	Norway	74.9
Norway	80.7	Netherlands	74.6
Netherlands	80.4	Italy	74.4
Greece	80.3	England and Wales	74.3
Finland	80.3	France	74.2
Austria	80.1	Spain	74.2
Germany	79.8	Austria	73.5
Belgium	79.8	Singapore	73.4
England and Wales	79.6	Germany	73.3
Israel	79.3	New Zealand	73.3
Singapore	79.0	Northern Ireland	73.1
United States	**78.9**	Belgium	73.0
		Cuba	73.0
		Costa Rica	73.0
		Finland	72.8
		Denmark	72.8
		Ireland	72.5
		United States	**72.5**

Sources: World Health Organization; United Nations; Centers for Disease Control and Prevention; National Center for Health Statistics; National Vital Statistics System 1990–95 and unpublished data.

Healthy People 2010 Goals

There are substantial differences in life expectancy among different population groups within the United States. For example, women outlive men by an average of 6 years. White women currently have the greatest life expectancy in the United States. The life expectancy for African American women has risen to be higher today than that for white men. People from households with an annual income of at least $25,000 live an average of 3 to 7 years longer, depending on gender and race, than do people from households with annual incomes of less than $10,000.

Quality of Life

Quality of life reflects a general sense of happiness and satisfaction with our lives and environment. General quality of life encompasses all aspects of life, including health, recreation, culture, rights, values, beliefs, aspirations, and the conditions that support a life containing these elements. *Health-related quality of life* reflects a personal sense of physical and mental health and the ability to react to factors in the physical and social environments. Health-related quality of life is more subjective than life expectancy and therefore can be more difficult to measure. Some tools, have been developed to measure health-related quality of life.

Global assessments, in which a person rates his or her health as "poor," "fair," "good," "very good," or "excellent," can be reliable indicators of one's perceived health. In 1996, 90 percent of people in the United States reported their health as good, very good, or excellent.

Healthy days is another measure of health-related quality of life that estimates the number of days of poor or impaired physical and mental health in the past 30 days. In 1998, adults averaged 5.5 days during the past month when their physical or mental health was not good—including 1.8 days when they were not able to do their usual activities. However, 52 percent of adults reported having good physical and mental health for the entire month in contrast with 10 percent of adults who were unhealthy for all 30 days. Typically, younger adults report more mentally unhealthy days while older adults report more physically unhealthy days.

Years of healthy life is a combined measure developed for the Healthy People initiative. The difference between life expectancy and years of healthy life reflects the average amount of time spent in less than optimal health because of chronic or acute limitations. Years of healthy life increased in 1996 to 64.2 years, a level that was only slightly above the 64.0 years at the beginning of the decade. During the same period, life expectancy increased a full year.

As with life expectancy, various population groups can show dramatic differences in quality of life. For example, people in the lowest income households are five times more likely to report their health as fair or poor than people in the highest income households (see figure 3). A higher percentage of women report their health as fair or poor compared to men. Adults in rural areas are 36 percent more likely to report their health status as fair or poor than are adults in urban areas.

Achieving a Longer and Healthier Life—the Healthy People Perspective

Healthy People 2010 seeks to increase life expectancy and quality of life over the next 10 years by helping individuals gain the knowledge, motivation, and opportunities they need to make informed decisions about their health. At the same time, Healthy People 2010 encourages local and State leaders to develop communitywide and statewide efforts that promote healthy behaviors, create healthy environments, and increase access to high-quality health care. Because individual and community health are virtually inseparable, both the individual and the community need to do their parts to increase life expectancy and improve quality of life.

Healthy People 2010 Goals

Figure 3. Percentage of persons with perceived fair or poor health status by household income, United States, 1995.

Relationship Between Household Income and Fair or Poor Health Status

Household income	Persons with perceived fair or poor health status
Less than $15,000	20.6%
$15,000-$24,999	13.1%
$25,000-$34,999	8.1%
$35,000-$49,999	5.9%
$50,000 or more	3.7%

Source: Centers for Disease Control and Prevention, National Center for Health Statistics. National Health Interview Survey. 1995.

Goal 2: Eliminate Health Disparities

The second goal of Healthy People 2010 is to eliminate health disparities among segments of the population, including differences that occur by gender, race or ethnicity, education or income, disability, geographic location, or sexual orientation. This section highlights ways in which health disparities can occur among various demographic groups in the United States.

Gender

Whereas some differences in health between men and women are the result of biological differences, others are more complicated and require greater attention and scientific exploration. Some health differences are obviously gender specific, such as cervical and prostate cancers.

Overall, men have a life expectancy that is 6 years less than that of women and have higher death rates for each of the 10 leading causes of death. For example, men are two times more likely than women to die from unintentional injuries and four times more likely than women to die from firearm-related injuries. Although overall death rates for women may currently be lower than for men, women have shown increased death rates over the past decade in areas where men have experienced improvements, such as lung cancer. Women are also at greater risk for Alzheimer's disease than men are and twice as likely as men to be affected by major depression.

Healthy People 2010 Goals

Race and Ethnicity

Current information about the biologic and genetic characteristics of African Americans, Hispanics, American Indians, Alaska Natives, Asians, Native Hawaiians, and Pacific Islanders does not explain the health disparities experienced by these groups compared with the white, non-Hispanic population in the United States. These disparities are believed to be the result of the complex interaction among genetic variations, environmental factors, and specific health behaviors.

Even though the Nation's infant mortality rate is down, the infant death rate among African Americans is still more than double that of whites. Heart disease death rates are more than 40 percent higher for African Americans than for whites. The death rate for all cancers is 30 percent higher for African Americans than for whites; for prostate cancer, it is more than double that for whites. African American women have a higher death rate from breast cancer despite having a mammography screening rate that is nearly the same as the rate for white women. The death rate from HIV/AIDS for African Americans is more than seven times that for whites; the rate of homicide is six times that for whites.

Hispanics living in the United States are almost twice as likely to die from diabetes as are non-Hispanic whites. Although constituting only 11 percent of the total population in 1996, Hispanics accounted for 20 percent of the new cases of tuberculosis. Hispanics also have higher rates of high blood pressure and obesity than non-Hispanic whites. There are differences among Hispanic populations as well. For example, whereas the rate of low birth weight infants is lower for the total Hispanic population compared with that of whites, Puerto Ricans have a low birth weight rate that is 50 percent higher than the rate for whites.

American Indians and Alaska Natives have an infant death rate almost double that for whites. The rate of diabetes for this population group is more than twice that for whites. The Pima of Arizona have one of the highest rates of diabetes in the world. American Indians and Alaska Natives also have disproportionately high death rates from unintentional injuries and suicide.

Asians and Pacific Islanders, on average, have indicators of being one of the healthiest population groups in the United States. However, there is great diversity within this population group, and health disparities for some specific segments are quite marked. Women of Vietnamese origin, for example, suffer from cervical cancer at nearly five times the rate for white women. New cases of hepatitis and tuberculosis are also higher in Asians and Pacific Islanders living in the United States than in whites.

Income and Education

Inequalities in income and education underlie many health disparities in the United States. Income and education are intrinsically related and often serve as proxy measures for each other (see figure 4). In general, population groups that suffer the worst health status are also those that have the highest poverty rates and the least education. Disparities in income and education levels are associated with differences in the occurrence of illness and death, including heart disease, diabetes, obesity, elevated blood lead level, and low birth weight. Higher incomes permit increased access to medical care, enable people to afford better housing and live in safer neighborhoods, and increase the opportunity to engage in health-promoting behaviors.

Healthy People 2010 Goals

Figure 4. Relationship between education and median household income among adults aged 25 years and older, by gender, United States, 1996.

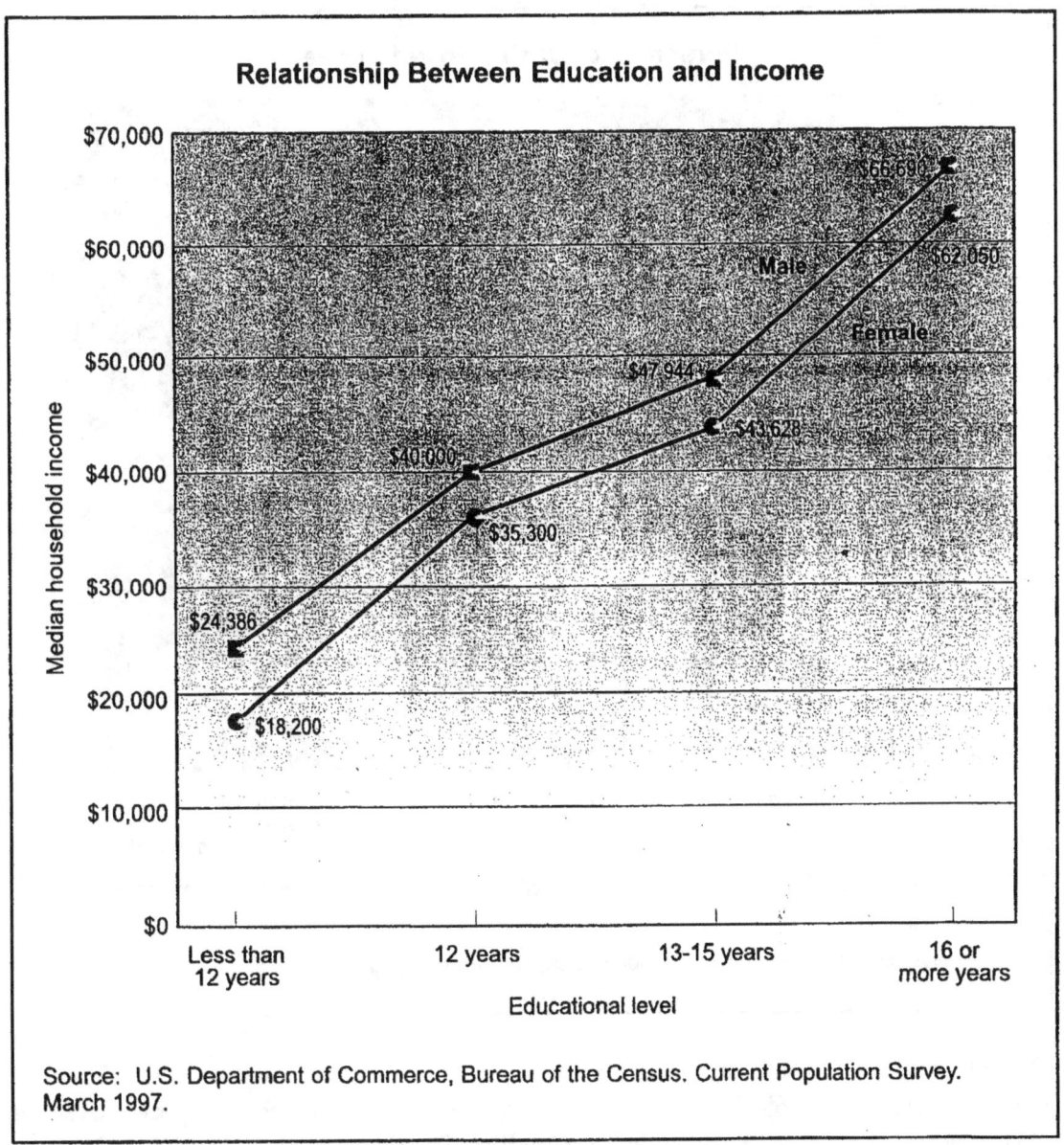

Source: U.S. Department of Commerce, Bureau of the Census. Current Population Survey. March 1997.

Income inequality in the United States has increased over the past three decades. There are distinct demographic differences in poverty by race, ethnicity, and household composition (see figure 5) as well as geographical variations in poverty across the United States. Recent health gains for the U.S. population as a whole appear to reflect achievements among the higher socioeconomic groups; lower socioeconomic groups continue to lag behind.

Healthy People 2010 Goals

Figure 5. Percentage of persons below the poverty level by race and ethnicity and type of household, United States, 1996.

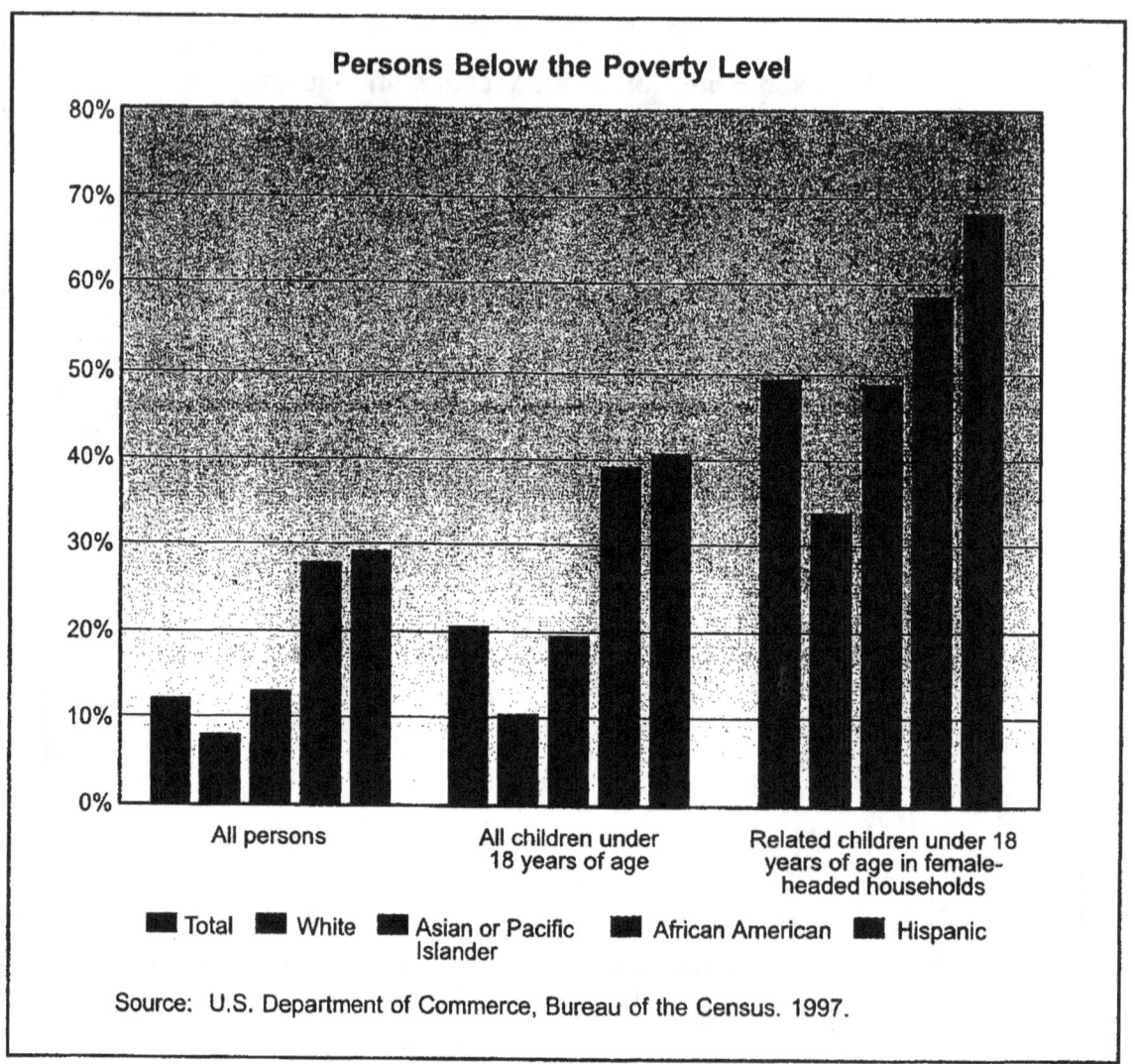

Source: U.S. Department of Commerce, Bureau of the Census. 1997.

Overall, those with higher incomes tend to fare better than those with lower incomes. For example, among white men aged 65 years, those in the highest income families could expect to live more than 3 years longer than those in the lowest income families. The percentage of people in the lowest income families reporting limitation in activity caused by chronic disease is three times that of people in the highest income families.

The average level of education in the U.S. population has increased steadily over the past several decades—an important achievement given that more years of education usually translate into more years of life. For women, the amount of education achieved is a key determinant of the welfare and survival of their children. Higher levels of education also may increase the likelihood of obtaining or understanding health-related information needed to develop health-promoting behaviors and beliefs in prevention. But again, educational attainment differs by race and ethnicity (see figure 6). Among people aged 25 to 64 years in the United States, the overall death rate for those with less than 12 years of education is more than twice that for people with 13 or more years of education. The infant mortality rate is almost double for infants of mothers with less than 12 years of education compared with those with an educational level of 13 or more years.

Figure 6. Percentage of adults aged 25 to 64 years by educational level and race and ethnicity, United States, 1996.

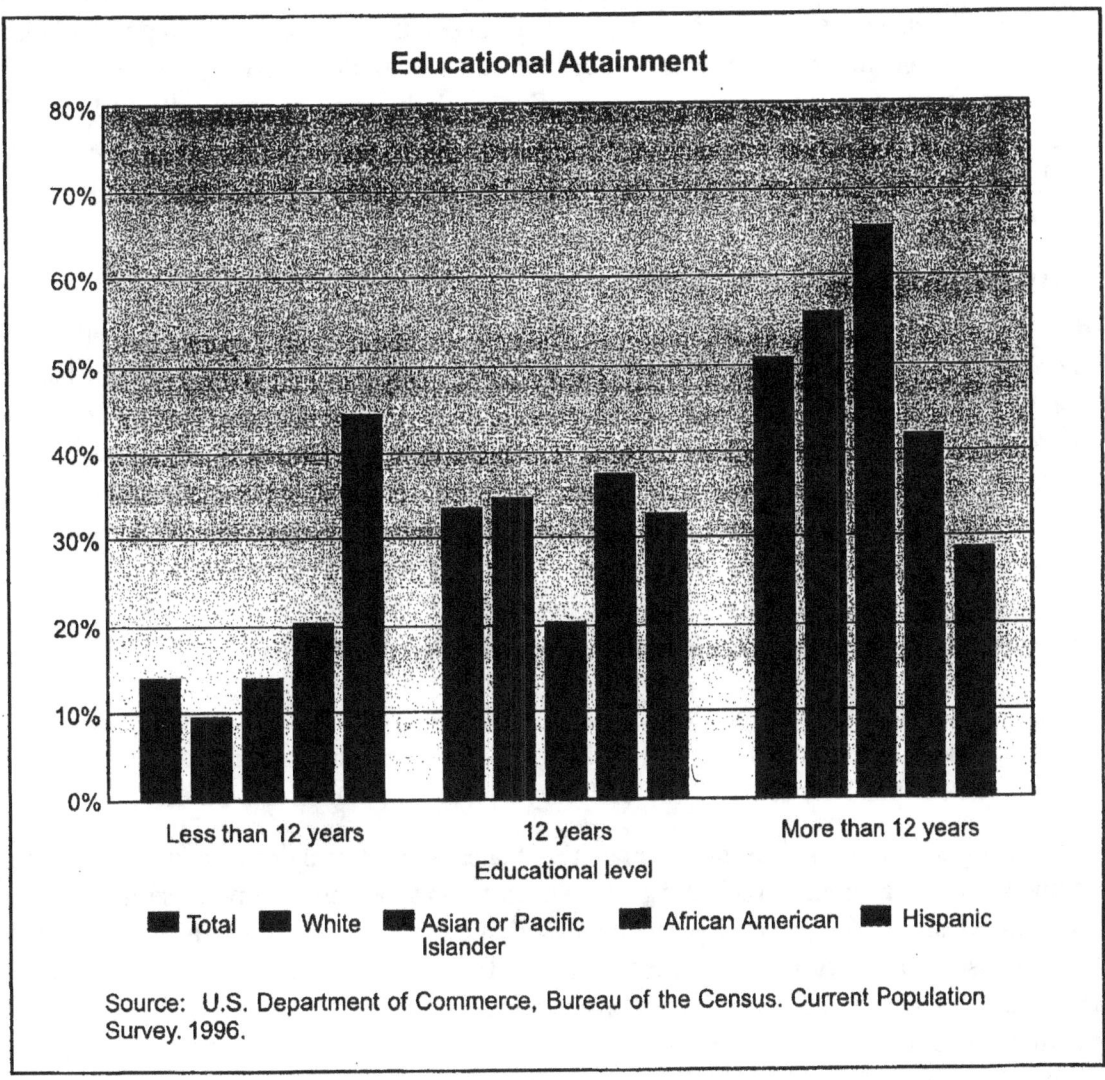

Disability

People with disabilities are identified as persons having an activity limitation, who use assistance, or who perceive themselves as having a disability. In 1994, 54 million people in the United States, or roughly 21 percent of the population, had some level of disability. Although rates of disability are relatively stable or falling slightly for people aged 45 years and older, rates are on the rise among the younger population. People with disabilities tend to report more anxiety, pain, sleeplessness, and days of depression and fewer days of vitality than do people without activity limitations. People with disabilities also have other disparities, including lower rates of physical activity and higher rates of obesity. Many people with disabilities lack access to health services and medical care.

Geographic Location

Twenty-five percent of Americans live in rural areas, that is, places with fewer than 2,500 residents. Injury-related death rates are 40 percent higher in rural populations than in urban populations. Heart disease, cancer, and diabetes rates exceed those for urban areas. People living in rural areas are less likely to use preventive screening services, exercise regularly, or wear safety belts. In 1996, 20 percent of the rural population was uninsured compared with 16 percent of the urban population. Timely access to emergency services and the availability of specialty care are other issues for this population group.

Sexual Orientation

America's gay and lesbian population comprises a diverse community with disparate health concerns. Major health issues for gay men are HIV/AIDS and other sexually transmitted diseases, substance abuse, depression, and suicide. Gay male adolescents are two to three times more likely than their peers to attempt suicide. Some evidence suggests lesbians have higher rates of smoking, overweight, alcohol abuse, and stress than heterosexual women. The issues surrounding personal, family, and social acceptance of sexual orientation can place a significant burden on mental health and personal safety.

Achieving Equity—The Healthy People Perspective

Although the diversity of the American population may be one of the Nation's greatest assets, it also represents a range of health improvement challenges—challenges that must be addressed by individuals, the community and State in which they live, and the Nation as a whole.

Healthy People 2010 recognizes that communities, States, and national organizations will need to take a multidisciplinary approach to achieving health equity—an approach that involves improving health, education, housing, labor, justice, transportation, agriculture, and the environment, as well as data collection itself. In fact, current data collection methods make it impossible to assess accurately the health status for some populations, particularly relatively small ones. However, the greatest opportunities for reducing health disparities are in empowering individuals to make informed health care decisions and in promoting communitywide safety, education, and access to health care.

Healthy People 2010 is firmly dedicated to the principle that—regardless of age, gender, race or ethnicity, income, education, geographic location, disability, and sexual orientation—every person in every community across the Nation deserves equal access to comprehensive, culturally competent, community-based health care systems that are committed to serving the needs of the individual and promoting community health.

Objectives

The Nation's progress in achieving the two goals of Healthy People 2010 will be monitored through 467 objectives in 28 focus areas. Many objectives focus on interventions designed to reduce or eliminate illness, disability, and premature death among individuals and communities. Others focus on broader issues, such as improving access to quality health care, strengthening public health services, and improving the availability and dissemination of health-related information. Each objective has a target for specific improvements to be achieved by the year 2010.

Together, these objectives reflect the depth of scientific knowledge as well as the breadth of diversity in the Nation's communities. More importantly, they are designed to help the Nation achieve Healthy People 2010's two overarching goals and realize the vision of healthy people living in healthy communities.

A list of the short titles of all Healthy People 2010 objectives by focus area can be found in the Appendix. In addition, *Healthy People 2010* provides an overview of the issues, trends, and opportunities for action in each of the 28 focus areas. It also contains detailed language of each objective, underlying rationale, target for the year 2010, and national data tables of its measures.

Healthy People 2010 Focus Areas

1. Access to Quality Health Services
2. Arthritis, Osteoporosis, and Chronic Back Conditions
3. Cancer
4. Chronic Kidney Disease
5. Diabetes
6. Disability and Secondary Conditions
7. Educational and Community-Based Programs
8. Environmental Health
9. Family Planning
10. Food Safety
11. Health Communication
12. Heart Disease and Stroke
13. HIV
14. Immunization and Infectious Diseases
15. Injury and Violence Prevention
16. Maternal, Infant, and Child Health
17. Medical Product Safety
18. Mental Health and Mental Disorders
19. Nutrition and Overweight
20. Occupational Safety and Health
21. Oral Health
22. Physical Activity and Fitness
23. Public Health Infrastructure
24. Respiratory Diseases
25. Sexually Transmitted Diseases
26. Substance Abuse
27. Tobacco Use
28. Vision and Hearing

Determinants of Health

Topics covered by the objectives in Healthy People 2010 reflect the array of critical influences that determine the health of individuals and communities.

For example, individual behaviors and environmental factors are responsible for about 70 percent of all premature deaths in the United States. Developing and implementing policies and preventive interventions that effectively address these determinants of health can reduce the burden of illness, enhance quality of life, and increase longevity.

Individual *biology* and *behaviors* influence health through their interaction with each other and with the individual's *social* and *physical environments*. In addition, *policies and interventions* can improve health by targeting factors related to individuals and their environments, including *access to quality health care* (see figure 7).

Figure 7. Determinants of health.

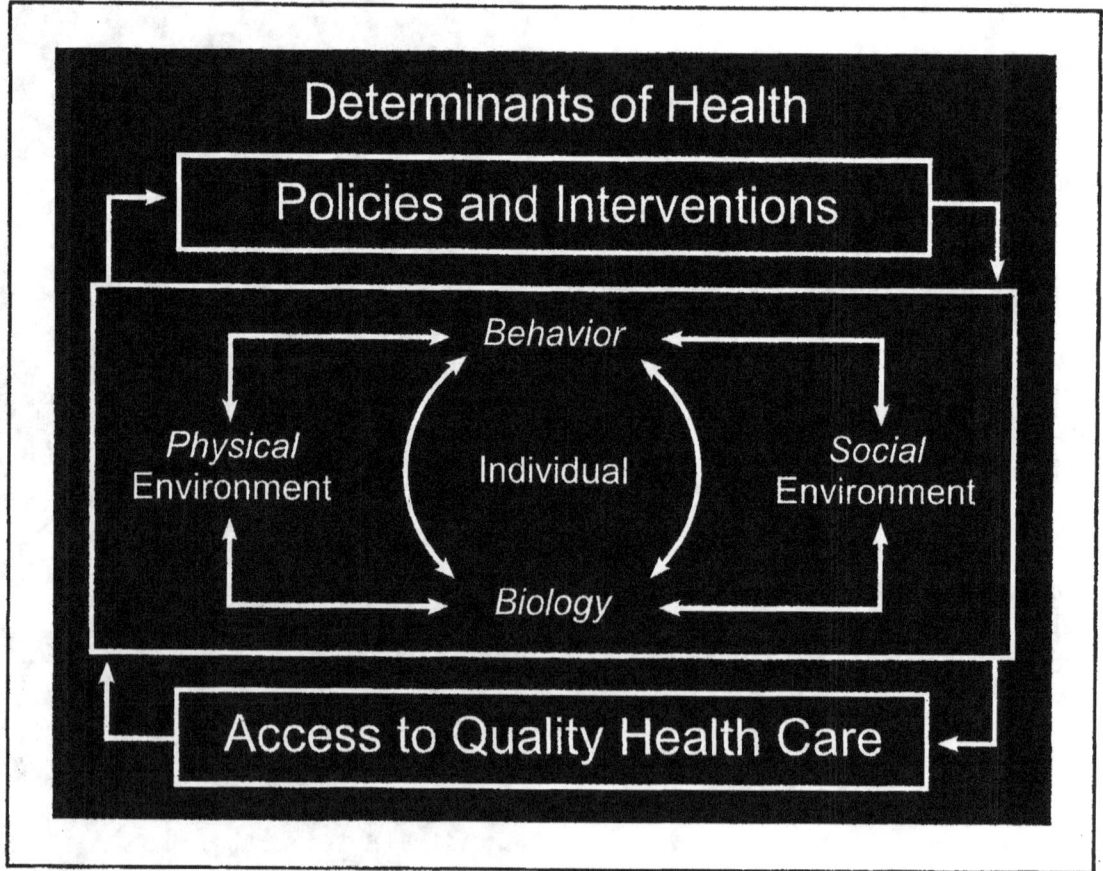

Biology refers to the individual's genetic makeup (those factors with which he or she is born), family history (which may suggest risk for disease), and the physical and mental health problems acquired during life. Aging, diet, physical activity, smoking, stress, alcohol or illicit drug abuse, injury or violence, or an infectious or toxic agent may result in illness or disability and can produce a "new" biology for the individual.

Behaviors are individual responses or reactions to internal stimuli and external conditions. Behaviors can have a reciprocal relationship to biology; in other words, each can react to the other. For example, smoking (behavior) can alter the cells in the lung and result in shortness of breath, emphysema, or cancer (biology) that then may lead an individual to stop smoking (behavior). Similarly, a family history that includes heart disease (biology) may motivate an individual to develop good eating habits, avoid tobacco, and maintain an active lifestyle (behaviors), which may prevent his or her own development of heart disease (biology).

Personal choices and the social and physical environments surrounding individuals can shape behaviors. The social and physical environments include all factors that affect the life of individuals, positively or negatively, many of which may not be under their immediate or direct control.

Social environment includes interactions with family, friends, coworkers, and others in the community. It also encompasses social institutions, such as law enforcement, the workplace, places of worship, and schools. Housing, public transportation, and the presence or absence of violence in the community are among other components of the social environment. The social environment has a profound effect on individual health, as well as on the health of the larger community, and is unique because of cultural customs; language; and personal, religious, or spiritual beliefs. At the same time, individuals and their behaviors contribute to the quality of the social environment.

Physical environment can be thought of as that which can be seen, touched, heard, smelled, and tasted. However, the physical environment also contains less tangible elements, such as radiation and ozone. The physical environment can harm individual and community health, especially when individuals and communities are exposed to toxic substances; irritants; infectious agents; and physical hazards in homes, schools, and worksites. The physical environment also can promote good health, for example, by providing clean and safe places for people to work, exercise, and play.

Policies and interventions can have a powerful and positive effect on the health of individuals and the community. Examples include health promotion campaigns to prevent smoking; policies mandating child restraints and safety belt use in automobiles; disease prevention services, such as immunization of children, adolescents, and adults; and clinical services, such as enhanced mental health care. Policies and interventions that promote individual and community health may be implemented by a variety of agencies, such as transportation, education, energy, housing, labor, justice, and other venues, or through places of worship, community-based organizations, civic groups, and businesses.

Determinants of Health

The health of individuals and communities also depends greatly on **access to quality health care**. Expanding access to quality health care is important to eliminate health disparities and to increase the quality and years of healthy life for all people living in the United States. Health care in the broadest sense not only includes services received through health care providers but also health information and services received through other venues in the community.

The determinants of health—individual biology and behavior, physical and social environments, policies and interventions, and access to quality health care—have a profound effect on the health of individuals, communities, and the Nation. An evaluation of these determinants is an important part of developing any strategy to improve health.

Our understanding of these determinants and how they relate to one another, coupled with our understanding of how individual and community health affects the health of the Nation, is perhaps the most important key to achieving our Healthy People 2010 goals of increasing the quality and years of life and of eliminating the Nation's health disparities.

Health Status

To understand the health status of a population, it is essential to monitor and evaluate the consequences of the determinants of health.

The health status of the United States is a description of the health of the total population, using information representative of most people living in this country. For relatively small population groups, however, it may not be possible to draw accurate conclusions about their health using current data collection methods. The goal of eliminating health disparities will necessitate improved collection and use of standardized data to identify correctly disparities among select population groups.

Health status can be measured by birth and death rates, life expectancy, quality of life, morbidity from specific diseases, risk factors, use of ambulatory care and inpatient care, accessibility of health personnel and facilities, financing of health care, health insurance coverage, and many other factors. The information used to report health status comes from a variety of sources, including birth and death records; hospital discharge data; and health information collected from health care records, personal interviews, physical examinations, and telephone surveys. These measures are monitored on an annual basis in the United States and are reported in a variety of publications, including *Health, United States* and *Healthy People Reviews*.

The leading causes of death are used frequently to describe the health status of the Nation. Over the past 100 years, the Nation has seen a great deal of change in the leading causes of death (see figure 8). At the beginning of the 1900s, infectious diseases ran rampant in the United States and worldwide and topped the leading causes of death. A century later, with the control of many infectious agents and the increasing age of the population, chronic diseases top the list.

A very different picture emerges when the leading causes of death are viewed for various population groups. Unintentional injuries, mainly motor vehicle crashes, are the fifth leading cause of death for the total population, but they are the leading cause of death for people aged 1 to 44 years. Similarly, HIV/AIDS is the 14th leading cause of death for the total population but the leading cause of death for African American men aged 25 to 44 years (see figure 9).

The leading causes of death in the United States generally result from a mix of behaviors; injury, violence, and other factors in the environment; and the unavailability or inaccessibility of quality health services. Understanding and monitoring behaviors, environmental factors, and community health systems may prove more useful to monitoring the Nation's *true* health, and in driving health improvement activities, than the death rates that reflect the cumulative impact of these factors. This more complex approach has served as the basis for developing the Leading Health Indicators.

Health Status

Figure 8. The leading causes of death as a percentage of all deaths in the United States, 1900 and 1997.

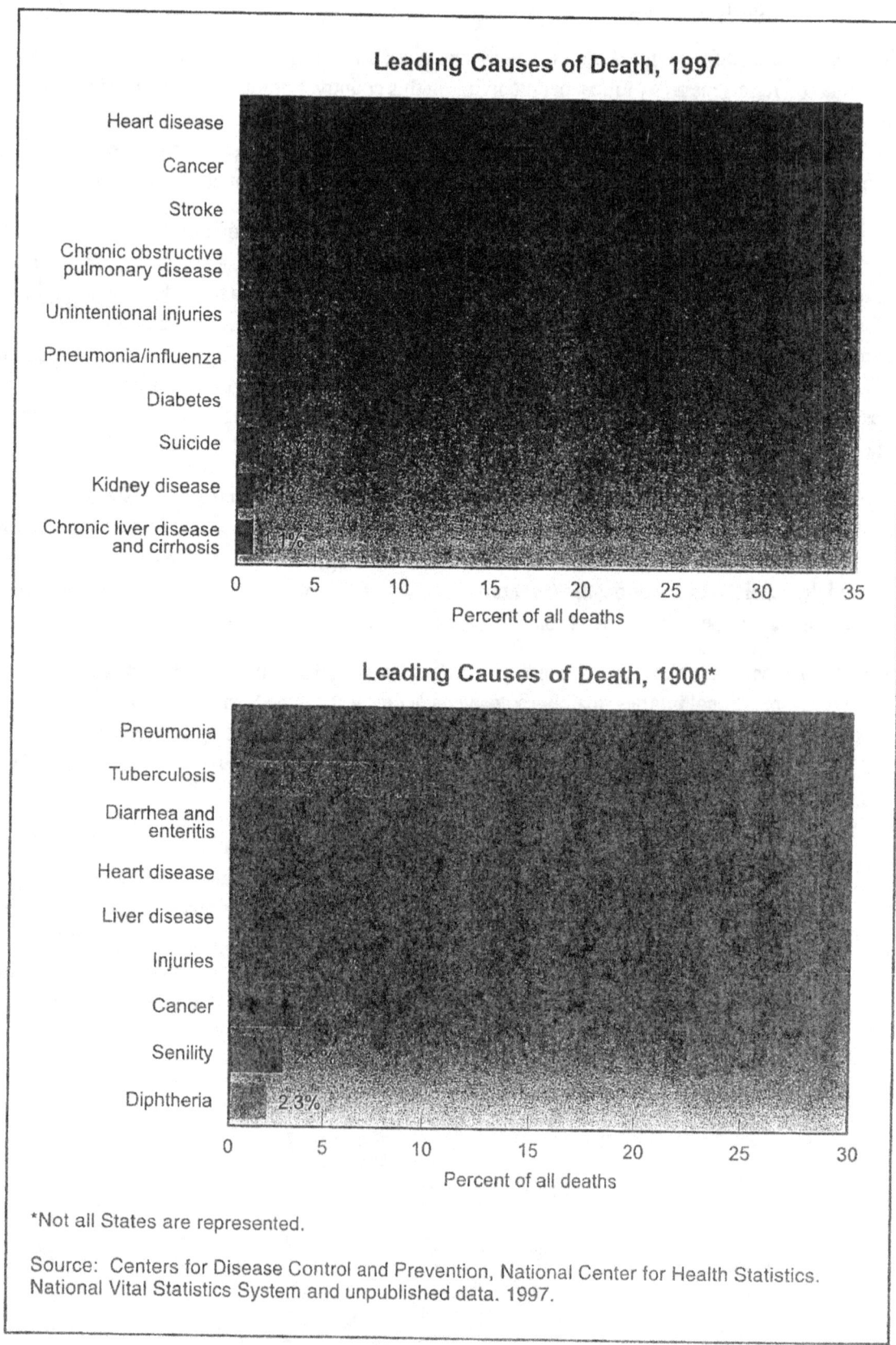

*Not all States are represented.

Source: Centers for Disease Control and Prevention, National Center for Health Statistics. National Vital Statistics System and unpublished data. 1997.

Health Status

Figure 9. The three leading causes of death by age group, United States, 1997.

Leading Causes of Death by Age Group

Under 1 Year	Number of Deaths
Birth defects	6,178
Disorders related to premature birth	3,925
Sudden infant death syndrome	2,991
1-4 Years	
■ Unintentional injuries	2,005
Birth defects	589
■ Cancer	438
5-14 Years	
■ Unintentional injuries	3,371
■ Cancer	1,030
Homicide	457
15-24 Years	
■ Unintentional injuries	13,367
Homicide	6,146
■ Suicide	4,186
25-44 Years	
■ Unintentional injuries	27,129
■ Cancer	21,706
■ Heart disease	16,513
45-64 Years	
■ Cancer	131,743
■ Heart disease	101,235
■ Unintentional injuries	17,521
65 Years and Older	
■ Heart disease	606,913
■ Cancer	382,913
■ Stroke	140,366

Bullets above link to the conditions listed in the charts in figure 8.

Source: Centers for Disease Control and Prevention, National Center for Health Statistics. National Vital Statistics System. 1999.

Leading Health Indicators

The Leading Health Indicators reflect the major public health concerns in the United States and were chosen based on their ability to motivate action, the availability of data to measure their progress, and their relevance as broad public health issues.

The Leading Health Indicators illuminate individual behaviors, physical and social environmental factors, and important health system issues that greatly affect the health of individuals and communities. Underlying each of these indicators is the significant influence of income and education (see Income and Education, page 12).

The process of selecting the Leading Health Indicators mirrored the collaborative and extensive efforts undertaken to develop Healthy People 2010. The process was led by an interagency work group within the U.S. Department of Health and Human Services. Individuals and organizations provided comments at national and regional meetings or via mail and the Internet. A report by the Institute of Medicine, National Academy of Sciences, provided several scientific models on

Leading Health Indicators

- Physical activity
- Overweight and obesity
- Tobacco use
- Substance abuse
- Responsible sexual behavior
- Mental health
- Injury and violence
- Environmental quality
- Immunization
- Access to health care

which to support a set of indicators. Focus groups were used to ensure that the indicators are meaningful and motivating to the public.

For each of the Leading Health Indicators, specific objectives derived from Healthy People 2010 will be used to track progress. This small set of measures will provide a snapshot of the health of the Nation. Tracking and communicating progress on the Leading Health Indicators through national- and State-level report cards will spotlight achievements and challenges in the next decade. The Leading Health Indicators serve as a link to the 467 objectives in *Healthy People 2010* and can become the basic building blocks for community health initiatives.

> **A major challenge throughout the history of Healthy People has been to balance a comprehensive set of health objectives with a smaller set of health priorities.**

The Leading Health Indicators are intended to help everyone more easily understand the importance of health promotion and disease prevention and to encourage wide participation in improving health in the next decade. Developing strategies and action plans to address one or more of these indicators can have a profound effect on increasing the quality of life and the years of healthy life and on eliminating health disparities—creating *healthy people in healthy communities*.

Physical Activity

Leading Health Indicator

Regular physical activity throughout life is important for maintaining a healthy body, enhancing psychological well-being, and preventing premature death.

In 1999, 65 percent of adolescents engaged in the recommended amount of physical activity. In 1997, only 15 percent of adults performed the recommended amount of physical activity, and 40 percent of adults engaged in no leisure-time physical activity.

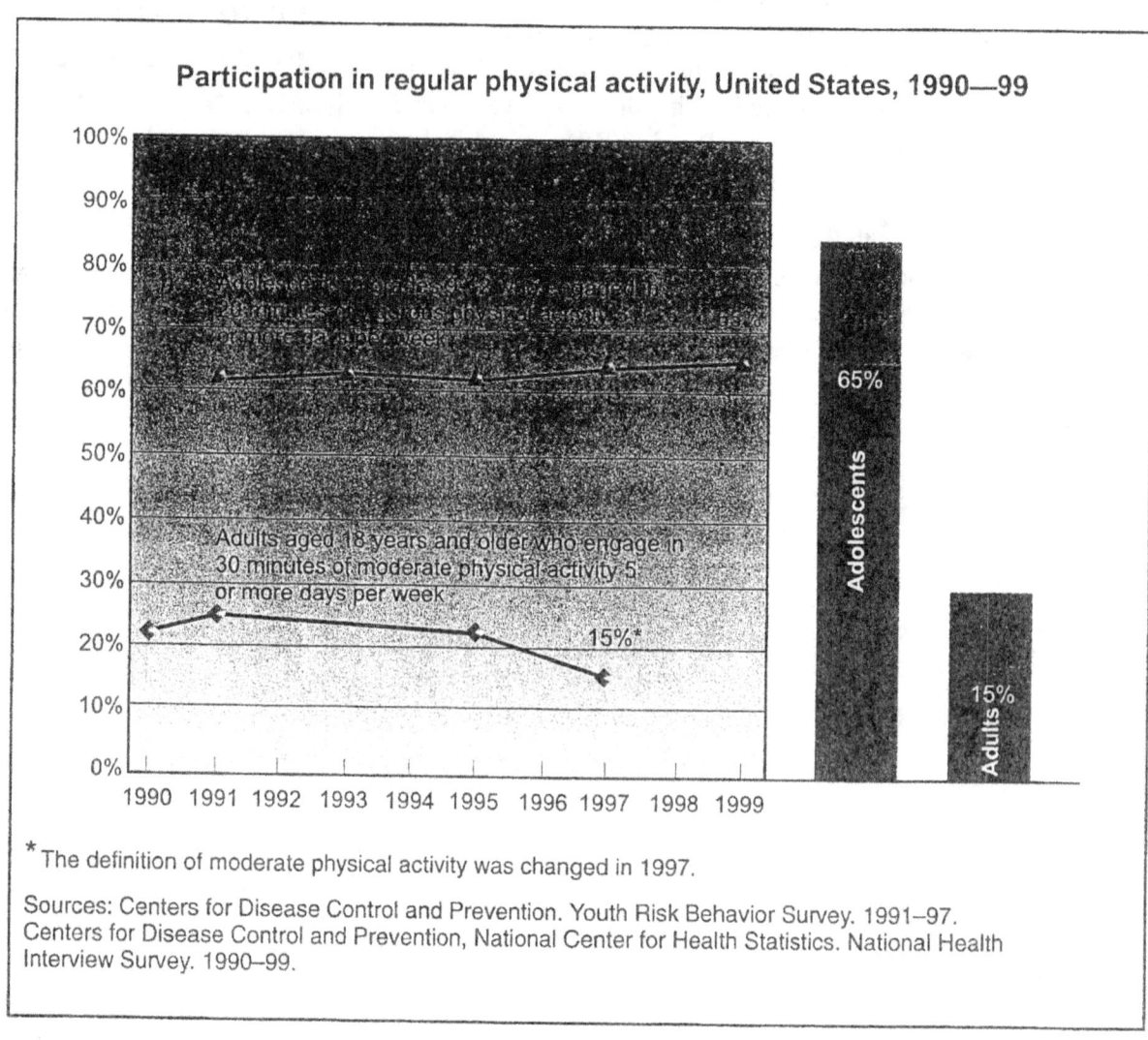

*The definition of moderate physical activity was changed in 1997.

Sources: Centers for Disease Control and Prevention. Youth Risk Behavior Survey. 1991–97. Centers for Disease Control and Prevention, National Center for Health Statistics. National Health Interview Survey. 1990–99.

The objectives selected to measure progress among adolescents and adults for this Leading Health Indicator are presented below. These are only indicators and do not represent all the physical activity and fitness objectives included in Healthy People 2010.

22-7. **Increase the proportion of adolescents who engage in vigorous physical activity that promotes cardiorespiratory fitness 3 or more days per week for 20 or more minutes per occasion.**

22-2. **Increase the proportion of adults who engage regularly, preferably daily, in moderate physical activity for at least 30 minutes per day.**

Leading Health Indicator

Health Impact of Physical Activity

Regular physical activity is associated with lower death rates for adults of any age, even when only moderate levels of physical activity are performed. Regular physical activity decreases the risk of death from heart disease, lowers the risk of developing diabetes, and is associated with a decreased risk of colon cancer. Regular physical activity helps prevent high blood pressure and helps reduce blood pressure in persons with elevated levels.

Regular physical activity also:

- Increases muscle and bone strength.
- Increases lean muscle and helps decrease body fat.
- Aids in weight control and is a key part of any weight loss effort.
- Enhances psychological well-being and may even reduce the risk of developing depression.
- Appears to reduce symptoms of depression and anxiety and to improve mood.

In addition, children and adolescents need weight-bearing exercise for normal skeletal development, and young adults need such exercise to achieve and maintain peak bone mass. Older adults can improve and maintain strength and agility with regular physical activity. This can reduce the risk of falling, helping older adults maintain an independent living status. Regular physical activity also increases the ability of people with certain chronic, disabling conditions to perform activities of daily living.

Populations With Low Rates of Physical Activity

- Women generally are less active than men at all ages.
- People with lower incomes and less education are typically not as physically active as those with higher incomes and education.
- African Americans and Hispanics are generally less physically active than whites.
- Adults in northeastern and southern States tend to be less active than adults in North-Central and Western States.
- People with disabilities are less physically active than people without disabilities.
- By age 75, one in three men and one in two women engage in *no* regular physical activity.

Other Issues

The major barriers most people face when trying to increase physical activity are lack of time, lack of access to convenient facilities, and lack of safe environments in which to be active.

Overweight and Obesity

Leading Health Indicator

Overweight and obesity are major contributors to many preventable causes of death. On average, higher body weights are associated with higher death rates. The number of overweight children, adolescents, and adults has risen over the past four decades. Total costs (medical cost and lost productivity) attributable to obesity alone amounted to an estimated $99 billion in 1995.

During 1988–94, 11 percent of children and adolescents aged 6 to 19 years were overweight or obese. During the same years, 23 percent of adults aged 20 years and older were considered obese.

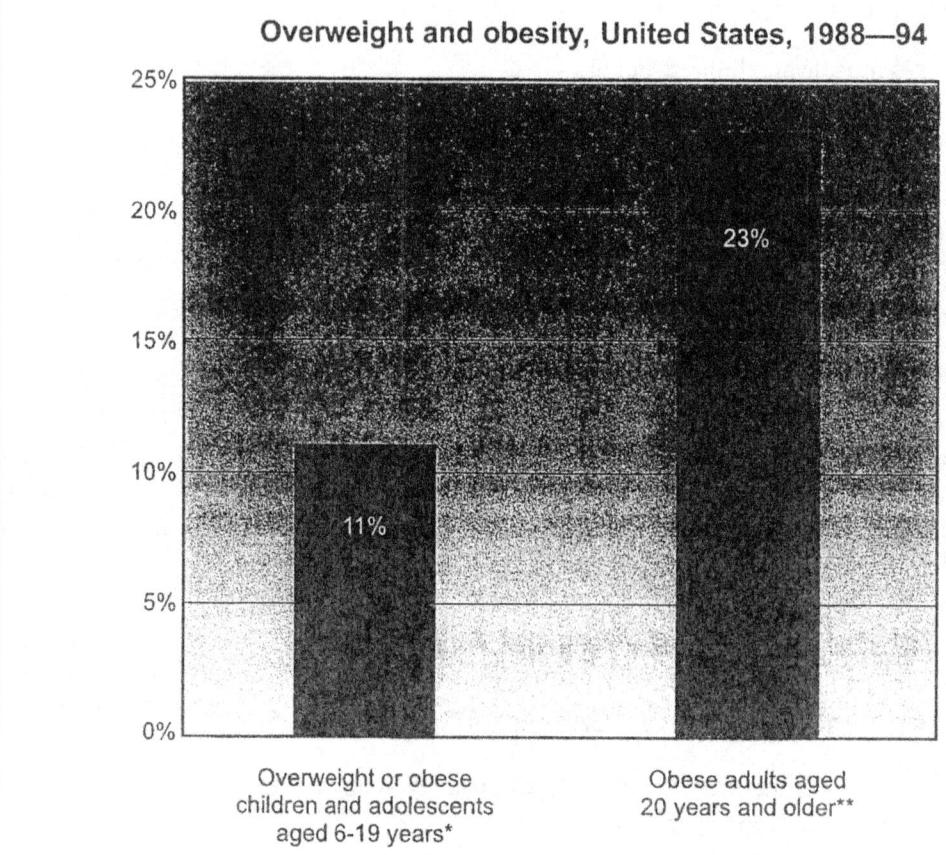

Overweight and obesity, United States, 1988—94

* In those aged 6 to 19 years, overweight or obesity is defined as at or above the sex- and age-specific 95th percentile of Body Mass Index (BMI) based on CDC Growth Charts: United States.

** In adults, obesity is defined as a BMI of 30 kg/m² or more; overweight is a BMI of 25 kg/m² or more.

Body mass index (BMI) is calculated as weight in kilograms (kg) divided by the square of height in meters (m²) (BMI = weight[kg]/height[m²]). To estimate BMI using pounds (lbs) and inches (in), divide weight in pounds by the square of height in inches. Then multiply the resulting number by 704.5 (BMI = weight[lbs]/height[in²] X 704.5).

Source: Centers for Disease Control and Prevention, National Center for Health Statistics. National Health and Nutrition Examination Survey. 1988–94.

The objectives selected to measure progress among children, adolescents, and adults for this Leading Health Indicator are presented below. These are only indicators and do not represent all the nutrition and overweight objectives included in Healthy People 2010.

19-3c. **Reduce the proportion of children and adolescents who are overweight or obese.**

19-2. **Reduce the proportion of adults who are obese.**

Leading Health Indicator

Health Impact of Overweight and Obesity

Overweight and obesity substantially raise the risk of illness from high blood pressure, high cholesterol, type 2 diabetes, heart disease and stroke, gallbladder disease, arthritis, sleep disturbances and problems breathing, and certain types of cancers. Obese individuals also may suffer from social stigmatization, discrimination, and lowered self-esteem.

Populations With High Rates of Overweight and Obesity

More than half of adults in the United States are estimated to be overweight or obese. The proportion of adolescents from poor households who are overweight or obese is twice that of adolescents from middle- and high-income households. Obesity is especially prevalent among women with lower incomes and is more common among African American and Mexican American women than among white women. Among African Americans, the proportion of women who are obese is 80 percent higher than the proportion of men who are obese. This gender difference also is seen among Mexican American women and men, but the percentage of white, non-Hispanic women and men who are obese is about the same.

Reducing Overweight and Obesity

Obesity is a result of a complex variety of social, behavioral, cultural, environmental, physiological, and genetic factors. Efforts to maintain a healthy weight should start early in childhood and continue throughout adulthood, as this is likely to be more successful than efforts to lose substantial amounts of weight and maintain weight loss once obesity is established.

A healthy diet and regular physical activity are both important for maintaining a healthy weight. Over time, even a small decrease in calories eaten and a small increase in physical activity can help prevent weight gain or facilitate weight loss. It is recommended that obese individuals who are trying to lose substantial amounts of weight seek the guidance of a health care provider.

Dietary and Physical Activity Recommendations

The *Dietary Guidelines for Americans* recommend that to build a healthy base, persons aged 2 years and older choose a healthful assortment of foods that includes vegetables; fruits; grains (especially whole grains); fat-free or low-fat milk products; and fish, lean meat, poultry, or beans. The guidelines further emphasize the importance of choosing foods that are low in saturated fat and added sugars most of the time and, whatever the food, eating a sensible portion size. It is recognized, however, that this guidance may be particularly challenging when eating out because the consumer may be offered large portion sizes with unknown amounts of saturated fat and added sugars.

The *Dietary Guidelines for Americans* recommend that all adults be more active throughout the day and get at least 30 minutes of moderate physical activity most, or preferably all, days of the week. Adults who are trying to maintain healthy weight after weight loss are advised to get even more physical activity. The guidelines also recommend that children get at least 60 minutes of physical activity daily and limit inactive forms of play such as television watching and computer games.

Tobacco Use

Leading Health Indicator

Cigarette smoking is the single most preventable cause of disease and death in the United States. Smoking results in more deaths each year in the United States than AIDS, alcohol, cocaine, heroin, homicide, suicide, motor vehicle crashes, and fires—combined.

Tobacco-related deaths number more than 430,000 per year among U.S. adults, representing more than 5 million years of potential life lost. Direct medical costs attributable to smoking total at least $50 billion per year.

In 1999, 35 percent of adolescents were current cigarette smokers. In 1998, 24 percent of adults were current cigarette smokers.

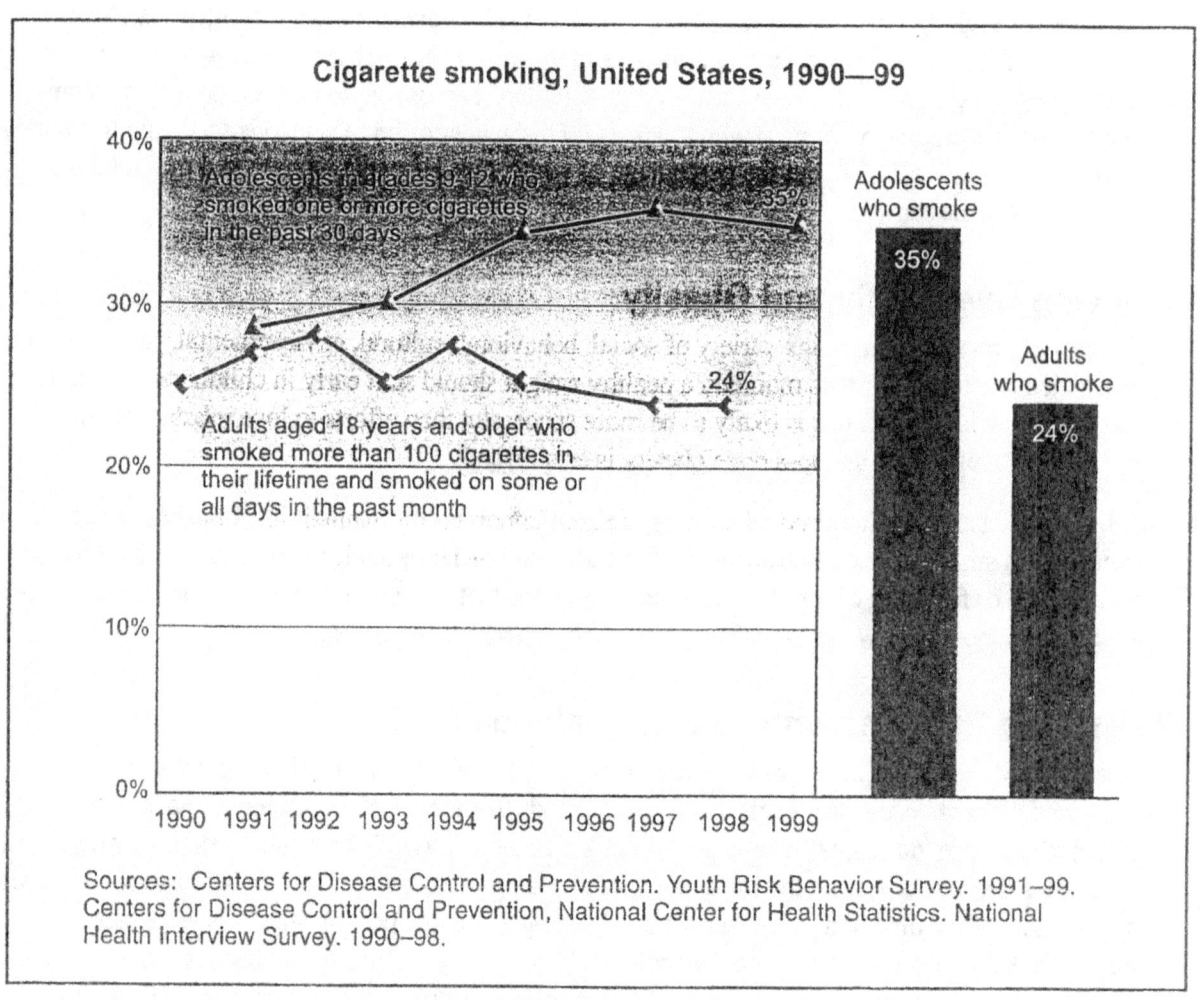

The objectives selected to measure progress among adolescents and adults for this Leading Health Indicator are presented below. These are only indicators and do not represent all the tobacco use objectives included in Healthy People 2010.

27-2b. Reduce cigarette smoking by adolescents.
27-1a. Reduce cigarette smoking by adults.

Leading Health Indicator

Health Impact of Cigarette Smoking

Smoking is a major risk factor for heart disease, stroke, lung cancer, and chronic lung diseases all leading causes of death. Smoking during pregnancy can result in miscarriages, premature delivery, and sudden infant death syndrome. Other health effects of smoking result from injuries and environmental damage caused by fires.

Environmental tobacco smoke (ETS) increases the risk of heart disease and significant lung conditions, especially asthma and bronchitis in children. ETS is responsible for an estimated 3,000 lung cancer deaths each year among adult nonsmokers.

Trends in Cigarette Smoking

Adolescents. Overall, the percentage of adolescents in grades 9 through 12 who smoked in the past month increased in the 1990s. Every day, an estimated 3,000 young persons start smoking. These trends are disturbing because the vast majority of adult smokers tried their first cigarette before age 18 years; more than half of adult smokers became daily smokers before this same age. Almost half of adolescents who continue smoking regularly will die eventually from a smoking-related illness.

Adults. Following years of steady decline, rates of smoking among adults appear to have leveled off in the 1990s.

Populations With High Rates of Smoking

Adolescents. Adolescent rates of cigarette smoking have increased in the 1990s among white, African American, and Hispanic high school students after years of declining rates during the 1970s and 1980s. In 1999, 39 percent of white high school students currently smoked cigarettes compared with 33 percent for Hispanics and 20 percent for African Americans. Among African Americans in 1999, only 19 percent of high school girls, compared with 22 percent of boys, currently smoked cigarettes.

Adults. Overall, American Indians and Alaska Natives, blue-collar workers, and military personnel have the highest rates of smoking in adults. Rates of smoking in Asian and Pacific Islander men are more than four times higher than for women of the same race. Men have only somewhat higher rates of smoking than women within the total U.S. population. Low-income adults are more likely to smoke than are high-income adults. The percentage of people aged 25 years and older with less than 12 years of education who are current smokers is nearly three times that for persons with 16 or more years of education.

Other Important Tobacco Issues

There is no safe tobacco alternative to cigarettes. Spit tobacco (chew) causes cancer of the mouth, inflammation of the gums, and tooth loss. Cigar smoking causes cancer of the mouth, throat, and lungs and can increase the risk of heart disease and chronic lung problems.

Substance Abuse

Leading Health Indicator

Alcohol and illicit drug use are associated with many of this country's most serious problems, including violence, injury, and HIV infection. The annual economic costs to the United States from alcohol abuse were estimated to be $167 billion in 1995, and the costs from drug abuse were estimated to be $110 billion.

In 1998, 79 percent of adolescents aged 12 to 17 years reported that they did *not* use alcohol or illicit drugs in the past month. In the same year, 6 percent of adults aged 18 years and older reported using illicit drugs in the past month; 17 percent reported binge drinking in the past month, which is defined as consuming five or more drinks on one occasion.

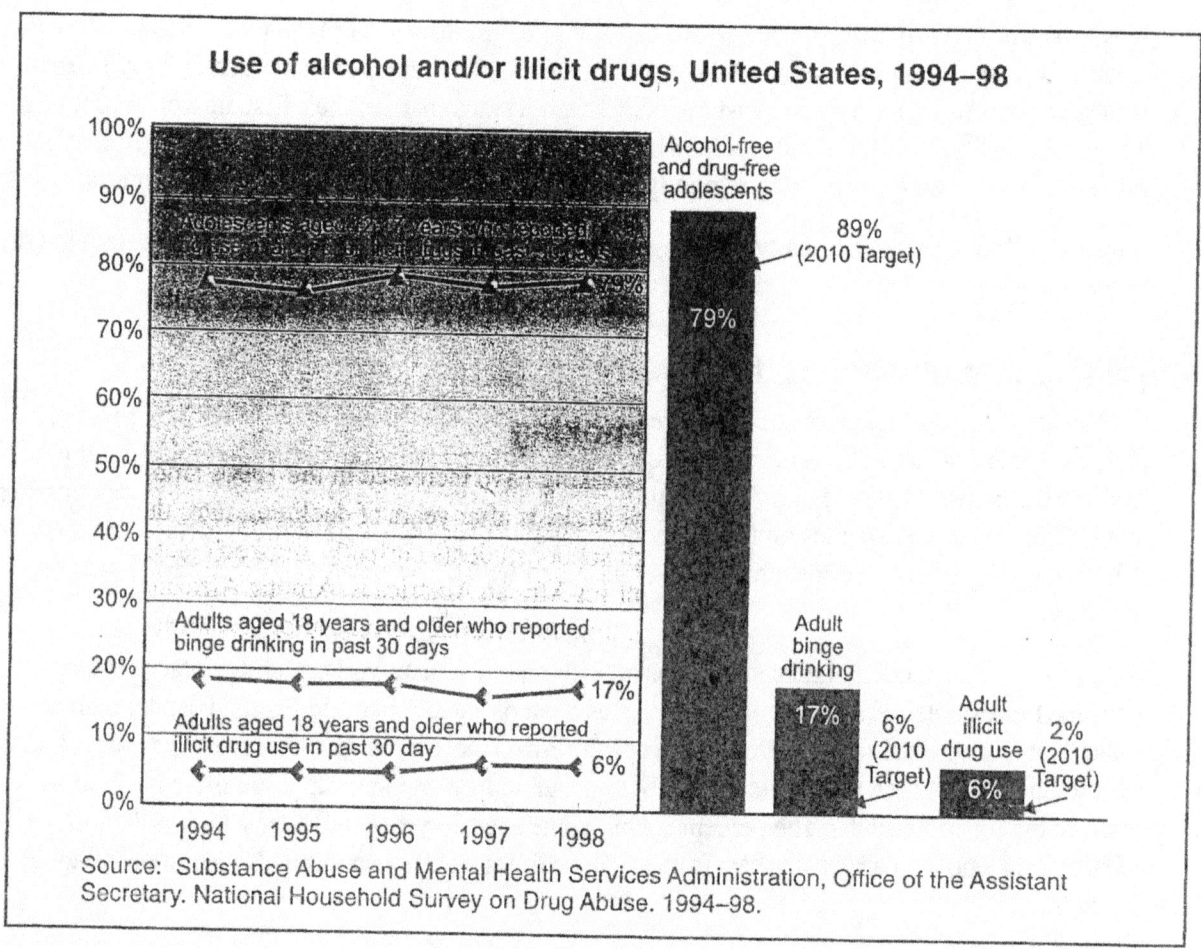

The objectives selected to measure progress among adolescents and adults for this Leading Health Indicator are presented below. These are only indicators and do not represent all the substance abuse objectives in Healthy People 2010.

26-10a. **Increase the proportion of adolescents not using alcohol or any illicit drugs during the past 30 days.**

26-10c. **Reduce the proportion of adults using any illicit drug during the past 30 days.**

26-11c. **Reduce the proportion of adults engaging in binge drinking of alcoholic beverages during the past month.**

Leading Health Indicator

Health Impact of Substance Abuse

Alcohol and illicit drug use are associated with child and spousal abuse; sexually transmitted diseases, including HIV infection; teen pregnancy; school failure; motor vehicle crashes; escalation of health care costs; low worker productivity; and homelessness. Alcohol and illicit drug use also can result in substantial disruptions in family, work, and personal life.

Alcohol abuse alone is associated with motor vehicle crashes, homicides, suicides, and drowning—leading causes of death among youth. Long-term heavy drinking can lead to heart disease, cancer, alcohol-related liver disease, and pancreatitis. Alcohol use during pregnancy is known to cause fetal alcohol syndrome, a leading cause of preventable mental retardation.

Trends in Substance Abuse

Adolescents. Although the trend from 1994 to 1998 has shown some fluctuations, about 77 percent of adolescents aged 12 to 17 years report being both alcohol-free and drug-free in the past month.

Alcohol is the drug most frequently used by adolescents aged 12 to 17 years. In 1998, 19 percent of adolescents aged 12 to 17 years reported drinking alcohol in the past month. Alcohol use in the past month for this age group has remained at about 20 percent since 1992. Eight percent of this age group reported binge drinking, and 3 percent were heavy drinkers (five or more drinks on the same occasion on each of 5 or more days in the past 30 days).

Data from 1998 show that 10 percent of adolescents aged 12 to 17 years reported using illicit drugs in the past 30 days. This rate remains well below the all-time high of 16 percent in 1979. Current illicit drug use had nearly doubled for those aged 12 to 13 years between 1996 and 1997 but then decreased between 1997 and 1998. Youth are experimenting with a variety of illicit drugs, including marijuana, cocaine, crack, heroin, acid, inhalants, and methamphetamines, as well as misuse of prescription drugs and other "street" drugs. The younger a person becomes a habitual user of illicit drugs, the stronger the addiction becomes and the more difficult it is to stop use.

Adults. Binge drinking has remained at the same approximate level of 17 percent for all adults since 1988, with the highest current rate of 32 percent among adults aged 18 to 25 years. Illicit drug use has been near the present rate of 6 percent since 1980. Men continue to have higher rates of illicit drug use than women have, and rates of illicit drug use in urban areas are higher than in rural areas.

Responsible Sexual Behavior

Leading Health Indicator

Unintended pregnancies and sexually transmitted diseases (STDs), including infection with the human immunodeficiency virus that causes AIDS, can result from unprotected sexual behaviors. Abstinence is the only method of complete protection. Condoms, if used correctly and consistently, can help prevent both unintended pregnancy and STDs.

In 1999, 85 percent of adolescents abstained from sexual intercourse or used condoms if they were sexually active. In 1995, 23 percent of sexually active women reported that their partners used condoms.

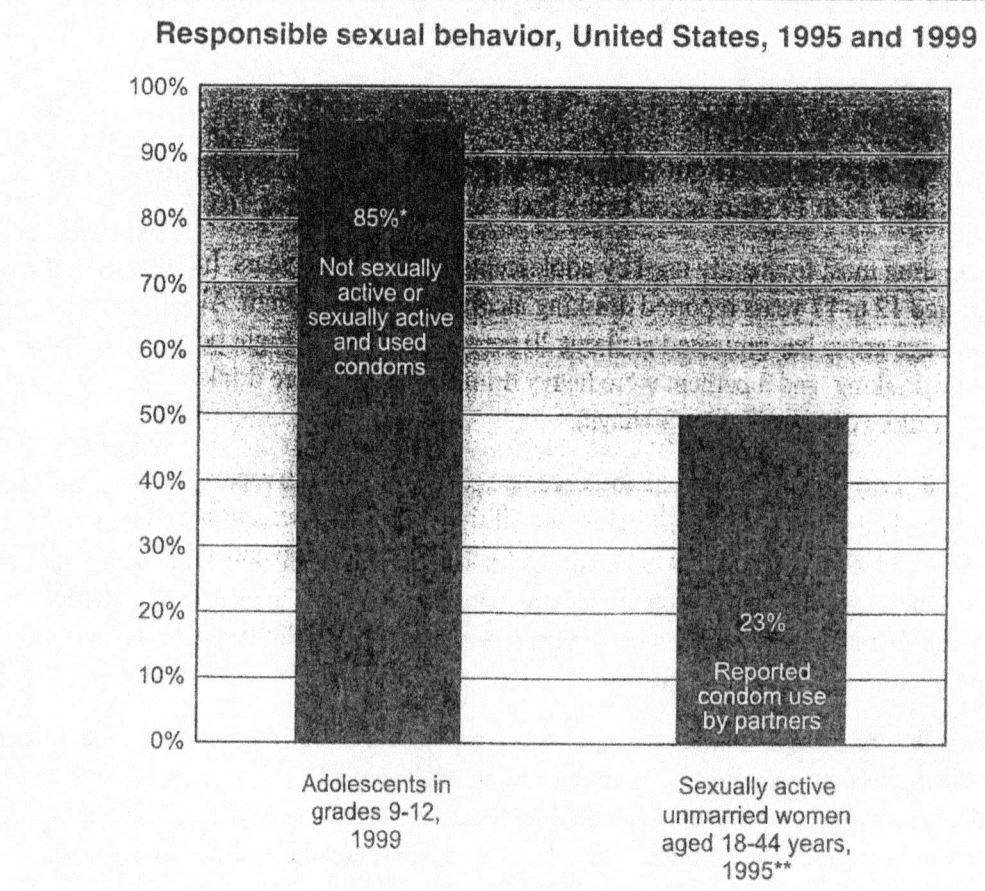

* This 85 percent includes 50 percent of students in grades 9-12 who were not ever sexually active, 14 percent who were not sexually active in the past 3 months, and 21 percent who were sexually active but used a condom at the last intercourse.

** Data on males aged 15 to 49 years will be collected in 2003.

Sources: Centers for Disease Control and Prevention. Youth Risk Behavior Survey. 1999. Centers for Disease Control and Prevention, National Center for Health Statistics. National Survey of Family Growth. 1995.

The objectives selected to measure progress among adolescents and adults for this Leading Health Indicator are presented below. These are only indicators and do not represent all the responsible sexual behavior objectives in Healthy People 2010.

25-11. **Increase the proportion of adolescents who abstain from sexual intercourse or use condoms if currently sexually active.**

13-6a. **Increase the proportion of sexually active persons who use condoms.**

Leading Health Indicator

Trends in Sexual Behavior

In the past 6 years there has been both an increase in abstinence among all youth and an increase in condom use among those young people who are sexually active. Research has shown clearly that the most effective school-based programs are comprehensive ones that include a focus on abstinence *and* condom use. Condom use in sexually active adults has remained steady at about 25 percent.

Unintended Pregnancies

Half of all pregnancies in the United States are unintended; that is, at the time of conception the pregnancy was not planned or not wanted. Unintended pregnancy rates in the United States have been declining. The rates remain highest among teenagers, women aged 40 years or older, and low-income African American women. Approximately 1 million teenage girls each year in the United States have unintended pregnancies. Nearly half of all unintended pregnancies end in abortion.

The cost to U.S. taxpayers for adolescent pregnancy is estimated at between $7 billion and $15 billion a year.

Sexually Transmitted Diseases

Sexually transmitted diseases are common in the United States, with an estimated 15 million new cases of STDs reported each year. Almost 4 million of the new cases of STDs each year occur in adolescents. Women generally suffer more serious STD complications than men, including pelvic inflammatory disease, ectopic pregnancy, infertility, chronic pelvic pain, and cervical cancer from the human papilloma virus. African Americans and Hispanics have higher rates of STDs than whites.

The total cost of the most common STDs and their complications is conservatively estimated at $17 billion annually.

HIV/AIDS

Nearly 700,000 cases of AIDS have been reported in the United States since the HIV/AIDS epidemic began in the 1980s. The latest estimates indicate that 800,000 to 900,000 people in the United States currently are infected with HIV. The lifetime cost of health care associated with HIV infection, in light of recent advances in HIV diagnostics and therapies, is $155,000 or more per person.

About one-half of all new HIV infections in the United States are among people under age 25 years, and the majority are infected through sexual behavior. HIV infection is the leading cause of death for African American men aged 25 to 44 years. Compelling worldwide evidence indicates that the presence of other STDs increases the likelihood of both transmitting and acquiring HIV infection.

Mental Health

Leading Health Indicator

Approximately 20 percent of the U.S. population is affected by mental illness during a given year; no one is immune. Of all mental illnesses, depression is the most common disorder. More than 19 million adults in the United States suffer from depression. Major depression is the leading cause of disability and is the cause of more than two-thirds of suicides each year.

In 1997, only 23 percent of adults diagnosed with depression received treatment.

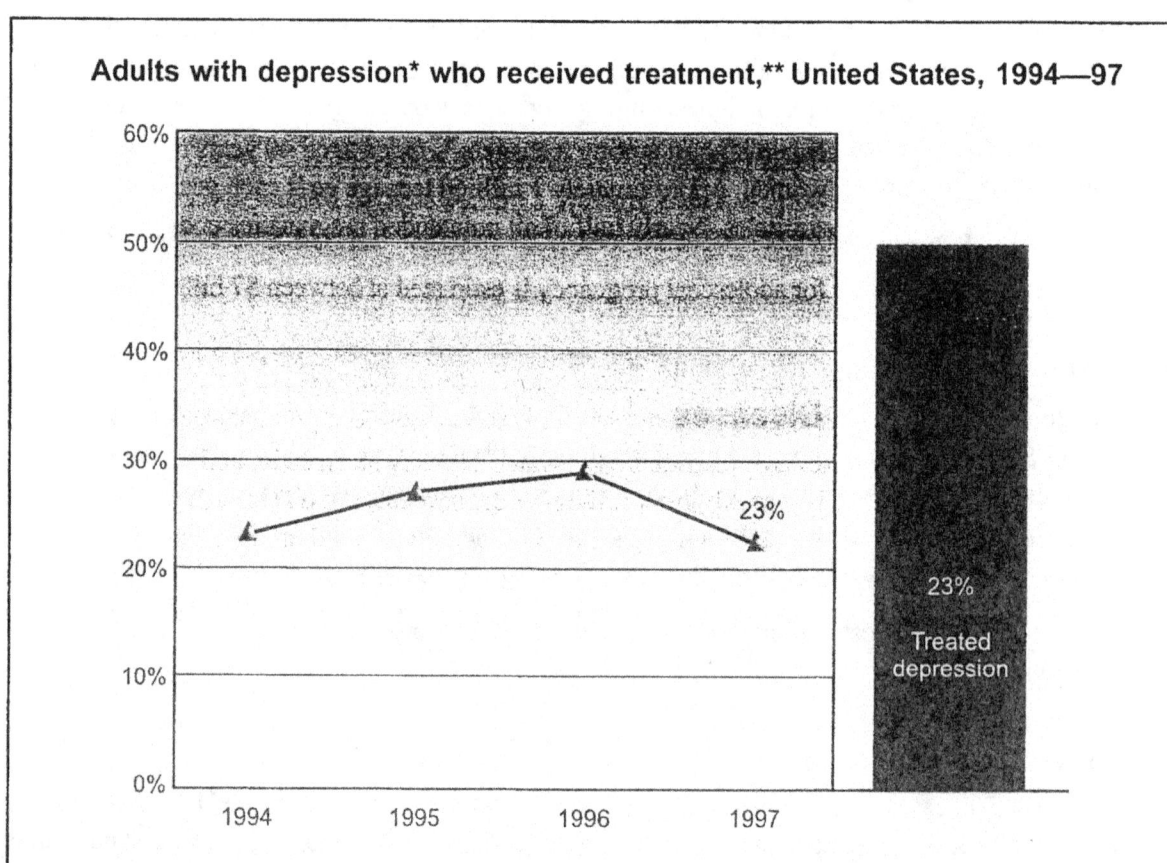

Adults with depression* who received treatment, United States, 1994—97**

* Depression is defined as major depressive episode in the past year.
** Treatment is defined as treatment in the past year for psychological problems or emotional difficulties at a mental health clinic or by a mental health professional on an outpatient basis or treatment for psychological or emotional difficulties at a hospital overnight or longer.

Source: Substance Abuse and Mental Health Services Administration, Office of Applied Studies. National Household Survey on Drug Abuse. 1994–97.

The objective selected to measure progress among adults for this Leading Health Indicator is presented below. This is only an indicator and does not represent all the mental health objectives in Healthy People 2010.

18-9b. Increase the proportion of adults with recognized depression who receive treatment.

Leading Health Indicator

Definition of Mental Health

Mental health is sometimes thought of as simply the absence of a mental illness but is actually much broader. Mental health is a state of successful mental functioning, resulting in productive activities, fulfilling relationships, and the ability to adapt to change and cope with adversity. Mental health is indispensable to personal well-being, family and interpersonal relationships, and one's contribution to society.

Impact of Depression

A person with a depressive disorder often is unable to fulfill the daily responsibilities of being a spouse, partner, or parent. The misunderstanding of mental illness and the associated stigmatization prevent many persons with depression from seeking professional help. Many people will be incapacitated for weeks or months because their depression goes untreated.

Depression is associated with other medical conditions, such as heart disease, cancer, and diabetes as well as anxiety and eating disorders. Depression also has been associated with alcohol and illicit drug abuse. An estimated 8 million persons aged 15 to 54 years had coexisting mental and substance abuse disorders within the past year.

The total estimated direct and indirect costs of mental illness in the United States in 1996 was $150 billion.

Treatment of Depression

Depression is treatable. Available medications and psychological treatments, alone or in combination, can help 80 percent of those with depression. With adequate treatment, future episodes of depression can be prevented or reduced in severity. Treatment for depression can enable people to return to satisfactory, functioning lives.

Populations With High Rates of Depression

Serious mental illness clearly affects mental health and can affect children, adolescents, adults, and older adults of all ethnic and racial groups, both genders, and people at all educational and income levels.

Adults and older adults have the highest rates of depression. Major depression affects approximately twice as many women as men. Women who are poor, on welfare, less educated, unemployed, and from certain racial or ethnic populations are more likely to experience depression. In addition, depression rates are higher among older adults with coexisting medical conditions. For example, 12 percent of older persons hospitalized for problems such as hip fracture or heart disease are diagnosed with depression. Rates of depression for older persons in nursing homes range from 15 to 25 percent.

Injury and Violence

Leading Health Indicator

More than 400 Americans die each day from injuries due primarily to motor vehicle crashes, firearms, poisonings, suffocation, falls, fires, and drowning. The risk of injury is so great that most persons sustain a significant injury at some time during their lives.

Motor vehicle crashes are the most common cause of serious injury. In 1998, there were 15.6 deaths from motor vehicle crashes per 100,000 persons.

Because no other crime is measured as accurately and precisely, homicide is a reliable indicator of all violent crime. In 1998, the murder rate in the United States fell to its lowest level in three decades—6.5 homicides per 100,000 persons.

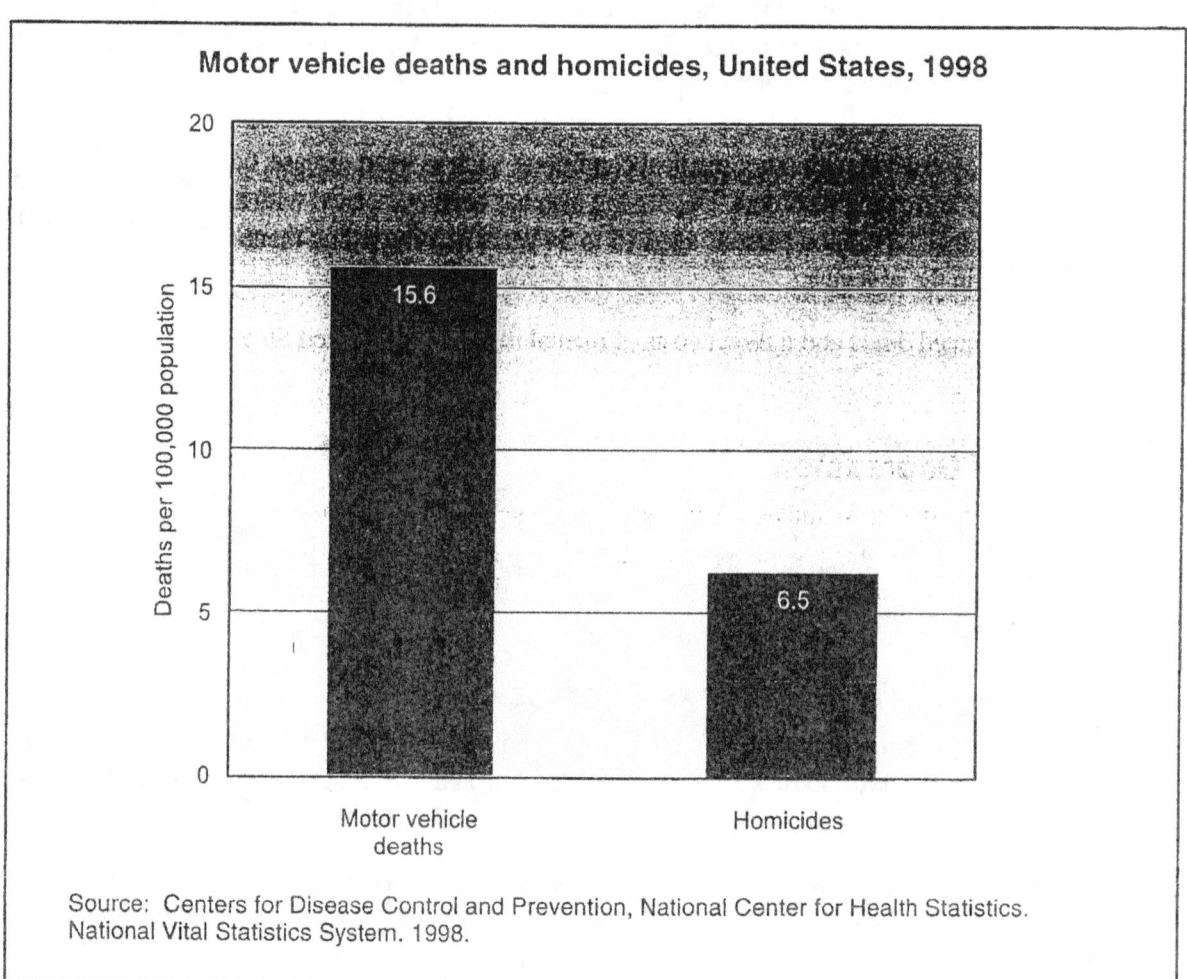

The objectives selected to measure progress for this Leading Health Indicator are presented below. These are only indicators and do not represent all the injury and violence prevention objectives in Healthy People 2010.

15-15a. Reduce deaths caused by motor vehicle crashes.
15-32. Reduce homicides.

Leading Health Indicator

Impact of Injury and Violence

In 1995, the cost of injury and violence in the United States was estimated at more than $224 billion per year. These costs include direct medical care and rehabilitation as well as productivity losses to the Nation's workforce. The total societal cost of motor vehicle crashes alone exceeds $150 billion annually.

Motor Vehicle Crashes

Motor vehicle crashes often are predictable and preventable. Increased use of safety belts and reductions in driving while impaired are two of the most effective means to reduce the risk of death and serious injury of occupants in motor vehicle crashes.

Death rates associated with motor vehicle-traffic injuries are highest in the age group 15 to 24 years. In 1996, teenagers accounted for only 10 percent of the U.S. population but 15 percent of the deaths from motor vehicle crashes. Those aged 75 years and older had the second highest rate of motor vehicle-related deaths.

Nearly 40 percent of traffic fatalities in 1997 were alcohol related. Each year in the United States it is estimated that more than 120 million episodes of impaired driving occur among adults. In 1996, 21 percent of traffic fatalities of children aged 14 years and under involved alcohol; 60 percent of the time the driver of the car in which the child was a passenger was impaired.

The highest intoxication rates in fatal crashes in 1995 were recorded for drivers aged 21 to 24 years. Young drivers who have been arrested for driving while impaired are more than four times as likely to die in future alcohol-related crashes.

Homicides

In 1997, 32,436 individuals died from firearm injuries; of this number, 42 percent were victims of homicide. In 1997, homicide was the third leading cause of death for children aged 5 to 14 years, an increasing trend in childhood violent deaths. In 1996, more than 80 percent of infant homicides were considered to be fatal child abuse.

Many factors that contribute to injuries are also closely associated with violent and abusive behavior, such as low income, discrimination, lack of education, and lack of employment opportunities.

Males are most often the victims and the perpetrators of homicides. African Americans are more than five times as likely as whites to be murdered. There has been a decline in the homicide of intimates, including spouses, partners, boyfriends, and girlfriends, over the past decade, but this problem remains significant.

Environmental Quality

Leading Health Indicator

An estimated 25 percent of preventable illnesses worldwide can be attributed to poor environmental quality. In the United States, air pollution alone is estimated to be associated with 50,000 premature deaths and an estimated $40 billion to $50 billion in health-related costs annually. Two indicators of air quality are ozone (outdoor) and environmental tobacco smoke (indoor).

In 1997, approximately 43 percent of the U.S. population lived in areas designated as nonattainment areas for established health-based standards for ozone. During the years 1988 to 1994, 65 percent of nonsmokers were exposed to environmental tobacco smoke (ETS).

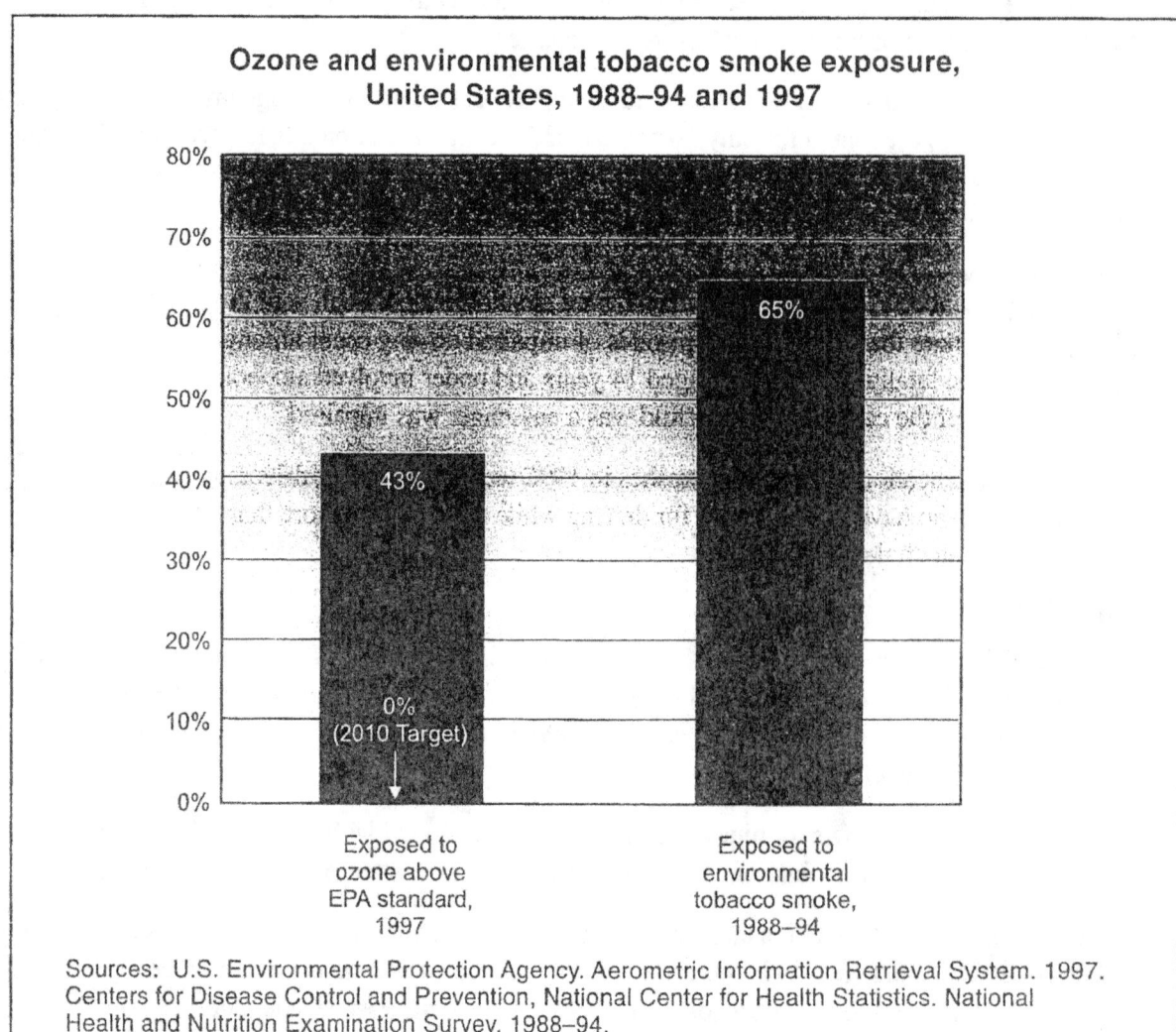

Ozone and environmental tobacco smoke exposure, United States, 1988–94 and 1997

Sources: U.S. Environmental Protection Agency. Aerometric Information Retrieval System. 1997. Centers for Disease Control and Prevention, National Center for Health Statistics. National Health and Nutrition Examination Survey. 1988–94.

The objectives selected to measure progress among children, adolescents, and adults for this Leading Health Indicator are presented below. These are only indicators and do not represent all the environmental quality objectives in Healthy People 2010.

8-1a. Reduce the proportion of persons exposed to air that does not meet the U.S. Environmental Protection Agency's health-based standards for ozone.

27-10. Reduce the proportion of nonsmokers exposed to environmental tobacco smoke.

Leading Health Indicator

Defining the Environment

Physical and social environments play major roles in the health of individuals and communities. The physical environment includes the air, water, and soil through which exposure to chemical, biological, and physical agents may occur. The social environment includes housing, transportation, urban development, land use, industry, and agriculture and results in exposures such as work-related stress, injury, and violence.

Global Concern

Environmental quality is a global concern. Ever-increasing numbers of people and products cross national borders and may transfer health risks such as infectious diseases and chemical hazards. For example, pesticides that are not registered or are restricted for use in the United States potentially could be imported in the fruits, vegetables, and seafood produced abroad.

Health Impact of Poor Air Quality

Poor air quality contributes to respiratory illness, cardiovascular disease, and cancer. For example, asthma can be triggered or worsened by exposure to ozone and ETS. The overall death rate from asthma increased 57 percent between 1980 and 1993, and for children it increased 67 percent.

Air Pollution. Dramatic improvements in air quality in the United States have occurred over the past three decades. Between 1970 and 1997, total emissions of the six principal air pollutants decreased 31 percent. Still, million of tons of toxic pollutants are released into the air each year from automobiles, industry, and other sources. In 1997, despite continued improvements in air quality, approximately 120 million people lived in areas with unhealthy air based on established standards for one or more commonly found air pollutants, including ozone. In 1996, a disproportionate number of Hispanics and Asian and Pacific Islanders lived in areas that failed to meet these standards compared with whites, African Americans, and American Indians or Alaska Natives.

Tobacco Smoke. Exposure to ETS, or secondhand smoke, among nonsmokers is widespread. Home and workplace environments are major sources of exposure. A total of 15 million children are estimated to have been exposed to secondhand smoke in their homes in 1996. ETS increases the risk of heart disease and respiratory infections in children and is responsible for an estimated 3,000 cancer deaths of adult nonsmokers.

Improvement in Environmental Quality

In the United States, ensuring clean water, safe food, and effective waste management has contributed greatly to a declining threat from many infectious diseases; however, there is still more that can be done. Work to improve the air quality and to understand better threats such as chronic, low-level exposures to hazardous substances also must continue.

Immunization

Leading Health Indicator

Vaccines are among the greatest public health achievements of the 20th century. Immunizations can prevent disability and death from infectious diseases for individuals and can help control the spread of infections within communities.

In 1998, 73 percent of children received all vaccines recommended for universal administration.

In 1998, influenza immunization rates were 64 percent in adults aged 65 years and older—almost double the 1989 immunization rate of 33 percent. In 1998, only 46 percent of persons aged 65 years and older had ever received a pneumococcal vaccine.

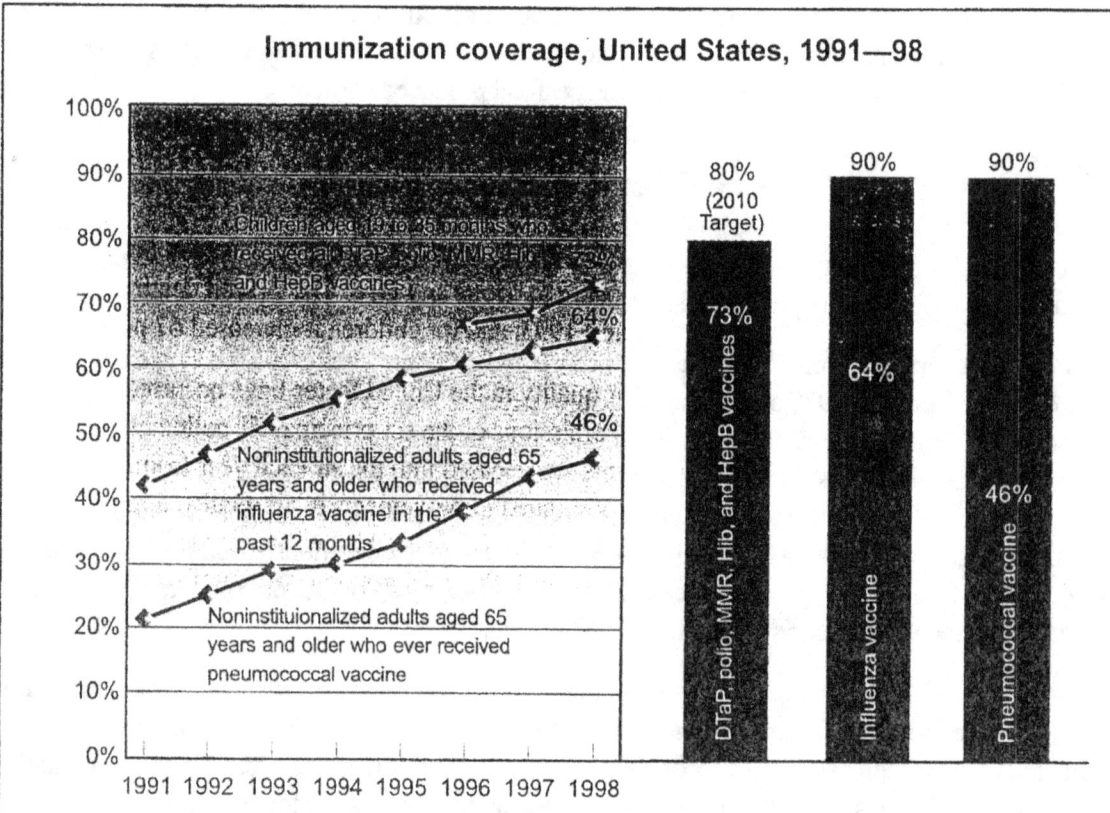

*Four or more doses of diphtheria/tetanus/acellular pertussis (DTaP) vaccine, three or more doses of polio vaccine, one or more dose of measles/mumps/rubella (MMR) vaccine, three or more doses of *Haemophilus influenzae* type b (Hib) vaccine, and three or more doses of hepatitis B (Hep B) vaccine.

Sources: Centers for Disease Control and Prevention, National Center for Health Statistics and National Immunization Program. National Immunization Survey. 1996–98. Centers for Disease Control and Prevention, National Center for Health Statistics. National Health Interview Survey. 1991–98.

The objectives selected to measure progress among children and adults for this Leading Health Indicator are presented below. These are only indicators and do not represent all the immunization and infectious diseases objectives in Healthy People 2010.

14-24a. **Increase the proportion of young children who receive all vaccines that have been recommended for universal administration for at least 5 years.**

14-29a, b. **Increase the proportion of noninstitutionalized adults who are vaccinated annually against influenza and ever vaccinated against pneumococcal disease.**

Leading Health Indicator

Impact of Immunization

Many once-common vaccine-preventable diseases now are controlled. Smallpox has been eradicated, poliomyelitis has been eliminated from the Western Hemisphere, and measles cases in the United States are at a record low.

Immunizations against influenza and pneumococcal disease can prevent serious illness and death. Pneumonia and influenza deaths together constitute the sixth leading cause of death in the United States. Influenza causes an average of 110,000 hospitalizations and 20,000 deaths annually; pneumococcal disease causes 10,000 to 14,000 deaths annually.

Recommended Immunizations

As of November 1, 1999, all children born in the United States (11,000 per day) should be receiving 12 to 16 doses of vaccine by age 2 years to be protected against 10 vaccine-preventable childhood diseases. This recommendation will change in the years ahead as new vaccines are developed, including combinations of current vaccines that may even reduce the number of necessary shots.

Recommended immunizations for adults aged 65 years and older include a yearly immunization against influenza (the "flu shot") and a one-time immunization against pneumococcal disease. Most of the deaths and serious illnesses caused by influenza and pneumococcal disease occur in older adults and others at increased risk for complications of these diseases because of other risk factors or medical conditions.

Trends in Immunization

National coverage levels in children now are greater than 90 percent for each immunization recommended during the first 2 years of life, except for hepatitis B and varicella vaccines. The hepatitis B immunization rate in children was 87 percent in 1998—the highest level ever reported. In 1998, 70 percent of children aged 19 to 35 months from the lowest income households received the combined series of recommended immunizations, compared with 77 percent of children from higher income households.

Both influenza and pneumococcal immunization rates are significantly lower for African American and Hispanic adults than for white adults.

Other Immunization Issues

Coverage levels for immunizations in adults are not as high as those achieved in children, yet the health effects may be just as great. Barriers to adult immunization include not knowing immunizations are needed, misconceptions about vaccines, and lack of recommendations from health care providers.

Access to Health Care

Leading Health Indicator

Strong predictors of access to quality health care include having health insurance, a higher income level, and a regular primary care provider or other source of ongoing health care. Use of clinical preventive services, such as early prenatal care, can serve as indicators of access to quality health care services.

In 1997, 83 percent of persons under age 65 years had health insurance. In 1998, 87 percent of persons of all ages had a usual source of health care. Also in that year, 83 percent of pregnant women received prenatal care in the first trimester of pregnancy.

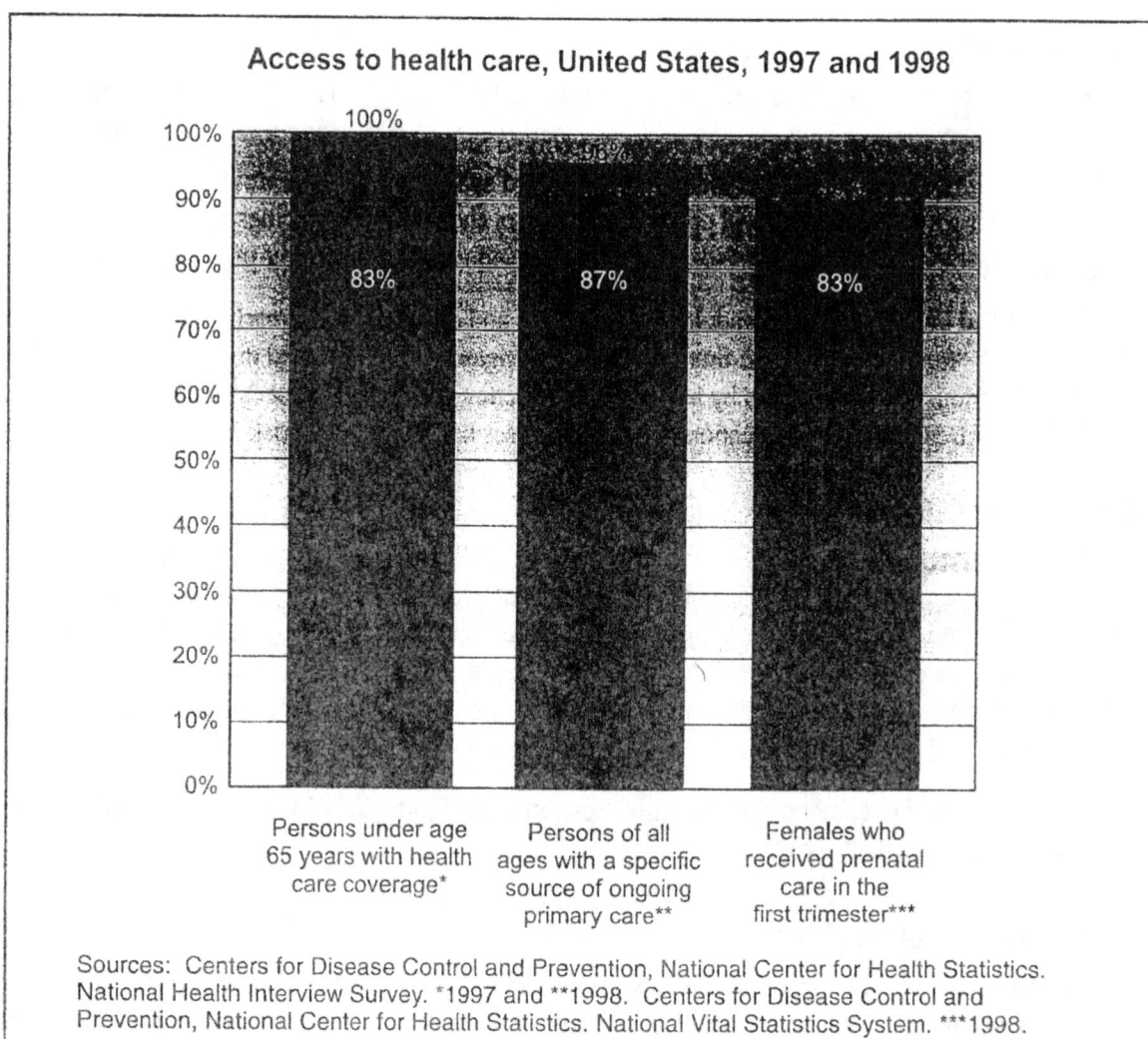

Access to health care, United States, 1997 and 1998

- Persons under age 65 years with health care coverage*: 83%
- Persons of all ages with a specific source of ongoing primary care**: 87%
- Females who received prenatal care in the first trimester***: 83%

Sources: Centers for Disease Control and Prevention, National Center for Health Statistics. National Health Interview Survey. *1997 and **1998. Centers for Disease Control and Prevention, National Center for Health Statistics. National Vital Statistics System. ***1998.

The objectives selected to measure progress for this Leading Health Indicator are presented below. These are only indicators and do not represent all the access to quality health services objectives in Healthy People 2010.

1-1. Increase the proportion of persons with health insurance.
1-4a. Increase the proportion of persons who have a specific source of ongoing care.
16-6a. Increase the proportion of pregnant women who begin prenatal care in the first trimester of pregnancy.

Leading Health Indicator

Health Insurance

Health insurance provides access to health care. Persons with health insurance are more likely to have a primary care provider and to have received appropriate preventive care such as a recent Pap test, immunization, or early prenatal care. Adults with health insurance are twice as likely to receive a routine checkup as are adults without health insurance.

More than 44 million persons in the United States do not have health insurance, including 11 million uninsured children. Over the past decade, the proportion of persons under age 65 years with health insurance remained steady at about 85 percent. About one-third of adults under age 65 years below the poverty level were uninsured. For persons of Hispanic origin, approximately one in three was without health insurance coverage in 1997. Mexican Americans had one of the highest uninsured rates at 40 percent.

Ongoing Sources of Primary Care

More than 40 million Americans do not have a particular doctor's office, clinic, health center, or other place where they usually go to seek health care or health-related advice. Even among privately insured persons, a significant number lacked a usual source of care or reported difficulty in accessing needed care due to financial constraints or insurance problems.

People aged 18 to 24 years were the most likely to lack a usual source of ongoing primary care. Only 80 percent of individuals below the poverty level and 79 percent of Hispanics had a usual source of ongoing primary care.

Barriers to Access

Financial, structural, and personal barriers can limit access to health care. Financial barriers include not having health insurance, not having enough health insurance to cover needed services, or not having the financial capacity to cover services outside a health plan or insurance program. Structural barriers include the lack of primary care providers, medical specialists, or other health care professionals to meet special needs or the lack of health care facilities. Personal barriers include cultural or spiritual differences, language barriers, not knowing what to do or when to seek care, or concerns about confidentiality or discrimination.

Appendix: Short Titles for Healthy People 2010 Objectives

1. Access to Quality Health Services

Goal: Improve access to comprehensive, high-quality health care services.

Objective Number and Short Title

Clinical Preventive Care
- 1-1 Persons with health insurance
- 1-2 Health insurance coverage for clinical preventive services
- 1-3 Counseling about health behaviors

Primary Care
- 1-4 Source of ongoing care
- 1-5 Usual primary care provider
- 1-6 Difficulties or delays in obtaining needed health care
- 1-7 Core competencies in health provider training
- 1-8 Racial and ethnic representation in health professions
- 1-9 Hospitalization for ambulatory-care-sensitive conditions

Emergency Services
- 1-10 Delay or difficulty in getting emergency care
- 1-11 Rapid prehospital emergency care
- 1-12 Single toll-free number for poison control centers
- 1-13 Trauma care systems
- 1-14 Special needs of children

Long-Term Care and Rehabilitative Services
- 1-15 Long-term care services
- 1-16 Pressure ulcers among nursing home residents

2. Arthritis, Osteoporosis, and Chronic Back Conditions

Goal: Prevent illness and disability related to arthritis and other rheumatic conditions, osteoporosis, and chronic back conditions.

Objective Number and Short Title

Arthritis and Other Rheumatic Conditions
- 2-1 Mean number of days without severe pain
- 2-2 Activity limitations due to arthritis
- 2-3 Personal care limitations
- 2-4 Help in coping
- 2-5 Employment rate
- 2-6 Racial differences in total knee replacement
- 2-7 Seeing a health care provider
- 2-8 Arthritis education

Osteoporosis
- 2-9 Cases of osteoporosis
- 2-10 Hospitalization for vertebral fractures

Chronic Back Conditions
- 2-11 Activity limitations due to chronic back conditions

3. Cancer

Goal: Reduce the number of new cancer cases as well as the illness, disability, and death caused by cancer.

Objective Number and Short Title

3-1	Overall cancer deaths
3-2	Lung cancer deaths
3-3	Breast cancer deaths
3-4	Cervical cancer deaths
3-5	Colorectal cancer deaths
3-6	Oropharyngeal cancer deaths
3-7	Prostate cancer deaths
3-8	Melanoma deaths
3-9	Sun exposure and skin cancer
3-10	Provider counseling about cancer prevention
3-11	Pap tests
3-12	Colorectal cancer screening
3-13	Mammograms
3-14	Statewide cancer registries
3-15	Cancer survival

4. Chronic Kidney Disease

Goal: Reduce new cases of chronic kidney disease and its complications, disability, death, and economic costs.

Objective Number and Short Title

4-1	End-stage renal disease
4-2	Cardiovascular disease deaths in persons with chronic kidney failure
4-3	Counseling for chronic kidney failure care
4-4	Use of arteriovenous fistulas
4-5	Registration for kidney transplantation
4-6	Waiting time for kidney transplantation
4-7	Kidney failure due to diabetes
4-8	Medical therapy for persons with diabetes and proteinuria

5. Diabetes

Goal: Through prevention programs, reduce the disease and economic burden of diabetes, and improve the quality of life for all persons who have or are at risk for diabetes.

Objective Number and Short Title

5-1	Diabetes education
5-2	New cases of diabetes
5-3	Overall cases of diagnosed diabetes
5-4	Diagnosis of diabetes
5-5	Diabetes deaths
5-6	Diabetes-related deaths
5-7	Cardiovascular disease deaths in persons with diabetes
5-8	Gestational diabetes
5-9	Foot ulcers
5-10	Lower extremity amputations
5-11	Annual urinary microalbumin measurement
5-12	Annual glycosylated hemoglobin measurement
5-13	Annual dilated eye examinations
5-14	Annual foot examinations
5-15	Annual dental examinations
5-16	Aspirin therapy
5-17	Self-blood-glucose-monitoring

6. Disability and Secondary Conditions

Goal: Promote the health of people with disabilities, prevent secondary conditions, and eliminate disparities between people with and without disabilities in the U.S. population.

Objective Number and Short Title

6-1	Standard definition of people with disabilities in data sets
6-2	Feelings and depression among children with disabilities
6-3	Feelings and depression interfering with activities among adults with disabilities
6-4	Social participation among adults with disabilities
6-5	Sufficient emotional support among adults with disabilities
6-6	Satisfaction with life among adults with disabilities
6-7	Congregate care of children and adults with disabilities
6-8	Employment parity
6-9	Inclusion of children and youth with disabilities in regular education programs
6-10	Accessibility of health and wellness programs
6-11	Assistive devices and technology
6-12	Environmental barriers affecting participation in activities
6-13	Surveillance and health promotion programs

7. Educational and Community-Based Programs

Goal: Increase the quality, availability, and effectiveness of educational and community-based programs designed to prevent disease and improve health and quality of life.

Objective Number and Short Title

School Setting

- 7-1 High school completion
- 7-2 School health education
- 7-3 Health-risk behavior information for college and university students
- 7-4 School nurse-to-student ratio

Worksite Setting

- 7-5 Worksite health promotion programs
- 7-6 Participation in employer-sponsored health promotion activities

Health Care Setting

- 7-7 Patient and family education
- 7-8 Satisfaction with patient education
- 7-9 Health care organization sponsorship of community health promotion activities

Community Setting and Select Populations

- 7-10 Community health promotion programs
- 7-11 Culturally appropriate and linguistically competent community health promotion programs
- 7-12 Older adult participation in community health promotion activities

8. Environmental Health

Goal: Promote health for all through a healthy environment.

Objective Number and Short Title

Outdoor Air Quality

- 8-1 Harmful air pollutants
- 8-2 Alternative modes of transportation
- 8-3 Cleaner alternative fuels
- 8-4 Airborne toxins

Water Quality

- 8-5 Safe drinking water
- 8-6 Waterborne disease outbreaks
- 8-7 Water conservation
- 8-8 Surface water health risks
- 8-9 Beach closings
- 8-10 Fish contamination

Toxics and Waste

- 8-11 Elevated blood lead levels in children
- 8-12 Risks posed by hazardous sites
- 8-13 Pesticide exposures
- 8-14 Toxic pollutants
- 8-15 Recycled municipal solid waste

Healthy Homes and Healthy Communities

- 8-16 Indoor allergens
- 8-17 Office building air quality
- 8-18 Homes tested for radon
- 8-19 Radon-resistant new home construction
- 8-20 School policies to protect against environmental hazards
- 8-21 Disaster preparedness plans and protocols
- 8-22 Lead-based paint testing
- 8-23 Substandard housing

Infrastructure and Surveillance

- 8-24 Exposure to pesticides
- 8-25 Exposure to heavy metals and other toxic chemicals
- 8-26 Information systems used for environmental health
- 8-27 Monitoring environmentally related diseases
- 8-28 Local agencies using surveillance data for vector control

Global Environmental Health

- 8-29 Global burden of disease
- 8-30 Water quality in the U.S.-Mexico border region

9. Family Planning

Goal: Improve pregnancy planning and spacing and prevent unintended pregnancy.

Objective Number and Short Title

- 9-1 Intended pregnancy
- 9-2 Birth spacing
- 9-3 Contraceptive use
- 9-4 Contraceptive failure
- 9-5 Emergency contraception
- 9-6 Male involvement in pregnancy prevention
- 9-7 Adolescent pregnancy
- 9-8 Abstinence before age 15 years
- 9-9 Abstinence among adolescents aged 15 to 17 years
- 9-10 Pregnancy prevention and sexually transmitted disease (STD) protection
- 9-11 Pregnancy prevention education
- 9-12 Problems in becoming pregnant and maintaining a pregnancy
- 9-13 Insurance coverage for contraceptive supplies and services

10. Food Safety

Goal: Reduce foodborne illnesses.

Objective Number and Short Title

10-1	Foodborne infections
10-2	Outbreaks of foodborne infections
10-3	Antimicrobial resistance of *Salmonella* species
10-4	Food allergy deaths
10-5	Consumer food safety practices
10-6	Safe food preparation practices in retail establishments
10-7	Organophosphate pesticide exposure

11. Health Communication

Goal: Use communication strategically to improve health.

Objective Number and Short Title

11-1	Households with Internet access
11-2	Health literacy
11-3	Research and evaluation of communication programs
11-4	Quality of Internet health information sources
11-5	Centers for excellence
11-6	Satisfaction with health care providers' communication skills

12. Heart Disease and Stroke

Goal: Improve cardiovascular health and quality of life through the prevention, detection, and treatment of risk factors; early identification and treatment of heart attacks and strokes; and prevention of recurrent cardiovascular events.

Objective Number and Short Title

Heart Disease

12-1	Coronary heart disease (CHD) deaths
12-2	Knowledge of symptoms of heart attack and importance of calling 911
12-3	Artery-opening therapy
12-4	Bystander response to cardiac arrest
12-5	Out-of-hospital emergency care
12-6	Heart failure hospitalizations

Stroke

12-7	Stroke deaths
12-8	Knowledge of early warning symptoms of stroke

Blood Pressure

12-9	High blood pressure
12-10	High blood pressure control
12-11	Action to help control blood pressure
12-12	Blood pressure monitoring

Cholesterol

12-13	Mean total blood cholesterol levels
12-14	High blood cholesterol levels
12-15	Blood cholesterol screening
12-16	LDL-cholesterol level in CHD patients

13. HIV

Goal: Prevent HIV infection and its related illness and death.

Objective Number and Short Title

13-1	New AIDS cases
13-2	AIDS among men who have sex with men
13-3	AIDS among persons who inject drugs
13-4	AIDS among men who have sex with men and who inject drugs
13-5	New HIV cases
13-6	Condom use
13-7	Knowledge of serostatus
13-8	HIV counseling and education for persons in substance abuse treatment
13-9	HIV/AIDS, STD, and TB education in State prisons
13-10	HIV counseling and testing in State prisons
13-11	HIV testing in TB patients
13-12	Screening for STDs and immunization for hepatitis B
13-13	Treatment according to guidelines
13-14	HIV-infection deaths
13-15	Interval between HIV infection and AIDS diagnosis
13-16	Interval between AIDS diagnosis and death from AIDS
13-17	Perinatally acquired HIV infection

14. Immunization and Infectious Diseases

Goal: Prevent disease, disability, and death from infectious diseases, including vaccine-preventable diseases.

Objective Number and Short Title

Diseases Preventable Through Universal Vaccination

14-1	Vaccine-preventable diseases
14-2	Hepatitis B in infants and young children
14-3	Hepatitis B in adults and high-risk groups
14-4	Bacterial meningitis in young children
14-5	Invasive pneumococcal infections

Diseases Preventable Through Targeted Vaccination
14-6 Hepatitis A
14-7 Meningococcal disease
14-8 Lyme disease

Infectious Diseases and Emerging Antimicrobial Resistance
14-9 Hepatitis C
14-10 Identification of persons with chronic hepatitis C
14-11 Tuberculosis
14-12 Curative therapy for tuberculosis
14-13 Treatment for high-risk persons with latent tuberculosis infection
14-14 Timely laboratory confirmation of tuberculosis cases
14-15 Prevention services for international travelers
14-16 Invasive early onset group B streptococcal disease
14-17 Peptic ulcer hospitalizations
14-18 Antibiotics prescribed for ear infections
14-19 Antibiotics prescribed for common cold
14-20 Hospital-acquired infections
14-21 Antimicrobial use in intensive care units

Vaccination Coverage and Strategies
14-22 Universally recommended vaccination of children aged 19 to 35 months
14-23 Vaccination coverage for children in day care, kindergarten, and first grade
14-24 Fully immunized young children and adolescents
14-25 Providers who measure childhood vaccination coverage levels
14-26 Children participating in population-based immunization registries
14-27 Vaccination coverage among adolescents
14-28 Hepatitis B vaccination among high-risk groups
14-29 Influenza and pneumococcal vaccination of high-risk adults

Vaccine Safety
14-30 Adverse events from vaccinations
14-31 Active surveillance for vaccine safety

15. Injury and Violence Prevention

Goal: Reduce injuries, disabilities, and deaths due to unintentional injuries and violence.

Objective Number and Short Title

Injury Prevention
15-1 Nonfatal head injuries
15-2 Nonfatal spinal cord injuries
15-3 Firearm-related deaths
15-4 Proper firearm storage in homes
15-5 Nonfatal firearm-related injuries
15-6 Child fatality review
15-7 Nonfatal poisonings
15-8 Deaths from poisoning
15-9 Deaths from suffocation
15-10 Emergency department surveillance systems
15-11 Hospital discharge surveillance systems
15-12 Emergency department visits

Unintentional Injury Prevention
15-13 Deaths from unintentional injuries
15-14 Nonfatal unintentional injuries
15-15 Deaths from motor vehicle crashes
15-16 Pedestrian deaths
15-17 Nonfatal motor vehicle injuries
15-18 Nonfatal pedestrian injuries
15-19 Safety belts
15-20 Child restraints
15-21 Motorcycle helmet use
15-22 Graduated driver licensing
15-23 Bicycle helmet use
15-24 Bicycle helmet laws
15-25 Residential fire deaths
15-26 Functioning smoke alarms in residences
15-27 Deaths from falls
15-28 Hip fractures
15-29 Drownings
15-30 Dog bite injuries
15-31 Injury protection in school sports

Violence and Abuse Prevention
15-32 Homicides
15-33 Maltreatment and maltreatment fatalities of children
15-34 Physical assault by intimate partners
15-35 Rape or attempted rape
15-36 Sexual assault other than rape
15-37 Physical assaults
15-38 Physical fighting among adolescents
15-39 Weapon carrying by adolescents on school property

16. Maternal, Infant, and Child Health

Goal: Improve the health and well-being of women, infants, children, and families.

Objective Number and Short Title

Fetal, Infant, Child, and Adolescent Deaths
- 16-1 Fetal and infant deaths
- 16-2 Child deaths
- 16-3 Adolescent and young adult deaths

Maternal Deaths and Illnesses
- 16-4 Maternal deaths
- 16-5 Maternal illness and complications due to pregnancy

Prenatal Care
- 16-6 Prenatal care
- 16-7 Childbirth classes

Obstetrical Care
- 16-8 Very low birth weight infants born at level III hospitals
- 16-9 Cesarean births

Risk Factors
- 16-10 Low birth weight and very low birth weight
- 16-11 Preterm births
- 16-12 Weight gain during pregnancy
- 16-13 Infants put to sleep on their backs

Developmental Disabilities and Neural Tube Defects
- 16-14 Developmental disabilities
- 16-15 Spina bifida and other neural tube defects
- 16-16 Optimum folic acid levels

Prenatal Substance Exposure
- 16-17 Prenatal substance exposure
- 16-18 Fetal alcohol syndrome

Breastfeeding, Newborn Screening, and Service Systems
- 16-19 Breastfeeding
- 16-20 Newborn bloodspot screening
- 16-21 Sepsis among children with sickle cell disease
- 16-22 Medical homes for children with special health care needs
- 16-23 Service systems for children with special health care needs

17. Medical Product Safety

Goal: Ensure the safe and effective use of medical products.

Objective Number and Short Title

- 17-1 Monitoring of adverse medical events
- 17-2 Linked, automated information systems
- 17-3 Provider review of medications taken by patients
- 17-4 Receipt of useful information about prescriptions from pharmacies
- 17-5 Receipt of oral counseling about medications from prescribers and dispensers
- 17-6 Blood donations

18. Mental Health and Mental Illness

Goal: Improve mental health and ensure access to appropriate, quality mental health services.

Objective Number and Short Title

Mental Health Status Improvement
- 18-1 Suicide
- 18-2 Adolescent suicide attempts
- 18-3 Serious mental illness (SMI) among homeless adults
- 18-4 Employment of persons with SMI
- 18-5 Eating disorder relapses

Treatment Expansion
- 18-6 Primary care screening and assessment
- 18-7 Treatment for children with mental health problems
- 18-8 Juvenile justice facility screening
- 18-9 Treatment for adults with mental disorders
- 18-10 Treatment for co-occurring disorders
- 18-11 Adult jail diversion programs

State Activities
- 18-12 State tracking of consumer satisfaction
- 18-13 State plans addressing cultural competence
- 18-14 State plans addressing elderly persons

19. Nutrition and Overweight

Goal: Promote health and reduce chronic disease associated with diet and weight.

Objective Number and Short Title

Weight Status and Growth
- 19-1 Healthy weight in adults
- 19-2 Obesity in adults
- 19-3 Overweight or obesity in children and adolescents
- 19-4 Growth retardation in children

Food and Nutrient Consumption
- 19-5 Fruit intake
- 19-6 Vegetable intake
- 19-7 Grain product intake
- 19-8 Saturated fat intake
- 19-9 Total fat intake
- 19-10 Sodium intake
- 19-11 Calcium intake

Iron Deficiency and Anemia
- 19-12 Iron deficiency in young children and in females of childbearing age
- 19-13 Anemia in low-income pregnant females
- 19-14 Iron deficiency in pregnant females

Schools, Worksites, and Nutrition Counseling
- 19-15 Meals and snacks at school
- 19-16 Worksite promotion of nutrition education and weight management
- 19-17 Nutrition counseling for medical conditions

Food Security
- 19-18 Food security

20. Occupational Safety and Health

Goal: Promote the health and safety of people at work through prevention and early intervention.

Objective Number and Short Title
- 20-1 Work-related injury deaths
- 20-2 Work-related injuries
- 20-3 Overexertion or repetitive motion
- 20-4 Pneumoconiosis deaths
- 20-5 Work-related homicides
- 20-6 Work-related assaults
- 20-7 Elevated blood lead levels from work exposure
- 20-8 Occupational skin diseases or disorders
- 20-9 Worksite stress reduction programs
- 20-10 Needlestick injuries
- 20-11 Work-related, noise-induced hearing loss

21. Oral Health

Goal: Prevent and control oral and craniofacial diseases, conditions, and injuries and improve access to related services.

Objective Number and Short Title
- 21-1 Dental caries experience
- 21-2 Untreated dental decay
- 21-3 No permanent tooth loss
- 21-4 Complete tooth loss
- 21-5 Periodontal diseases
- 21-6 Early detection of oral and pharyngeal cancers
- 21-7 Annual examinations for oral and pharyngeal cancers
- 21-8 Dental sealants
- 21-9 Community water fluoridation
- 21-10 Use of oral health care system
- 21-11 Use of oral health care system by residents in long-term care facilities
- 21-12 Dental services for low-income children
- 21-13 School-based health centers with oral health component
- 21-14 Health centers with oral health service components
- 21-15 Referral for cleft lip or palate
- 21-16 Oral and craniofacial State-based surveillance system
- 21-17 Tribal, State, and local dental programs

22. Physical Fitness and Activity

Goal: Improve health, fitness, and quality of life through daily physical activity.

Objective Number and Short Title

Physical Activity in Adults
- 22-1 No leisure-time physical activity
- 22-2 Moderate physical activity
- 22-3 Vigorous physical activity

Muscular Strength/Endurance and Flexibility
- 22-4 Muscular strength and endurance
- 22-5 Flexibility

Physical Activity in Children and Adolescents
- 22-6 Moderate physical activity in adolescents
- 22-7 Vigorous physical activity in adolescents
- 22-8 Physical education requirement in schools
- 22-9 Daily physical education in schools
- 22-10 Physical activity in physical education class
- 22-11 Television viewing

Access
- 22-12 School physical activity facilities
- 22-13 Worksite physical activity and fitness
- 22-14 Community walking
- 22-15 Community bicycling

23. Public Health Infrastructure

Goal: Ensure that Federal, Tribal, State, and local health agencies have the infrastructure to provide essential public health services effectively.

Objective Number and Short Title

Data and Information Systems
- 23-1 Public health employee access to the Internet
- 23-2 Public access to information and surveillance data
- 23-3 Use of geocoding in health data systems
- 23-4 Data for all population groups
- 23-5 Data for Leading Health Indicators, Health Status Indicators, and Priority Data Needs at Tribal, State, and local levels
- 23-6 National tracking of Healthy People 2010 objectives
- 23-7 Timely release of data on objectives

Workforce
- 23-8 Competencies for public health workers
- 23-9 Training in essential public health services
- 23-10 Continuing education and training by public health agencies

Public Health Organizations
- 23-11 Performance standards for essential public health services
- 23-12 Health improvement plans
- 23-13 Access to public health laboratory services
- 23-14 Access to epidemiology services
- 23-15 Model statutes related to essential public health services

Resources
- 23-16 Data on public health expenditures

Prevention Research
- 23-17 Population-based prevention research

24. Respiratory Diseases

Goal: Promote respiratory health through better prevention, detection, treatment, and education efforts.

Objective Number and Short Title

Asthma
- 24-1 Deaths from asthma
- 24-2 Hospitalizations for asthma
- 24-3 Hospital emergency department visits for asthma
- 24-4 Activity limitations
- 24-5 School or work days lost
- 24-6 Patient education
- 24-7 Appropriate asthma care
- 24-8 Surveillance systems

Chronic Obstructive Pulmonary Disease (COPD)
- 24-9 Activity limitations due to chronic lung and breathing problems
- 24-10 Deaths from COPD

Obstructive Sleep Apnea (OSA)
- 24-11 Medical evaluation and followup
- 24-12 Vehicular crashes related to excessive sleepiness

25. Sexually Transmitted Diseases

Goal: Promote responsible sexual behaviors, strengthen community capacity, and increase access to quality services to prevent sexually transmitted diseases (STDs) and their complications.

Objective Number and Short Title

Bacterial STD Illness and Disability
- 25-1 Chlamydia
- 25-2 Gonorrhea
- 25-3 Primary and secondary syphilis

Viral STD Illness and Disability
- 25-4 Genital herpes
- 25-5 Human papillomavirus infection

STD Complications Affecting Females
- 25-6 Pelvic inflammatory disease (PID)
- 25-7 Fertility problems
- 25-8 Heterosexually transmitted HIV infection in women

STD Complications Affecting the Fetus and Newborn
25-9   Congenital syphilis
25-10 Neonatal STDs

Personal Behaviors
25-11 Responsible adolescent sexual behavior
25-12 Responsible sexual behavior messages on television

Community Protection Infrastructure
25-13 Hepatitis B vaccine services in STD clinics
25-14 Screening in youth detention facilities and jails
25-15 Contracts to treat nonplan partners of STD patients

Personal Health Services
25-16 Annual screening for genital chlamydia
25-17 Screening of pregnant women
25-18 Compliance with recognized STD treatment standards
25-19 Provider referral services for sex partners

26. Substance Abuse

Goal: Reduce substance abuse to protect the health, safety, and quality of life for all, especially children.

Objective Number and Short Title

Adverse Consequences of Substance Use and Abuse
26-1   Motor vehicle crash deaths and injuries
26-2   Cirrhosis deaths
26-3   Drug-induced deaths
26-4   Drug-related hospital emergency department visits
26-5   Alcohol-related hospital emergency department visits
26-6   Adolescents riding with a driver who has been drinking
26-7   Alcohol- and drug-related violence
26-8   Lost productivity

Substance Use and Abuse
26-9   Substance-free youth
26-10 Adolescent and adult use of illicit substances
26-11 Binge drinking
26-12 Average annual alcohol consumption
26-13 Low-risk drinking among adults
26-14 Steroid use among adolescents
26-15 Inhalant use among adolescents

Risk of Substance Use and Abuse
26-16 Peer disapproval of substance abuse
26-17 Perception of risk associated with substance abuse

Treatment for Substance Abuse
26-18 Treatment gap for illicit drugs
26-19 Treatment in correctional institutions
26-20 Treatment for injection drug use
26-21 Treatment gap for problem alcohol use

State and Local Efforts
26-22 Hospital emergency department referrals
26-23 Community partnerships and coalitions
26-24 Administrative license revocation laws
26-25 Blood alcohol concentration (BAC) levels for motor vehicle drivers

27. Tobacco Use

Goal: Reduce illness, disability, and death related to tobacco use and exposure to secondhand smoke.

Objective Number and Short Title

Tobacco Use in Population Groups
27-1 Adult tobacco use
27-2 Adolescent tobacco use
27-3 Initiation of tobacco use
27-4 Age at first tobacco use

Cessation and Treatment
27-5 Smoking cessation by adults
27-6 Smoking cessation during pregnancy
27-7 Smoking cessation by adolescents
27-8 Insurance coverage of cessation treatment

Exposure to Secondhand Smoke
27-9   Exposure to tobacco smoke at home among children
27-10 Exposure to environmental tobacco smoke
27-11 Smoke-free and tobacco-free schools
27-12 Worksite smoking policies
27-13 Smoke-free indoor air laws

Social and Environmental Changes
27-14 Enforcement of illegal tobacco sales to minors laws
27-15 Retail license suspension for sales to minors
27-16 Tobacco advertising and promotion targeting adolescents and young adults
27-17 Adolescent disapproval of smoking
27-18 Tobacco control programs
27-19 Preemptive tobacco control laws
27-20 Tobacco product regulation
27-21 Tobacco tax

28. Vision and Hearing

Goal: Improve the visual and hearing health of the Nation through prevention, early detection, treatment, and rehabilitation.

Objective Number and Short Title

Vision

- 28-1 Dilated eye examinations
- 28-2 Vision screening for children
- 28-3 Impairment due to refractive errors
- 28-4 Impairment in children and adolescents
- 28-5 Impairment due to diabetic retinopathy
- 28-6 Impairment due to glaucoma
- 28-7 Impairment due to cataract
- 28-8 Occupational eye injury
- 28-9 Protective eyewear
- 28-10 Vision rehabilitation services and devices

Hearing

- 28-11 Newborn hearing screening, evaluation, and intervention
- 28-12 Otitis media
- 28-13 Rehabilitation for hearing impairment
- 28-14 Hearing examination
- 28-15 Evaluation and treatment referrals
- 28-16 Hearing protection
- 28-17 Noise-induced hearing loss in children
- 28-18 Noise-induced hearing loss in adults

www.ingramcontent.com/pod-product-compliance
Lightning Source LLC
Chambersburg PA
CBHW080320020526
44117CB00035B/2454